Metaphorically Speaking

CSLI LECTURE NOTES NUMBER 93

Metaphorically Speaking

Patti D. Nogales

CSLI PUBLICATIONS
Center for the Study of Language and Information
Stanford, California

© 1999
CSLI Publications
Center for the Study of Language and Information
Leland Stanford Junior University
03 02 01 00 99   1 2 3 4 5

Library of Congress Cataloging-in-Publication Data

Nogales, Patti D.
Metaphorically speaking / Patti D. Nogales.
p.   cm. — (CSLI lecture notes : 93)
Includes bibliographical references and index.
ISBN 1-57586-159-3 (alk. paper) —
ISBN 1-57586-158-5 (pbk. : alk. paper)
1. Metaphor.   2. Semantics (Philosophy).   3. Concepts.
I. Title.   II. Series.

B840.N64   1999
121'.68—dc21   98-54375
                                                CIP

Acknowledgments

First of all, I want to thank the people at Stanford University, in particular my editors, Dikran Karagueuzian and John Feneron. I am also grateful to my advisor, Julius Moravcsik, and the other members of my reading committee, John Perry and Dagfinn Follesdal, for keeping in touch and providing comments while I was in Chicago. I also thank Herb Clark and Rob Robinson for being willing to join a committee to discuss topics of concern to philosophers.

At the University of Chicago, I want to give special thanks to Josef Stern, for many hours in fruitful discussion of metaphor, for being willing to exchange sources with me, and for his confirmation that part of what a theory of metaphor requires is an assumption of the distinction between meaning and content. I also thank Boaz Keysar for his willingness to exchange materials and ideas.

My thanks also to Kathy Felts and Tricia Boggs, without whose help this work would not have been possible.

Finally, I want to thank family and friends (with an extra nod to my husband), who have provided an abundance of examples of natural language use, and who have put up with a wife/mother/friend who has always has one ear listening to *how* they communicate what they say.

Contents

Figures and Tables

Metaphorically Speaking

Introduction

Why Metaphor

Consider an utterance of "Steve is a sheepdog" by a woman to her mother. In the absence of contextual information, it is not clear whether the utterance is metaphorical or not and what the speaker intends to convey. However, given the information that Steve is the name of the woman's husband, most people would call this utterance *metaphorical* and would observe, as evidence for this classification, that the main point of the utterance has nothing to do with dogs. In fact, as our experience tells us and the work of psychologists confirms, ordinary speakers are almost always able to distinguish metaphorical utterances from literal utterances, even in the absence of an explicit context, and are even able to rank them according to degree of metaphoricity. As a result, one of the tasks for a theory of communication is that of accounting for metaphoricity, that which distinguishes metaphorical utterances from literal utterances.

Philosophers, psychologists, and linguists of different bents have attempted to account for the way we understand metaphors, what we grasp when we understand them, and what knowledge enters into our processing of them. The process is of particular interest because it seems (at least to most people)[1] to be different from the process of understanding the class of literal utterances. For example, in the case of a literal utterance, if the subject is being assigned to a class or identified with an individual, the subject must be thought to have all the characteristics of that class or individual designated by the term in order for the utterance to be considered

---

[1] David Rumelhart disputes this in "Some Problems with the Notion of Literal Meaning," in *Metaphor and Thought*, ed. A. Ortony (Cambridge: Cambridge University Press, 1979), pp. 78–90.

true. However, this does not seem to be so in the case of metaphorical ut-terances. That is, despite the fact that the woman's husband obviously lacks many of the traits of sheepdogs (such as being a member of the ca-nine species), we can imagine circumstances in which an utterance of the sentence in question could make a true assertion about a man named Steve. In fact, although their interpretations of what exactly the utterance conveys might vary (i.e. Steve has a job guiding people vs. Steve is always telling people what to do, etc.), most people would agree that the utter-ance expresses a proposition (or thought) that the mother can agree with, learn from, or openly debate. That is, most people have the intuition that a metaphorical utterance expresses a metaphorical content which is capable of being judged true or false.

In fact, to communicate effectively, it is essential to be able to compre-hend a metaphorical utterance, a process which seems, at the very least, to result in a different message than if the same utterance were taken literally. In other words, if the mother were to take the utterance literally she would fail to understand what the speaker was trying to communicate. So too when a child too young to conceive of or recognize nonliteral speech in-terprets a metaphorical utterance literally, that child has failed to under-stand the utterance.[2] The parties have in all cases failed in their communi-cative task because of their inability to interpret an utterance metaphori-cally rather than literally.[3] Yet the problem of comprehension can work in the other direction, one can mistakenly take an utterance intended literally as a metaphor. For example, consider the following conversation:

> *Dena:* The man lives without a doorbell or any windows.
> *Diane:* He's hard to get in touch with, huh?
> *Dena:* No, seriously, his house doesn't have a door or any windows.

In this conversation Diane interprets the utterance *metaphorically*, in that she thinks Dena is describing the man's character rather than the features of his house. In doing so, she is misinterpreting the utterance; that is, she is not deriving the appropriate message. This example shows not only that interpreting an utterance metaphorically is different than interpreting it

---

[2]Donald Davidson, "What Metaphors Mean," in *The Philosophy of Language*, ed. A. P. Martinich, 2nd ed. (Oxford: Oxford University Press, 1990), pp. 430–41, p. 433.

[3]Note that analysis leaves room for cases in which the person successfully inter-prets an utterance metaphorically *without* identifying it as metaphorical (i.e. knowl-edge of whether something is metaphorical is not a prerequisite to being able to inter-pret an utterance metaphorically).

literally, but also that the process of interpreting a metaphorical utterance depends upon contextual information. In other words, the fact that this metaphor can be taken either metaphorically or literally (with different results) indicates that the metaphoricity and metaphorical content of an utterance depends on the context in which it appears, including such diverse features as other information in the linguistic context and the role a certain object plays in a cultural community.

If metaphors were a tiny subset of ordinary language use, one might dismiss their eccentricities as interesting but irrelevant. However, despite a positivist tradition which dismisses metaphor as irrelevant to the study of language, simple observation and recent work by many theorists[4] show the ubiquity of metaphor. In fact, in some realms, such as literature, rhetoric, science, and education, it is difficult to find language that is free of metaphor. The ubiquity of metaphor in literature is most well known. Indeed, the presence of metaphor (and other figures) in literature has often been cited by philosophers of a certain bent (i.e. logical positivism) as a reason for disregarding the intellectual value of literature. The role of metaphor in literature has been almost equally well established. On the one hand, the emotive power of metaphor makes it a powerful tool for provoking catharsis or some other desired emotional reaction. On the other hand, the ability of metaphor to cause the audience to view a known entity from a different perspective is also regarded as important to any field which seeks to provoke insight. These two functions of metaphor have also served to establish metaphor as a traditional tool of both rhetoric, with its goal of persuasion, and education, with its goal of provoking insight and the integration of new knowledge with old. Most recently, metaphor has also established an important role in science. While the emotive aspect of metaphor would be deemed useless in this context, its capacity for offering a different perspective on a known entity and so connecting entities (as defined by their relationships) within different domains is clearly of interest to science.

Beyond the pervasiveness of metaphor in the fields listed above, much of existing literal language use seems to have had metaphorical origins. For example, although the term "hood" now literally refers to the hood of a car, it is likely that it was metaphorical when first used in this way. Similarly, the way we describe such abstract processes of thought, as in "gathering one's thoughts," seems metaphorical in that this process of

---

[4]George Lakoff and Mark Johnson's work is representative of this group. *Metaphors We Live By* (Chicago: The University of Chicago Press, 1980).

gathering, while structurally similar to the process of gathering grain, also seems subsidiary to it. In other words, it seems as though the process of gathering wheat was part of our theory of the world before our understanding of what we do with thoughts, such that we use our understanding of the former to guide our understanding of the latter. As a result, the study of metaphor would seem to aid in the creation of a model of how certain terms acquire meaning or how certain objects become part of the extension of a term.

If the ubiquity of metaphorical utterances, along with the fact that competent speakers must be able to distinguish and interpret metaphors, ensures the place of metaphor as a part of a theory of communication, the use of the study of metaphor as a model of how certain words acquire meaning also ensures its place as part of a theory of language. However, even if we reduce our domain of investigation to linguistic metaphors, it is unclear where metaphor falls within the field of philosophy of language, which has traditionally been subdivided into the study of syntax, semantics, and pragmatics. Thus one of the fundamental questions that emerges regarding metaphor is, At what level it should be analyzed? According to the traditional taxonomy, metaphorical utterances are a subclass of the class of nonliteral or figurative utterances. However, the question remains whether this distinction is semantic, such that metaphors are semantic phenomena and the knowledge their processing requires is semantic or whether it is pragmatic. Most traditional theories of metaphor (such as that of Black) hold metaphor to be a matter of semantics. However, as we shall see in Chapter 2, these theories use the terminology of semantics in a way that seems to be inconsistent with traditional semantics (i.e. they violate the constraints on meaning specified by semantics such as that of relative context independence). As a result, more recent theories of metaphor analyze metaphor as a matter of pragmatics, mostly within the framework of speech act theory originated by Austin[5] and subsequently developed by Grice and Searle. For example, Searle analyzes metaphorical utterances as a subclass of the class of indirect speech acts, itself a subset of the class of speech acts.[6]

By definition, the same facts that establish metaphor as an issue of language also provide reasons for a philosopher of language to study metaphor. However, there are other reasons to study metaphor besides those

[5]J. L. Austin, *How to Do Things with Words* (Oxford: Oxford University Press, 1962).

[6]John Searle, "Metaphor," in *The Philosophy of Language*, ed. Martinich, p. 408.

just cited. For one thing, the study of metaphor presents a challenge to the traditional way of conceiving of the distinction between semantics and pragmatics. That is, as we shall see in our examination, metaphorical content possesses some of the attributes of what we consider semantically defined phenomena and some of the attributes of what we consider pragmatically defined phenomena. As a result, metaphor poses a challenge to the usefulness and significance of this distinction between semantics and pragmatics.

Another reason metaphorical utterances are of particular interest to philosophers is that, as with indirect speech acts, the force or ultimate impact of metaphorical utterances cannot be explained solely from the literal meaning of the terms, even though the force is somehow related to that meaning. One indication of a gap between the ultimate force of a metaphorical utterance and its literal meaning is the proposition it seems to convey. That is, metaphors (like indirect speech acts) seem to convey propositional content beyond or instead of that expressed according to the rules of the language. While in some cases it seems easy to express this content using a paraphrase, in other cases a paraphrase seems to elude us. However, even if we grant that a metaphorical utterance expresses a proposition other than the one it would express if taken literally, many claim that even this special or metaphorical interpretation fails to capture the full impact of the metaphor. In fact, most theorists hold that while the paraphrase of a metaphorical utterance may capture the truth conditions of that utterance, the metaphor conveys something more and different, whether or not this difference is cognitive.[7] This difference or special metaphorical quality seems particularly important in the fields in which metaphor is most often employed, namely, literature, rhetoric, science, and education. In all these fields metaphors seem to be employed because of the insight they provide, either in giving a new way of looking at an existing entity or in explaining a new entity in such a way as to incorporate it into an existing schema.

In this work I argue that an analysis of metaphor as reconceptualization explains both the special impact of metaphor and its resulting use in literature, rhetoric, science, and education. In literature, authors typically seek to draw the audience into a new way of seeing the world and the entities within it such that characteristics ordinarily thought necessary to a

---

[7]This phenomenon is often characterized as the nonparaphrasability of metaphor. I discuss it in more depth in Chapter 2 (Davidson's analysis) and Chapter 3 (my own analysis).

thing are seen as irrelevant while other characteristics are seen as definitive. For example, Wallace Stevens's poem "An Ordinary Evening in New
Haven"[8] helps us see that the ordinary activities of one's daily existence
are, in a sense a search for reality which is as essential as the search for
God. Yet the process the author seeks to induce is nothing other than the
process of reconceptualization. Both perception and literal language depend fundamentally upon the conceptualizations we make in an attempt
to comprehend what is around us. Thus it makes sense that the task of the
poet (or other writer) be that of reconceptualization which both highlights
our current conceptualization, challenges it, and presents an alternative.
In the case of education, the fact that metaphors prompt the audience (or
student) to reconceptualize an entity so that certain properties are seen as
essential and others are not, while tying new domains to old ones, help
students abstract (derive the essential properties of a thing) and integrate
their knowledge, both of the essence to education. In rhetoric, (1) the emotional impact of the metaphor vehicle, together with (2) the necessity that
people processing metaphors must derive the characteristics involved and
(3) the fact that the lack of explicitness of what is said allows the speaker
to slip in other propositions without scrutiny, all help the rhetorician. Finally, the fact that metaphor is based on reconceptualization of entities often in terms of a system of relationships allows it to assist science as it postulates new entities (via conceptualization and reconceptualization) in order to explain various phenomena and attempts to incorporate these
entities into a theory of the world.

Some accounts of metaphor essentially explain metaphoricity away by
arguing that the metaphorical is not fundamentally different from the literal. And indeed, as I will argue, the metaphorical and the literal form a
continuum rather than existing as noncontinguous sets. Other accounts of
metaphor analyze metaphoricity in semantic, pragmatic, or essentially
nonlinguistic terms. I explain metaphoricity in terms of reconceptualization, something which straddles the options previously considered in that
while reconceptualization is essentially a prelinguistic phenomenon that
underlies language use, a metaphorical utterance contains components
(such as that of metaphorical content) which follow semantic and pragmatic rules. As a result, metaphor can be fruitfully studied within a study
of language that embraces both semantic and pragmatic notions (such as

[8]Wallace Stevens, ed., *The Palm at the End of the Mind* (New York: Knopf, 1971),
p. 331.

the notion of meaning, content, and speaker intention). At the same time, since metaphor requires an examination of reconceptualization and, concomitantly, of the conceptualization underlying literal language use, the study of metaphor ultimately yields insight into the origins of literal language.

This work has two main goals: (1) to present and justify an analysis of metaphor based on reconceptualization and (2) to establish a list of criteria against which a theory of metaphor can be measured. Since the best way to evaluate a theory of metaphor is to see whether it accounts for the major attributes of metaphorical utterances, the latter goal serves the first. After Chapter 1, which presents my analysis of metaphor in terms of reconceptualization, each chapter not only argues for the major claims of my analysis but also contributes to a list of criteria against which to measure both my own analysis and more traditional analyses of metaphors. Some of the criteria I list are already an established part of the theory. For example, almost all theories of metaphor begin with the announced task of explaining (1) metaphoricity (i.e. what distinguishes the metaphorical from the literal) and (2) how metaphors are understood (i.e. metaphor comprehension), both of which are needed to explain the role of metaphor in communication. Certain features of metaphor are easily demonstrated, simply by examining metaphorical utterances in general or by considering particular metaphorical utterances. For example, we have noted (3) the intuition that metaphors express a metaphorical content (i.e. are potentially true), (4) the difficulty of determining the content of some or all metaphors (i.e. apparent nonparaphrasability), (5) the context dependence of metaphor, requiring that the audience go beyond linguistic competence to comprehend the metaphorical content of a metaphor, and (6) the ubiquity of metaphor (i.e. why it is used). Finally, additional conditions have been added to the list by various theorists. For example, it is thought that a theory of metaphor should be able to account for: (7) the relationship between metaphor and the other figures (specifically, the relationship between metaphor and simile), and (8) the different types of metaphor (i.e. novel vs. common, simple vs. complex, alive vs. dead, nominative vs. nonnominative).[9] One further condition I must add to the list of desiderata for a theory of metaphor is that (9) it account for the incorporation of some metaphors into the language. In the course of examining traditional se-

---

[9]Ina Loewenberg discusses some of these types in "Truth and Consequences of Metaphor," *Philosophy and Rhetoric* 6 (1973): 30–45, p. 36.

mantic and nonsemantic theories of metaphor (such as that of Black, Davidson, Grice, Martinich, Searle, and Fogelin), I elaborate on the need to meet these conditions and I add a few more to the list.

The remainder of this book is devoted to presenting and arguing for my analysis of metaphor in terms of reconceptualization. In Chapter 1 I present the major claims of my analysis in terms of reconceptualization and examine and argue for some of its underlying assumptions. In Chapters 2–6 I argue for the major claims of the analysis, via an evaluation of existing theories of metaphor. Finally, in Chapter 7 I use the list of conditions established in this introduction and in Chapters 2–5 to evaluate my analysis of metaphor.

1

Metaphor as Reconceptualization

Consider the following utterances:

(1) That [pointing to a sheep dog] is a sheep dog.
(2) I think I'll visit the bank tomorrow.
(3) He lives without a doorbell or any windows.
(4) Steve is a sheep dog.
(5) Margaret Thatcher is a bulldozer.
(6) Shirley Temple is a bulldozer.
(7) Mom, my sock has a hangnail.
(8) I promise to give the butterfly [speaking of one's daughter] a real talking to.
(9) The philosopher is the city's pilot.
(10) In the days that came after my father's death, I walked the halls of my memories day and night.
(11) A semicolon is a period.
(12) The ham sandwich wants a cup of coffee.

The Analysis

When presented with utterances of the sentences above, most people would identify utterances of the sentences (4) through (10) as metaphorical, as opposed to literal. They would probably also classify utterances of sentences (1) through (3) as literal, (11) as false or anomalous, and (12) as either literal and elliptical or, perhaps, as metaphorical. In this book I propose and describe an analysis of metaphor that accounts for the differences between these utterances by appealing to the notion of *reconceptualization,* based on *conceptualization,* something I believe underlies all language use, embodied in a naive metaphysics and challenged by figurative language use.[1] According to my analysis, the utterances that are literal are so because comprehension of the utterances is consistent with a standardized conceptualization that underlies the use of the terms, one which reflects the naive metaphysics embedded in the standardized taxonomy. Because of this consistency, the features one uses to derive what the speaker is saying (i.e. the proposition expressed by the utterance) are either (1) specified directly by the rules of the language (i.e. the meanings of the terms), (2) derivative from the meanings of the terms, or (3) supplied by contextual clues but still consistent with the standardized conceptualization.[2] For example, in comprehending an utterance of (1), the features one uses to derive the proposition expressed by the utterance are those according to which a sheep dog is ranked within the traditional taxonomy, namely, such features as being a member of a certain biological species, performing a certain function, etc.

In contrast, the utterances that are metaphorical (i.e. 4–10) are so because comprehension of them is *not* consistent with the standardized taxonomy. Instead, the comprehension of a metaphorical utterance requires a reconstruction of the concepts underlying the use of the terms, a *reconceptualization*. That is, one must alter one's conception of the entities—in the case of (5), of bulldozers and a particular person—in order to grasp what is being said. As a result of this reconceptualization, to comprehend the utterances that are *metaphorical*, the features to which one must attend are generally *not* specified by the rules of the language or by the concepts embodied in the underlying taxonomy. In fact, for an utterance to be metaphorical at all, these features must be inconsistent with the conception underlying language use. For example, to comprehend an utterance of (5) we must leave behind the features specified by a literal interpretation of bulldozer (such as being inanimate and a mechanical object), since these are clearly inconsistent with features specified by a literal interpretation of the term "Margaret Thatcher" (such as being animate and a human). Thus to process the utterance, the audience must reconceptualize, first the meta-

---

[1]Heidegger reminds us that, in many cases, we become aware of a tool we use (such as conceptualization), a tool that has become an extension of us, only when it is varied or fails to work.

[2]Sometimes the features associated with an entity and referenced by an utterance may not be required by the definition of the object (i.e. part of it meaning) but can be derived from the meaning. For example, the color of a sheep dog is not specified by the meaning of the term "sheep dog," yet we are able, using collected facts about the biological species of sheep dogs, to rule out certain colors as belonging to sheep dogs.

phor vehicle (i.e. bulldozers) and then the metaphor subject (i.e. Margaret Thatcher). This process of reconceptualization (i.e. of selection and suppression of features to individuate a thing) is guided by the *role* played by the entities within a *system* and with respect to their relationships within the system. For example, in order to comprehend an utterance of (5) one must conceive of a bulldozer (or the class of bulldozers) in terms of the relationships a bulldozer has to dirt, grass, limbs, and other things in its path, without attending to its individual characteristics. What emerges, epiphenomenally, from the network of relationships, is a role.

Finally, sentences such as (11) and (12), which don't seem to be metaphorical but are obviously false if taken literally, can be explained in different ways, depending upon one's analysis of metaphor and the contexts in which the utterances appear. Because of the complexity of what makes an utterance metaphorical, there are many ways an utterance can fail to be metaphorical. For example, an utterance of sentence (11) could be explained as a failed metaphor in that it is impossible to reconceptualize a semicolon and a period in such a way as to result in their being in the same class (i.e. there is no role). Another way of explaining this failure is to say that the metaphor fails because the interpreter cannot generate a class of which the comma is a prototypical representative and to which the semicolon can be assigned. This might seem strange, because semicolons and periods actually have more properties in common than the other metaphor subjects and vehicles on the list (i.e. being a part of speech and being used to punctuate independent clauses). However, it is precisely this great degree of similarity between the metaphor subject and vehicle that causes the utterance to fail to be metaphorical, rather than some general inability on the part of the metaphor subject to be reconceptualized. Note, for example, that in the utterance "Her tasteless remark was a period" the audience can easily reconceptualize a period in terms of the role it plays in language (i.e. that of putting an end to something) and then extrapolate that the person's remark ended the conversation. That is, while it is possible to reconceptualize a period in some contexts (i.e. with the right metaphor subject), it may not be possible in the wrong context. In the example given, the obvious contrast between in the metaphor vehicle (a part of speech) and the metaphor subject (tasteless remark) causes the audience to reconceptualize the metaphor vehicle, that is, to seek a way of understanding the metaphor vehicle in terms of the role it plays, rather than as a collection of individual features. In other words, the audience is forced to take a nonliteral perspective in order to comprehend the utterance.[3] In contrast, in an utterance of sentence (11), the metaphor subject and vehicle share so many features that the audience wants to take it literally. However, if the utterance is taken literally the utterance must be false due to the few features the metaphor subject and vehicle do not share. Thus the utterance seems anomalous. On the other hand, an utterance of sentence (12) does not seem anomalous, in that it is possible to generate a proposition the utterance can be said to express (i.e. that the man who ordered the ham sandwich wants a cup of coffee). However, since this proposition seems to emerge from adding the phrase "The customer who ordered" in front of the sentence, rather than by reconceptualizing a ham sandwich in terms of its role and then applying this to the customer, my analysis would say that this utterance is elliptical rather than metaphorical.[4]

Terminology

Analyzing the metaphorical in terms of reconceptualization (which has yet to be justified) has several interesting consequences, both for theories of metaphor and for theories of language. However, before examining the major claims of this analysis, their justification, and their consequences, we should set forth some of the relevant definitions. Within this analysis, some of the terms are part of an established terminology of philosophy of language, linguistics, and theories of metaphor. From philosophy of language I adopt the notion of *the proposition expressed* (according to Frege's use of the term) and *content* (according to Kaplan), used interchangeably to represent what the speaker says using an utterance (i.e. *what is said*). At the same time I distinguish between what an utterance says and what it *implies* (Gricean *implicature*), which is thought to be deduced from what is said. In accordance with the standard terminology of linguistics, I refer to sentences in which the subject of the sentence is being assigned to a certain class (sentence 4) as *nominative* and metaphors that do not have this pattern (sentence 7) as *non-nominative*. (One of the strengths of this analysis of metaphor is that it accounts for non-nom-

----

[3]Note that there is the phenomenon of mixed metaphors that jolt the audience by forcing them to take different perspectives within the process of trying to understand the comprehension of one idea.

[4]I thank Herb Clark for bringing up this example as a challenge to my analysis. An analysis that defines metaphoricity as utterances in which what is said (i.e. speaker meaning) is different from sentence meaning would not differentiate between the two and would thus classify (12) as metaphorical. Searle's theory would fall into this category.

inative metaphors as well as nominative metaphors, unlike some existing theories of metaphor, which base their analyses on metaphors being class inclusion statements.[5]) Another concept borrowed from philosophy of language is that of an *utterance*, intended to represent a sentence in a context. Since, as we have seen, a given sentence (such as 3) can be interpreted either metaphorically or not, it would be a fallacy to assert that metaphoricity occurs at the level of a sentence (regardless of context). Thus, in this analysis, utterances (sentences-in-a-context), are classified as metaphorical, not mere sentences.

From more traditional analyses of metaphor, I adopt the terms *metaphor subject* (or *topic*) and *metaphor vehicle*. According to this usage, the *metaphor subject* is the object being metaphorically presented or the object we are trying to understand via the metaphorical utterance.[6] In nominative metaphors (such as 4), the subject of the sentence (Steve) is the metaphor subject. In non-nominative metaphors such as (10), the subject of the metaphor need not be the subject of the sentence. For example, the metaphor subject of an utterance of (10) would be the process of experiencing memories that the speaker is attempting to describe by using a metaphor. In contrast, the *metaphor vehicle* is the entity used by the speaker to convey an understanding of the metaphor subject. In other words, the metaphor vehicle (in Black's terms, the *focus*) is the term being applied metaphorically. The entity to which it refers can also be described as the prototypical representative of the class to which the metaphor subject is assigned via reconceptualization.[7] In nominative metaphors, the metaphor vehicle is the prototypical representative of the class to which the metaphor subject is being assigned. For example, the metaphor vehicle

---

[5]Glucksberg and Keysar's theory falls into this category. See, for example, Sam Glucksberg and Boaz Keysar, "Understanding Metaphorical Comparisons: Beyond Similarity," *Psychological Review*, 97, no. 1 (1990): 3–18.

[6]Note that the metaphor subject can refer to an entity or to a term that refers to an entity.

[7]See Glucksburg and Keysar's theory. Note that the metaphor vehicle has several notions associated with it. For example, the metaphor vehicle in (8) has a term associated with it ("butterfly") and an entity or class to which it literally refers. Once the notion of conceptualization is introduced, the list increases. In addition to the entity as traditionally conceived (i.e. the biologically determined butterfly), we also have the entity or class as reconceptualized (i.e. the entity or class of flighty things). For the purpose of this work, it is not necessary to define each notion separately. In general, the term "metaphor vehicle" refers to the entity associated with the term, *prior* to the issue of reconceptualization. If a more specific distinction is needed (i.e. that between the metaphor vehicle as traditionally conceived and as metaphorically conceived), it is made clear in that context.

in an utterance of sentence (4) is a sheep dog, which is the prototypical representative of a class of entities which bear a certain relationship to other entities within a system. Another entity in this class might be a teacher and a tour guide. In non-nominative metaphors, the metaphor vehicle still represents the reconceptualizing class, but the metaphor subject is *assumed* to be a member of the class rather than explicitly assigned to it in the utterance in question. For example, in an utterance of (8), the speaker assumes that the metaphor subject belongs to the class represented by the metaphor vehicle (i.e. that of butterflies).

Within this analysis I also introduce terms of my own and refashion existing terms according to the needs of the analysis. One of the terms I refashion is that of interpretation. In my analysis, an *interpretation* of an utterance is the resulting product of the audience's attempt to grasp what the speaker said by uttering a sentence (in other words, a proposition). Although any given utterance expresses only one proposition, a sentence or utterance may be interpreted in many ways, and each interpretation may be either metaphorical or literal. For example, one can derive both a metaphorical and a literal interpretation of sentence (3). Given Kaplan's use of the term "content," the *literal content* of an utterance is the proposition one would derive by interpreting the utterance literally. Contrarily, the *metaphorical content* of an utterance is the proposition one would derive by interpreting the utterance metaphorically.

An utterance is accordingly said to be *metaphorical* if the interpretation which best fits in with the information provided by the context is metaphorical. For example, given a conversation about the former prime minister of the United Kingdom, an utterance of sentence (5) in our list would be considered metaphorical. (Note that while it may be verifiable that an utterance has a certain interpretation that is metaphorical, it may *not* be decidable whether or not the context uniquely requires that interpretation so that the utterance can definitively said to be metaphorical. That is, whether or not a particular interpretation is metaphorical and whether the utterance itself is metaphorical are two different issues, decided on the basis of different factors.)[8]

A *metaphorical context* is one which favors a metaphorical interpretation of the utterance in question. That is, a context that highlights proper-

---

[8]Note that the speaker's intention to speak metaphorically is not sufficient to make the utterance metaphorical. As in literal speech, the speaker is responsible for controlling features of context in such a way as to facilitate the interpretation of the utterance the speaker intends to communicate.

ties either not present or suppressed in the ordinary conception of the denoted entities or encourages a look toward relational properties is metaphorical. For example, a discussion about people's ways of interacting with other people favors a metaphorical reading of "Margaret Thatcher is a bulldozer." Since relational properties of entities (i.e. the role they play in a given system) are less likely to be specified in an ordinary conception than individual attributes (i.e. being solid, animate, etc.), metaphors are often used to attribute relational properties to the subject of the metaphor (as well as to those with which the subject interacts). This is accomplished as follows: since the individual properties of the metaphor subject and vehicle are in such obvious conflict, they rule each other out so that functional and/or relational properties are highlighted. For example, in (4), since the material properties of Steve and sheep dogs are clearly in conflict, we dismiss them as irrelevant and focus on relational properties. Any given context or situation is only metaphorical relative to a particular utterance. For example, a situation in which the speaker is discussing the character of a person provides a metaphorical context for an utterance of sentences (3) and (4) above. However, it would provide a literal context for an utterance of another sentence, such as "He gets frustrated easily."

An interpretation of an utterance is a *metaphorical interpretation* if, rather than being tied to it by linguistic convention (i.e. the rules of the language), it stands in a metaphorical relation to it such that its comprehension requires a different way of conceiving of some or all of the entities referenced in the utterance.

Two terms that take on a technical role in this analysis are the terms "system" and "role." In my analysis, a *system* is a related group of entities, where the entities in question are those that are part of our naive metaphysics (a *schema* or, in Goodman's terms, a *realm*). For example, since midwives often appear with laboring mothers and babies struggling to be born, we can say that these entities constitute a system. Likewise, sheep dogs and the sheep they herd form a system. A given entity or group of entities might form many different systems, and the boundaries of a system need not be clearly defined.[9] For example, the midwife also has a certain relationships with doctors and hospitals (typically one of exclusion)

---

[9]As we shall see later, the fact that any given entity can be part of different systems and can play different roles provides difficulty for an account (such as that of Glucksberg and Keysar) which takes the metaphor vehicle as a static representative of a certain class, via prototypicality. It is precisely the variety of ways in which any given entity can be conceived, based on its role in a system, which gives metaphor its power and open-ended quality.

and thus can be used to evoke a different system. Also, in the case of sheep dogs, one might define a system to include the sheepherder, or not. The term *"role"* refers to the part an entity plays within a certain system, the relationships it has with the other entities. For example, the midwife has a certain role in the system of labor and delivery, as defined by the relationship the midwife bears to the mother and the infant. The notion of a role is critical to my analysis in that it is according to the role the metaphor vehicle is thought to represent that the selection of features, the determination of what is relevant or irrelevant, takes place. That is, the role serves as a basis for reconceptualizing first the metaphor vehicle and then the metaphor subject. As a result, metaphors with metaphor vehicles whose role is preeminent are much easier to understand than those in which it is not. Thus the comparative ease of understanding "Steve is a sheep dog" vs. "John's mind is a meadow in winter."[10]

Finally, the notion most critical to my analysis is that of *reconceptualization*, itself based on the notion of *conceptualization*. Logical positivists, together with another band of twentieth-century thinkers, have argued against intensional notions such as conceptualization, and their arguments have greatly shaped the modern study of language. However, the increasingly large number of phenomena which cannot be accounted for by purely extensional theories of language, together with the clear incompatibility of some of the assumptions of their view of natural language (we consider this in Chapter 2) force another approach on us. Although we begin to explain and justify the notion of reconceptualization in this chapter, the most compelling justification of the notion of reconceptualization lies in the analysis of metaphor it enables, which in turn accounts for the features of metaphor we uncover throughout this work. As a result, arguments directed to support the analysis as a whole also substantiate the use of reconceptualization as its basis.

At a basic level, to reconceptualize something is to change one's conception of what that thing is. Thus to the extent that the notion of conceptualization is critical to the notion of reconceptualization, we must also present an account of conceptualization. However, must account for it *only* to this extent, in the way one can identify a rerun of a movie without knowing the details of the movie or how it was made. That is, if we are

---

[10]In fact, metaphor vehicles of this type seem likely to become incorporated into the language in that the (literal) meaning of the term might shift over time to leave behind individual characteristics of the entity (such as being a dog) and come to represent the role.

able to establish that conceptualization underlies literal language use and that this conceptualization is overhauled in metaphorical language use, without completely accounting for the nature of conceptualization, this would be sufficient for our purposes.

Central to the notion of conceptualization (and reconceptualization) is the differentiation of objects (or individuation) and the creation of classes or kinds. In other words, we conceive of a thing in terms of features, both individual and relational (i.e. in terms of relationships with others). This individuation and creation of classes is a cognitive process that underlies all language and, in the case of most language use, goes unnoticed, inasmuch as we take the features of the entity referred to to be specified by the meaning of the term. However, in metaphorical utterances, in which most individual attributes of the entity are irrelevant, we are forced to reexamine the attributes of a thing that our naive metaphysics predicts, search out those that are relevant, and discard those that are not. That is, in processing a metaphor we take the entities of our naive metaphysics and reconceptualize them, thus also changing the taxonomy that underlies and guides language processing and the chain of inferences that follow from processing a certain utterance. The result of this is a new concept, a new way of individuating the entity in question and a new class of entities based on the new concept. It is important to note that the type of reconceptualization which occurs in metaphorical (and other figurative utterances) is radically different from that which occurs in the process of abstraction, despite superficial similarities. For example, consider what happens when we process the utterance "Apples and pears are fruit." In assigning an entity to a super-ordinate class using a literal class inclusion statement, we ignore certain features of the individual entities (those different) and focus on others (those in common). However, although we ignore certain features temporarily and focus on others, we do not restructure the standardized metaphysics or taxonomy but only temporarily focus on certain parts and, in the case of class inclusion statements, add a node or so to the standardized tree.[11]

AN EXAMPLE

Given this terminology, we are equipped to describe an analysis of metaphorical utterances. In the case of nominative metaphors, such as an utterance of "Steve is a sheep dog," the grammatical form of the utterance

[11]For more on the distinction between the metaphorical and literal, see the second assumption discussed later in this chapter.

dictates that the audience assign the subject of the sentence (and the metaphor) to the class represented by the metaphor vehicle. Since the utterance is metaphorical, the class represented by the metaphor vehicle is *not* the class dictated by the meaning of the term. Instead, the audience must reconceptualize the metaphor vehicle to determine the intended class. In other words, the audience must leave behind certain features of sheep dogs and select others in order to arrive at a class of which the metaphor vehicle is a prototypical representative. The process of reconceptualization is bounded by contextual information, such as the metaphor subject, the topic of conversation, and other aspects concerning the metaphor vehicle mentioned in the conversation. Most immediately, the obvious contrast between the metaphor subject and vehicle in terms of individual characteristics (reflected also in the distance between the two in any ordinary taxonomy) indicates that the audience is speaking in terms of role and relational properties rather than in terms of individual characteristics (as is done in literal speech); thus the latter immediately become irrelevant.[12] As a result, the audience uses contextual information to derive the system in which the metaphor vehicle plays a role, by determining the other entities to which the metaphor vehicle is typically related and the relationships it bears to those entities. In the case of sheep dogs, a system of sheep dogs and sheep immediately comes to mind, where sheep dogs behave in a certain way toward sheep. This system can then be used to generate syllogisms which can be used to determine what is being said about the metaphor subject (i.e. Steve). For example, the metaphor in question produces the syllogism: Sheep dogs : sheep :: Steve : ? Applying analogical reasoning, the audience can use this syllogism, along with information provided either in the immediate conversational context or from past conversations, to infer the entities toward which Steve behaves as sheep dogs do toward sheep. The final task is to deduce the particular relationships Steve bears toward the other entities in the relevant system. That is, the audience infers how to reconceptualize the metaphor subject (i.e. what features to

[12]The way these characteristics become irrelevant is different from the way certain characteristics are irrelevant in certain instances of literal speech. For example, in processing an utterance of "A whale is a mammal" certain features of the whale are irrelevant to an understanding of what is being said. For example, you don't need to know how much whales weigh or what color they are. However, this does not mean that to understand the utterance, the audience must conceive of a whale as colorless or weightless. In fact, to do so would be counter-productive. In contrast, in the case of metaphorical utterances, the features that are deemed irrelevant become counterproductive to a proper conception of the metaphor subject.

attribute to it). One thing to keep in mind is that while metaphorical utterances are typically cited in the absence of context, they usually appear in rich conversational or written contexts in which the speaker and audience exchange further information in pursuit of the relevant reconceptualization. For example, the utterance cited would probably be followed by the question "Is he like that at work, or with family and friends?"

In the case of non-nominative metaphors, while the surface form is different, the underlying processes (involving the selection of the relevant systems, the construction of a new class in terms of the role the metaphor vehicle plays in the relevant system, and the reconceptualization of the metaphor vehicle and subject) are the same. For example, in an utterance of sentence (7), the subject of the utterance (the sock) is not being assigned to a class. Nor is the subject of the utterance the subject of the metaphor. Instead the metaphor subject is some part of the sock that the speaker is referring to as a hangnail, while the metaphor vehicle is the hangnail. However, while the structure is different from that of a nominative metaphor, to comprehend the utterance one must undergo the same processes. First one must reconceptualize the metaphor vehicle (hangnail) in terms of the role a hangnail plays in a system. In this case, neither the role nor the system comes easily to mind as in the case of bulldozers and sheep dogs. In this case the system consists mainly of the hangnail and the foot to which it is attached. Thus the following syllogism emerges: Hangnail : foot :: X : sock. Since the most obvious feature of hangnails is that they protrude and, given the confinement of a shoe, need to be clipped, the audience must conclude that this is the relevant feature of the item in question. In this case the metaphor is used only to refer to an item whose name the speaker does not know.[13]

In other non-nominative metaphors, the process may be more difficult. For example, consider an utterance of sentence (10). In this utterance the speaker is describing an event or process, specifically, something the speaker went through in the days that came after their father's death. In this metaphor, unlike the previous one, more than one entity is mentioned (i.e. halls and memories), yet they are ostensibly from different systems, the former a concrete system and the latter an abstract state. To understand the utterance, the audience must reconceptualize the entities in such

---

[13]Despite the apparent triviality of this metaphor, it is still metaphorical. In contrast, if the speaker had said, instead "Mom, my sock has a thingamajig," the utterance would *not* have been metaphorical. What makes the utterance metaphorical is that the audience must reconceptualize hangnails in order to determine what item is being mentioned.

a way as to be able to compare the process to something involving memories. One syllogism the audience might use is one in which rooms have been plugged in as a means of fleshing out the physical system that serves as a model for the process the speaker is trying to describe: walking halls : rooms :: X : memories.

MAJOR CLAIMS OF THE ANALYSIS

Underlying this analysis of metaphor are the following major claims. I propose that (1) metaphor is *not* a matter of meaning. However, in opposition to Davidson, I am committed to: (2) the fact that a metaphorical utterance has a metaphorical content which has satisfaction conditions different from those that the same utterance would have if it were taken literally, (3) the identification of the metaphorical content of a metaphorical utterance in a metaphorical context as the proposition it expresses, and (4) the classification of this metaphorical content as semantic (as the proposition expressed).[14] Finally, and most importantly, I propose that (5) metaphoricity, that which distinguishes metaphorical utterances from literal utterances, is not determined by the speaker's intention to speak metaphorically but stems from the relationship between the class represented by the metaphor vehicle (using Black's terminology) when interpreted literally and the class to which the term refers when used metaphorically. That is, in my analysis the metaphoricity of a given utterance consists of the reconstruction of the concepts appealed to within the utterance. As a result, the metaphorical content of a metaphor is one which is different from the literal interpretation of the utterance but is related to it in that it is produced by a change in one's conception of some or all of the entities (literally) referenced by the utterance. One of the results of this claim is that what distinguishes metaphorical content from literal content in my analysis is the fact that the properties (and classes) predicted or assumed of the subject of the metaphor are not those accessed via (and consistent with) either linguistic or conceptual (taxonomic) convention. As a result, the metaphorical content of a particular metaphorical utterance is the product of reconceptualization, rather than either the content of an elliptical simile (as Fogelin would hold) or an encoded message created from the interaction of the literal meanings (as Black would hold).[15] These

[14]Rumelhart, Glucksberg and Keysar, Moravcsik, and others have begun to debate the issue of whether the proposition expressed by an utterance is completely determined semantically, that is, by the information provided by linguistic competence.

[15]Comparativists analyze metaphorical content by claiming that it is actually the

claims constitute the backbone of my analysis of metaphor, and the remaining chapters are devoted to arguing for them (as well as to expanding the list of conditions a theory of metaphor must satisfy).

Outline

In the introduction to this book I establish 9 criteria for judging a theory of metaphor. In Chapter 2 I argue that metaphorical utterances have a metaphorical content which is different from their literal content (Claim 2). I also argue for the existence of metaphorical content and truth (Criterion 3) and establish the need for a theory of metaphor to be consistent with the framework provided by semantics (Criterion 10). In Chapter 3 I argue against an analysis of metaphor as a matter of meaning (Claim 1). I also establish three additional criteria with which to judge a theory of metaphor: the dependence of the metaphorical on literal meaning (Criterion 11), the lack of conventionality of metaphor (Criterion 12), and the fact that metaphors are about the world (Criterion 13). In Chapter 4 I argue against speaker intention as a creator of metaphoricity (Criterion 14). I also argue in favor of the existence of a distinct metaphorical content (Claim 2), one which constitutes the proposition expressed by the utterance (Claim 3). In Chapter 5 I argue against an identification of metaphorical content as a conversational implicature (Grice and Martinich) or the content of ironic utterances (Searle's speaker meaning) and, on these grounds, against its classification as use-based or pragmatic. Instead, I argue that metaphorical content plays the role of the proposition expressed by the metaphorical utterance (Claim 3), and if the proposition expressed by an utterance is considered to be semantic rather than pragmatic, then so too must we classify metaphorical content (Claim 4). In Chapter 6 I argue against a classification of metaphorical as the indirect content of an indirect speech act (Claims 3 and 4) and examine and argue for the proposed analysis of the metaphorical as a matter of reconceptualization, that is, of metaphoricity as a relation between the proposition actually expressed and that produced by a literal interpretation of the utterance

---

content of a comparison statement. In other words, the content of "Steve is a sheep dog" is actually the proposition that compares Steve to a sheep dog. In my analysis, there is no transformation of the form of the utterance. As a result, a nominative metaphor (such as most of those above) remains a class inclusion statement, that is, a statement that assigns the subject of the metaphor to a certain class. In this respect, my analysis is similar to that of Glucksberg and Keysar. However, it goes beyond theirs in that it accounts for all types of metaphors, be they nominative or not.

(Claim 5). In Chapter 7 I evaluate my analysis according to the criteria we have established to evaluate theories of metaphor. In the remainder of this chapter I will examine and argue for some of the major assumptions that underlie this analysis of metaphor.

Assumptions

Because metaphorical utterances are communicative acts, any theory of metaphor is inevitably connected to a theory of such acts. Inasmuch as a theory of communicative acts depends upon the notion of meaning, a theory of metaphor must also assume a theory of semantics. For the purposes of this work, I assume a theory of semantics similar to the Fregean, holding (1) that meaning is compositional, (2) that propositions are the same as Fregean thoughts or content (i.e. what is capable of being true or false), and (3) that the content of an utterance is the proposition expressed by that utterance. In addition, I assume a distinction between meaning and content like that of Kaplan, such that while the meaning of an utterance may be context-independent, its content may be context-dependent.[16]

Another of my primary linguistic or semantic assumptions is that utterances (i.e. sentences in a context) can be interpreted in more than one way and that each different interpretation of an utterance produces a different proposition with different truth (or satisfaction) conditions. For example, I hold that an utterance of sentence (3) expresses a different proposition depending upon whether it is interpreted literally or metaphorically. If interpreted literally, an utterance of (3) will be true if and only if the person in question has no doorbell. However, if the utterance is interpreted metaphorically, the presence of a doorbell is irrelevant to the truth value of the utterance. Given this definition of interpretation, the act of interpreting a term or proposition becomes the act of deriving either the contribution a particular term makes to the proposition expressed or the proposition itself.[17] (Note that this terminology is intended to correspond to and substitute for the common way of describing the same phenomenon as that of "taking" an utterance either literally or metaphorically.)[18] This is not to

[16]Thanks to Josef Stern for this point.

[17]Note that this position distinguishes this analysis from Davidson's and from most of traditional semantics in that it denies that the proposition expressed by an utterance is determined solely by the rules of the language. However, the position is compatible with some of the work done by philosophers such as Kaplan, Donnellan, Perry, and Moravcsik and by psychologists such as Carston and Recanati.

[18]This use of the term "metaphorical interpretation" is consistent with Good-

say, however, that in opening the door to the possibility that an utterance may be interpreted in different ways I am claiming that there are no constraints on the possible interpretations. One constraint on possible interpretations is provided by the meanings of the terms. (This is confirmed by the fact that we cannot process a metaphor if we do not know the literal meaning of its terms.) Others, as Moravcsik points out, are provided by the society, the culture, and information given in the context either directly ("What I mean by emergency is . . .") or indirectly ("She's such a princess. She has to have her own way and she never does any work").

It is important to note that the possibility that an utterance may have more than one interpretation does not mean that it is metaphorical. That is, there are utterances with more than one possible literal interpretation as well, such as cases of utterances containing ambiguous expressions (sentence 2). For example, given an utterance of "I think I'll visit the bank tomorrow," the speaker could be saying (1) that she intends to go to the bank of the river, where she usually goes to fish (literal); (2) that she intends to go to her bank (First Arizona); (3) that she intends to visit her inscrutable, rich uncle; or (4) that she intends to get her money out from under the mattress of her bed. Neither are cases of ambiguity the only types of literal utterances which have more than one possible interpretation and whose truth conditions are not completely determined by semantic factors. A case in point is the now familiar case of utterances containing indexicals, whose interpretation requires that the speaker have certain contextual information.

Another case in point is that of utterances containing terms like "emergency," whose truth conditions, as Moravcsik points out, are not determined by the meaning of the term but rather only constrained by them so that the speaker and audience need to spell them out and reach an agreement upon each occasion of use (unless the immediate context or history of use can substitute for this).[19]

One final example of utterances whose content is not determined semantically is cases of the kind Donnellan cites in which definite descriptions are successfully used to refer to certain objects even though those objects fail to uniquely satisfy the criteria specified by the definition.[20]

---

man's. As an extensionalist, Goodman does not speak of metaphorical meaning but rather of the metaphorical application of a term.

[19]Julius Moravcsik, "Between Reference and Meaning," *Midwest Studies in Philosophy*, 14 (1989): 68–83.

[20]Keith Donnellan, "Reference and Definite Descriptions," *Philosophical Review* 75 (1966): 281–304.

Since no one would claim that the previous examples[21] are cases of metaphorical or even figurative utterances, an analysis of metaphor must not only account for the similarities between metaphor and these phenomena but also for the differences between them.[22] Some theorists, while accepting the inability of the rules of the language (i.e. the meanings of the terms and the rules of composition) to completely determine the proposition expressed by an utterance, challenge the very notion of metaphoricity by claiming that there is little difference between literal and metaphorical utterances. In fact, many of these theorists use the fact that the proposition expressed by both literal and metaphorical utterances is not determined by the rules of the language but requires both contextual information and knowledge of how the world works as evidence to support the claim that there is no distinction between the literal and the metaphorical. (To further substantiate this claim they also cite the results of their studies as evidence that the comprehension process of literal and metaphorical utterances is identical.)[23]

Among the factors that determine the diversity of ways of interpreting an utterance is the diversity of ways of conceptualizing the world and the objects within it (as represented within the utterance). For example, different ways of conceptualizing bulldozers (i.e. as a class of land-moving equipment rather than a class of pushy beings that interact with others in a steadily aggressive manner) produce different propositions (with different truth conditions). Accordingly, another important assumption of this

---

[21]Note that the ability of a certain sentence type to have different interpretations in a given context can also be described in terms of context dependence.

[22]Note that this task is different than the task of distinguishing between the metaphorical and phenomena of use (such as implicatures) in that the latter is a defense of the metaphorical as an issue of the proposition expressed by an utterance and the former a defense of that which is figurative, as opposed to literal.

[23]David Rumelhart makes this claim in "Some Problems with Literal Meanings," in *Metaphor and Thought*, ed. A. Ortony (Cambridge: Cambridge University Press, 1979), pp. 78–90. Raymond Gibbs uses his studies of conventionalized indirect speech acts and metaphors in appropriate contexts to claim that there is no difference between the processing of literal and metaphorical utterances and to propose a new model of comprehension. "A Critical Examination of the Contribution of Literal Meaning to Understanding Nonliteral Discourse," *Text* 2, nos. 1–3 (1982): 9–27. Dan Sperber and Deirdre Wilson claim that what we call metaphorical utterances are, in fact, merely instances of what they call "loose talk." In their conception, speakers are not committed, as Grice and most of the tradition believes, by a conversational principle that guarantees the truth of the proposition expressed by each utterance; instead, they are bound to the maximum informativeness of the utterance, which includes both the proposition expressed and its implicatures. "Loose Talk," in *Pragmatics*, ed. Steven Davis (Oxford: Oxford University Press, 1991), pp. 540–49.

analysis is that underlying language use is our naive notion of what it is to be a certain thing which, for the purpose of this work, I call the conception of a thing. For example, underlying our comprehension of an utterance of (1) is the understanding of a sheep dog as a certain kind of thing, that is, our conception of a sheep dog. In my analysis, the conception of a thing is the result of a process of conceptualization, in which certain features of a thing are taken as relevant to that thing and others are taken as irrelevant. Within the realm of language use, the practical consequence of conceptualization is that it determines which features are relevant to determining the referent of a term or to understanding an utterance. Conceptualization can be described in either extensional or intensional terms. That is, we can describe what it is to be a bulldozer by saying that it belongs in a certain class of objects or by attempting to list the features an object must have to be considered a bulldozer. The conceptualization underlying language use is reflected in the meanings associated with terms in our language, but is not necessarily limited to it. That is, we may attribute many features to a particular sheep dog that we would not claim are required by the definition of a term or part of its meaning. For example, we can refer to the weight of a sheep dog or the fact that it maintains a distinct boundary between itself and other objects. The process of conceptualization (or differentiation of kinds) is attached to what I call a pretheoretic or naive metaphysics concerning what exists in the world and what features we note in existing entities that we deem relevant to their existence.

One of the problems with associating conceptualization with a theory of language is that any one object can be conceived of in a number of ways. For example, we can conceive of a given sheep dog as this particular sheep dog, as a sheep dog with blue eyes, as a dog, as an animal, as a mammal, or as an animate being. Each type of conception places the sheep dog within a different level of abstraction which, in turn, allows one to associate certain features with it and make certain inferences about it.[24] However, within the multiplicity of ways of conceiving of a thing we can distinguish two fundamental types. On the one hand, we can conceive of a thing in terms of the features it has as an entity existing independently within what we consider to be an objective world. On the other, we can conceive of an entity in terms of the role it plays within a system of relationships, itself a subset of what we consider to be the objective world. For

[24]The multiplicity of levels of conception is one of the things that makes it extremely difficult to determine what a child knows when s/he points to a glass and says "juice."

example, the class of sheep dogs can be conceived of as a certain species bred and trained to perform a certain function or it can be conceived of solely in terms of the relationships sheep dogs bear to other entities in their workplace. As a result, being a sheep dog can require and predict different features and inferences depending on how it is conceived. Likewise, a given person can be conceived as an individual member of a certain species with a certain historical background or s/he can be conceived solely in terms of relationships s/he bears to others in her/his workplace.

Given our existence in the world as physical entities, we tend to characterize entities and create classes of entities (types) in terms of individual and physical features and our pretheoretic or naive metaphysics postulates entities as objectively existing independently of our perception of them. As a result, the traditional taxonomy of physical beings is based upon individual (usually physical) features. For example, the criteria for being in the class of sheep dogs are physical features that serve to distinguish sheep dogs from other biological entities. As a result, the conceptualization that underlies literal language use is that which defines entities in terms of the features they are thought to have as independently existing objects. This does not necessarily mean that sheep dogs are defined in terms of genetics, although certain species are such that the test of whether they are members of the class is in the hands of experts. In contrast, in some cases, as with sheep dogs, being trained in the behavior of sheep dogs is sufficient to make that individual qualify as a sheep dog. Yet in both cases, despite the breadth or narrowness of the genetic definition (i.e. requiring that the individual be a dog or a certain kind of dog), the criterion for being members of these classes is based upon individual and physical characteristics of the entities. Literal speech draws upon this conceptualization. However, sometimes in our pursuit of coming to know a certain entity or event, what is relevant is not the individual characteristics of that thing, according to its existence in the world generated by our naive metaphysics. Instead, what is relevant is the role the object plays among other objects that are significant to us. (The philosopher's view of reality behind the appearances.) In these cases metaphorical speech is often appropriate and reconceptualization is called for.

The final major assumption of this theory that there *is* a fundamental difference between the metaphorical and the literal, despite a strong connection between the two and an abundance of data that fall between them. In fact, the key task of any analysis of metaphor is to account for metaphoricity, that which serves to differentiate metaphors (1) from literal utterances (even those whose interpretation is not semantically determined) and (2) from anomalous utterances (or category mistakes). Under this analysis, the difference between the two, what makes one utterance of a class inclusion statement literal and one metaphorical is based upon the relationship between the class to which the term literally refers and that to which it refers within the metaphor (i.e. such that the latter is a reconceptualization of the first) and upon the reconceptualization of the metaphor subject into this class.

One of the most immediate differences between the metaphorical and the literal interpretations of an utterance lies in the fact that they appear to have different truth conditions. For example, if the interpreter takes the utterance "He lives in a structure without a doorbell or any windows" to be literal, the truth conditions will be very different than if they take it to be metaphorical. That is, if one takes the utterance literally, whether the person's house has a door with a doorbell is relevant whereas, if one takes the utterance metaphorically, this does not matter, while certain personality traits of the person do matter. However, since the truth conditions of a class inclusion statement clearly depend on the class to which the subject is assigned membership, and since the terms referring to the class are the same whether one takes the utterance literally or metaphorically, the truth conditions of both interpretations should be the same. The analysis I propose accounts for this difference by claiming that under different interpretations (i.e. literal vs. metaphorical and within each category among the different possibilities), the class represented by the term used metaphorically is different. In other words, what makes the class inclusion statement in (1) literal is the fact that the class to which the subject of the sentence is being assigned is the class assigned to that term under the rules of the language. In contrast, in a metaphorical interpretation, the class to which the subject of the class inclusion statement is assigned is not the class assigned to it by the rules of the language but rather must be derived by the speaker using some other means (so far unspecified). Given this analysis, the truth conditions of a metaphorical interpretation of an utterance are different from the truth conditions of its literal interpretation because the class to which the subject is assigned is different in each case.

Since the term that refers to the class is the same in each case, one might want to attempt to explain the variety of classes referenced by classifying the term used metaphorically as semantically ambiguous. However, as we shall see in Chapter 3, terms used metaphorically are *not* ambiguous in such a way that the metaphorical meaning (or referent) of the term is one of many literal meanings of that term. In fact, as soon as the metaphorical meaning becomes one of the literal meanings of a term, that meaning ceases to be metaphorical. Instead, under this analysis, the difference between the interpretations lies in the fact that we can conceptualize entities in different ways. That is, while an object may be a member of a class in that its name assigns it to that class and it has all the features of that class, it may also belong or be a prototypical member of another ad hoc category, which may conflict with the common taxonomy by grouping supposedly unlike entities together.[25]

Under this analysis, in metaphorical utterances of the nominative form the subject of the metaphor is assigned to an ad hoc category of which the metaphor vehicle is a prototypical member. For example, in the case of the metaphorical utterance "Margaret Thatcher is a bulldozer," Margaret Thatcher is proclaimed to be in a class of which bulldozers are prototypical exemplars. The utterance is metaphorical because the class to which Margaret Thatcher is being assigned is not the class to which the term "bulldozer" literally refers (that is, refers according to the rules of the language). Instead, the class to which Margaret Thatcher is assigned is an ad hoc category of which bulldozers are considered to be prototypical member. As a result, in order to process the utterance, the audience must decide what ad hoc category bulldozers represent in this situation in order to decide what it means for Margaret Thatcher to belong in that class (i.e. what proposition is being conveyed) before even attempting to evaluate the truth value of the utterance. Thus the metaphoricity of the utterance stems from the fact that in order to correctly understand the utterance, we must change some of the categories through which we conceptualize the world so that Margaret Thatcher and bulldozers can be said to be in the same category.[26] That is, implicit in metaphorical utterances is the proposal of a new category scheme such that objects that were previously not considered of the same group, now are.[27] In the present analysis, this proposal is what makes the utterance figurative, differentiating it from a class inclusion statement with the same truth conditions as the metaphorical utterance. That is, it is neither the actual proposition expressed by the utterance (that Margaret Thatcher is pushy) nor the fact that an ad hoc cate-

---

[25]My thanks to Sam Glucksberg and Boaz Keysar for pointing out to me that the metaphor vehicle tends to be the prototypical member of the new class.

[26]This description is similar to Black's in that Black explains metaphor as seeing one thing through another. However, this analysis explains what it means to see one thing in terms of another in terms of the use of a different category scheme or taxonomy.

[27]This feature of this analysis is reminiscent of Goodman.

gory is used in the class inclusion statement that makes the utterance metaphorical. To see this, we need only consider a literal utterance that expresses the same proposition as the metaphor. For example, we can compare the metaphor about Margaret Thatcher with the literal utterance of "Margaret Thatcher is the kind of person who gets her way in any encounter with other people, even if they make strenuous objections to what she wants. No one can win in an encounter with her." A literal utterance that expresses the same proposition as the metaphor is essentially a literal paraphrase of the metaphor in that it expresses the same content and thus has the same truth conditions. In the example given, while most would agree this proposition has the same truth conditions as the metaphor in question (given an appropriate context), and it makes use of an ad hoc category, it is not metaphorical. Since the category which is the subject of the sentence is the same in each case, it cannot be this that makes the utterance metaphorical. Nor can it be the content itself, since this too is the same in both the metaphorical interpretation and its literal paraphrase. Neither can the metaphoricity stem from the fact that the truth conditions of this utterance are spelled out rather than given indirectly via the category name, since sentences that contain ad hoc categories are not considered to be metaphorical for this reason alone.

The difference between a metaphorical interpretation of an utterance and its literal paraphrase arises, at least in part, from the difference in the way the category in question is accessed. In the literal paraphrase, the category accessed by a description of its truth conditions via the rules of the language in such a way that truth conditions of the utterance depends upon the fact that any properties hinted at or explicitly mentioned in the description must be instantiated in any object. For example, whether or not an utterance of "X is the kind of person who gets their way in any encounter with other people, even if they make strenuous objections to what that person wants" is true depends upon whether X has all the properties explicitly mentioned (such as getting their way) as well as those hinted at (such as being human). In contrast, in the case of metaphor the term that represents the class in question refers (via the rules of the language) to an object that instantiates all the properties given in the definition of the term, many of which are considered to be irrelevant to the ad hoc category which it is used in this context to represent. As a result, the truth conditions of the metaphorical utterance are not given by the rules of the language and the audience must derive the definition of the class and the resulting truth conditions of the utterance by reconceptualizing their view of the metaphorical vehicle using an abstraction process. At the same time, we also change our view of the subject of the metaphor since the category to which it is assigned emphasizes certain properties (such as the way it interacts with other entities and leaves out others entirely (such as one's genus, species, proper name, etc.). Another way of describing what makes the utterance metaphorical is to appeal to the fact that a new category scheme, with its corresponding inclusion, accentuating, exclusion and de-emphasis of features, is proposed as the means for understanding the subject of the metaphor. The biologist, in presenting his taxonomy of reptiles, is saying not only that the animals can be distinguished from each other in the way shown but also that this particular way of dividing things up and the resulting selection and emphasis of certain properties is the best way of understanding the entities in question.[28] In the same way, when Socrates describes the philosopher as the pilot of the city he is saying that the category scheme underlying his description (in which the city is a cohesive entity that requires guiding by a human being, namely the philosopher) allows a better understanding of the philosopher and her/his role (and of the other entities in question, such as the city) than a category scheme that classifies philosophers as nonworking talkers or even as students of philosophical works.

Background: Class Inclusion Theory

According to the analysis we propose in this chapter, metaphorical utterances are utterances in which reconceptualization alters the class inclusion that is either explicit (if the statement is nominative) or implicit (if not). As a result, before proceeding with my analysis of metaphor I should explain some of the basic concepts of class inclusion or categorization theory. Class inclusion statements claim that the subject of the sentence falls into the class described in the predicate. In other words, class inclusion statements answer the implicit question of what *kind* of thing the subject is. One of the ways we reach or communicate an understanding of a thing, its essential features, is by appealing to classification, as embodied in class inclusion statements. Given the philosophical insight that the properties of any entity are potentially infinite, no two things can really be identified. As a result, in order to group things together or say that they are of the same kind, we must make decisions about what features of a

---

[28]Keysar and Glucksberg seem to take the fact that metaphoricity is based on a proposal of a new category scheme as evidence that it is a matter of use, which they contrast with one of processing or comprehension.

thing are essential enough to count as a way of individuating that thing. For example, in creating the category of apple, we must leave aside certain features (such as coming from a tree with the same number of leaves) and select certain others that can serve as a way of determining whether or not something is an apple.[29] One way of appealing to classification is to make use of the categories that underlie class inclusion statements (as embodied by literal statements of the form "A is a B") and, indeed, all language use in general.[30] For example, in saying that a whale is a mammal we convey the proposition that all whales fall into a certain category, that designated by the term "mammal" according to the rules of the language. However, as the study of metaphor reveals, there is more than one way of appealing to classification.

The Basic Picture

Neither class inclusion statements nor the categories that underlie them exist in a vacuum. That is, class inclusion statements of the sort described presuppose a *taxonomy*, a hierarchy or structure of categories organized in such a way that, depending on where they fall in the structure, individual objects have specific relationships with others within the same structure. The most common way of depicting a taxonomy is via a *category tree*, that is, as sketch in which categories are represented as nodes in a tree connected by lines. Category trees such as the one in Figure 1 represent the organization of the objects of our world as members of groups, each of which corresponds to a category. For example, the category tree in Figure 1 shows where Margaret Thatcher and bulldozers fit into a taxonomy of concrete objects.

As a result, a category tree can be described in terms of a group membership in which each member of a group at a certain location within the tree is also a member of any group above it in the tree and connected to it by lines. (Such groups can be called *"ancestor groups."*) For example, a bulldozer is a member of the group of inanimate objects, as well as a

[29]Note that biologists make take classes created by ordinary speakers differentiated by features accessible without the benefit of microscopic analysis and redefine the same class in terms of different features. A frequently cited example of this is the case of water, which, as Putnam points out, creates certain dilemmas for a theory of semantics.

[30]Note that while categories can include different syntactic categories (i.e. verb phrases as well as noun phrases), they are only associated with denoting terms. However, in our conception, categories need not possess individuation and persistence criteria.

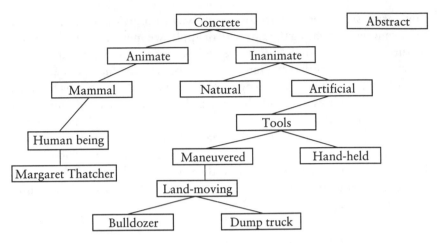

FIG. I. *A Typical Category Tree.*

member of the group of artificial things. Furthermore, each category or group within a tree is typically thought to correspond to a concept. For example, all members of the group bulldozer are thought to instantiate or meet the criteria of the concept of bulldozer, held to be a mental entity of some kind.

The traditional or classical way of defining concepts, as specified by what is known as the Classical View, has both an intensional and an extensional component. On the one hand each concept can be defined in terms of the features an object must possess in order to fall under that concept. On the other hand, a concept can also be defined extensionally in terms of the objects that fall under it. A second assumption of the Classical View is that of *summary representation*. That is, the specification of the features of a concept is not thought to be an exhaustive description of all objects or even of one object under the concept, but serves rather the kind of description of the entire class that applies to all possible members. For example, the representation of the concept of bulldozer need not specify the color of bulldozers, even though all bulldozers have color. A third assumption of the Classical View is that the features or properties that define a concept are singly necessary and jointly sufficient. For example, for an object to qualify as a bulldozer, it must have each one of the properties specified in its definition, that is, it must be a piece of construction equipment used to displace large quantities of dirt quickly and efficiently. In addition, if an object meets all the conditions necessary for being a bulldozer, then it must be a bulldozer. The fourth and final assumption of the Classical View is the existence of the class inclusion relation among the groups in a tree such that if an object in A is a member of B, then all the features of B are present in A. That is, any given object must also possess the features of its ancestor groups and not just those of the group in which it has immediate membership. As a result, bulldozers are typically thought to be both concrete, inanimate, and non–self-propelling.[31]

These two ways of describing category trees (i.e. in terms of group membership or the possession of features) parallel each other in that any relation which can be described in terms of group membership can also be described in terms of the possession of properties. For example, in any category tree there is a vertical ordering that can be expressed both in terms of group membership and in terms of the possession of features. Using the former, we can say that each group is a member of those above it that are connected via membership lines. Using the latter, we can say that each member of a given node has all the properties of its ancestor nodes, as well as others unique to its location. The ordering within a tree results in the fact that groups or nodes at the top are different from those at the bottom. Using each of the two methods, we can describe this difference by saying (1) that categories at the top of the tree include more members than those at the bottom or (2) that the categories at the top of the tree are less differentiated or more abstract than those at the bottom. For example, consider the category "concrete" in the tree in Figure 1. Since all categories below it are included within it, it clearly has more members than they do. At the same time, since what allows its members to gain membership is only the possession of the property of concreteness, its representative concept is less differentiated than that of tools. According to where a category falls within the ordering, it can be identified as super-ordinate or subordinate relative to others in the tree. A category that is above another in a tree so that members of the latter are members of the former while the reverse is not the case is said to be *super-ordinate* to that category. For example, the category "mammal" is super-ordinate to the category "human being." By the same token, a category that is underneath another in the hierarchy such that its members are members of the latter but not vice-versa, is *subordinate* to that category. For example, the category "human being" is subordinate to the category "mammal." Class inclusion statements typi-

---

[31]As technology advances, of course, the properties of an object may change (e.g. bulldozers may become self-propelling) and then one would have to decide whether to change the specifications of the class or create a new class.

cally reflect this ordering in that in statements of the form "A is a B," A represents a member of a class that is subordinate to B. (Note that in metaphorical utterances this does not seem to be the case, as we shall explore later in this chapter.) In addition, the truth conditions of class inclusion statements mirror that of membership in any group in the taxonomy. That is, in all statements of the grammatical form "A is a B," what is being said is that the subject of the class assignment (A) possesses all the qualities of the class to which the subject is assigned (B). As a result, the truth conditions (and resulting truth value) of a class inclusion statement are based on whether or not the subject of the sentence meets the necessary conditions for membership in the class to which it is being assigned.

Given a certain category structure, one can specify the relationship between two objects within that structure according to their location in it. For example, according to the taxonomy in Figure 1, Margaret Thatcher and bulldozers are less closely related than dump trucks and bulldozers since the first two are related only via membership in the group of concrete objects while the latter two are in the same group within the tree.

Modifications

The Classical View has many advantages, not the least of which is its intuitive appeal, simplicity, and the ease with which it explains many important issues. For one thing, its intensional/extensional definition of concepts provides the basis for an intuitively compelling account of reference in that it specifies that the intension determines the extension. Another advantage of the Classical View is the support it provides the epistemological distinction between the a priori and the a posteriori. However, the basic picture provided by the Classical View has been challenged on a number of fronts by philosophers, psychologists, and linguists.

For one thing, the view that category membership is determined by singly necessary and jointly sufficient properties (the heart of the Classical View) leads to a series of difficulties insofar as it is incompatible both with the existence of unclear cases and with our seeming inability to produce a definition of certain concepts. The most famous example of the latter is Wittgenstein's example of the concept "game," which resists a comprehensive definition despite the fact that we all recognize a game when we see one.[32]

---

[32]As an alternative way of representing concepts, Wittgenstein introduced the notion of family resemblance, in which class membership is determined not strictly by the possession of certain properties (a deterministic procedure) but rather through

Another problem with the Classical View is that it seems to provide no means of acknowledging that some members of a group are more representative of that group than others, despite the fact that both meet the conditions for group membership. For example, a robin is considered to be more "birdlike" than a penguin. In response to this inadequacy, Rosch and Mervis and others have proposed that, in addition to the structure shown in a category tree, categories also typically have an internal structure (called graded). Having *graded structure* is thought to involve three features: (1) some members of the class are thought to be more representative of the class than others; (2) there are some unclear cases (i.e. it is not clear whether some entities fall into the group or not); and (3) among nonmembers of the group, some entities are closer to being a member than others.[33] Members of a class that are thought to typify of a class are called *prototypes* of that class. That is, a robin is considered a prototypical exemplar or prototype of the class of birds.

Another difficulty with the picture presented by the Classical View of conceptualization stems from the additional assumption held by many philosophers (such as Goodman) that any given object has infinitely many properties. Since categories can be identified by groupings of properties, it seems that there should be infinitely many ways of categorizing things, with no one way better than any other. However, as common sense tells us and the recent work of psychologists confirms, while theory may predict an infinite number of equally good category schemes, this is not consistent with experience. This view contains two different components and is thus inadequate in at least two ways. For one thing, as the work of many psychologists has shown,[34] it is simply not true that the world is an unstructured place that forms a set of stimuli in which all possible stimulus attrib-

family resemblance, that is, through similarity to prototypical members of the class. Putnam challenges the assumption that intensions determine extensions, and both Putnam and Kripke suggest an alternate theory of reference, a causal theory which explains how terms refer to objects by appealing to an initial baptism and subsequent intentions to maintain the initial connection. Hilary Putnam, "Is Semantics Possible?" in *Language, Belief and Metaphysics*, ed. H. E. Kiefer and M. K. Munitz (New York: State University of New York Press, 1970), pp. 50–63. Putnam, "Meaning and Reference," *The Journal of Philosophy* 70 (Nov. 8, 1973): 699–711. Saul Kripke, "Identity and Necessity," *Identity and Individuation* (New York: New York University Press, 1971), pp. 135–64.

[33] Eleanor Rosch and C. B. Mervis, "Family Resemblances: Studies in the Internal Structure of Categories," *Cognitive Psychology* 7 (1975): 573–605.

[34] See, e.g., Eleanor Rosch, C. B. Mervis, W. D. Gray, D. M. Johnson, and P. Boyes-Braem, "Basic Objects in Natural Categories," *Cognitive Psychology* 8 (1976): 382–439

utes occur with equal probability combined with all other possible attributes. Instead, the world is such that certain properties are much more likely to accompany others. For example, something that swims is much more likely to have gills than something that does not. This fact leads to the proposition that the world has what psychologists calls a certain *correlational structure*, which leads to the next correction of the classical picture. If the world has a certain correlational structure, then our category schemes or taxonomies should reflect this. That is, every taxonomy is not created equal but will be more appropriate to the extent that it mirrors the correlational structure of the environment.

A final inadequacy of the classical model of conceptualization is one of incompleteness in that it does not acknowledge that while any given object may belong to any number of groups and represented thus more or less abstractly, each level is not equal. That is, as Rosch and her colleagues have shown,[35] categories at certain level of abstraction stand out from the others. For example, a given chair may be categorized or represented as a blue channel-backed chair, a channel-backed chair, a chair, a piece of furniture, an artificial object, or a concrete object. However, to classify it as a chair (i.e. at that particular level of abstraction) is to say more about it than to classify it in any of the other ways. In other words, certain levels of abstraction are more basic. In the terminology of psychologists, basic categories are those which (1) carry the most information, (2) possess the highest category cue validity, and thus (3) are the most differentiated from one another.[36] Studies by Rosch et al. have shown that basic categories (1) are the most inclusive categories for which a concrete image of the category as a whole can be formed; (2) are the first categorizations made during perception of the environment; (3) are the earliest categories sorted and earliest named by children; and (4) are the categories most codable, most coded, and most necessary in language.

The first criticism of the Classical View is severe enough to have led to the formation of an alternative theory based on family resemance. The last three merely seem to call for minor additions. For our purposes here it suffices to point out that category schemes are essentially functional, created to help us achieve goals.[37] If we assume that the world does have a

[35]Rosch et al., "Basic Objects."
[36]Ibid., p. 382.
[37]This does not rule out categories and even category schemes that exist independently of human existence and desires. That is, while mathematical schemes exist, they seem to exist independently of human desire. However, granted the existence of such categories, the purposefulness of the category schemes that underlie our language al-

correlational structure, then it is clearly in our best interest for our language and the categorization that underlies it to mirror that structure. (For example, it would be unhelpful for the word "rabbit" to include the air around Quine's rabbit at a particular time since it is the physically and concretely delineated rabbit that persists in time and can be referred to more than once.) The functionality of categorization explains why category schemes are highly determined, mirror the correlational structure of the environment, and possess basic levels of categorization.

For our language to be useful to us, it must embody classes defined in such a way as to serve our needs. Since we are physical entities and interact with other physical entities, these needs are most often physically defined. Two clear prerequisites of communication are: (1) the ability to draw attention to an entity that is corporeal, which itself presupposes that the entity be physically delineated from other and (2) that the term used to identify that object refer to the entity so delineated. Since we are creatures of needs and desires, and language is but one tool to meet these needs and desires, our categories are functionally designed even beyond the need to distinguish corporeal entities. For example, since color is irrelevant to our needs, we do not include color in the definition of bulldozers. Instead, the features that define a certain class of objects in the traditional taxonomy (i.e. those features that characterize things like bulldozers) tend to be physical and pertain to the functionality of that entity. For example, in most situations in which we think about or speak about bulldozers, we are interested in objects with precisely the features and properties that characterize the class literally referred to by the term "bulldozer" (as opposed to those which define the class it represents during metaphorical use). When the equipment manager of a construction firm orders three bulldozers, he wants three land-moving machines and would look in disbelief at the delivery of two land-moving machines and one pushy person.

Common Categories vs. Ad Hoc Categories

In the category tree shown in Figure 1, each category is represented by a term in the language (e.g. inanimate, mammal, bulldozer). This type of category, that is, categories that are represented by a term in the language, are called *common categories*. However, all categories need not be so rep-

---

most guarantees that our category schemes will incorporate these independently occurring categories

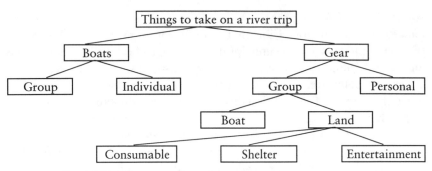

FIG. 2. *An Ad Hoc Category Tree.*

resented. That is, in addition to common categories there are categories that are not represented by a term in language but instead must be described. Such categories, called *ad hoc categories*, can be as well delineated as common categories. For example, studies have shown that people are typically able to distinguish members of such categories as "things to take on a camping trip or river trip."[38] In some respects, there seem to be few differences between common and ad hoc categories. That common categories are named whereas ad hoc categories are not seems inconsequential in that the names of common categories can be regarded as merely abbreviations for the descriptions that actually define the category. Like common categories, ad hoc categories also constitute category trees, such as that shown in Figure 2, which has all the features as category trees of common categories.

In addition, as the work of Barsalou has confirmed, ad hoc categories also feature graded structure, one of the principal properties of common categories. For example, within the ad hoc category of things to take on a river trip, some members (e.g. a kayak) are thought to be more representative than others. According to Barsalou, the difference between ad hoc categories and common categories is that (1) ad hoc categories violate the correlational structure of the environment and (2) ad hoc categories are not well established in memory in terms of (a) category concept recognition, (b) associations from instance to concept, and (c) associations from concept to instance.[39] (Barsalou seems to find an explanation for the fact

[38]For studies on ad hoc categories, see Lawrence Barsalou, "Ad Hoc Categories," *Memory & Cognition* 11, no. 3 (1983): 211–27.
[39]Ibid., pp. 213–14.

that ad hoc categories are not well established in memory in the fact that those categories are usually constructed as they are used and not established beforehand. A simpler explanation, however, is that they are not encoded in the language, in that they are not named. Since the act of naming a group of entities delineates the members of that group as identical in some way, perhaps functionally identical, it would seem that being named reinforces the features of the group in memory. This is probably a chicken/egg situation.)

Barsalou also seems to differentiate between ad hoc categories and common categories when he claims that the former are created in order to serve a goal.[40] While this implies (perhaps unintentionally on Barsalou's part) that common categories are *not* created to serve a purpose, this does not seem to be the case. One obvious goal served by common categories stems from the fact that common categories (supposedly) mirror the correlational structure of the environment. That is, categories such as those of human beings and birds actually group together entities that are similar enough (for most purposes) to make their grouping productive. For example, if we are told before meeting George that George is a bird rather than a human being we will not expect to shake hands or exchange pleasantries when we are introduced. The correlation between the structure of common categories and the entities in our world makes common categories enormously useful in all kinds of ways since it entails that in speaking our language we will group things in a manner that predicts functionally relevant behaviors and similarities.

To summarize, our analysis of metaphor should take into the underlying functionality of category formation, the existence of graded structure and basic categories, and the differences between common and ad hoc categories.

Summary

The theory presented in this chapter is semantic in that it claims that the propositional content expressed by a metaphorical utterance is its metaphorical content, and it is pragmatic in that it acknowledges that extralinguistic knowledge is required for the derivation of this content. According to this analysis, what makes an utterance metaphorical is that (1) to process it one must change one conception of the classes involved in a way in-

[40]Ibid., p. 214.

TABLE 1

Features of My Analysis

Metaphoricity	Shifted conceptualization of entities and relations resulting from a or imposition of new category scheme
Comprehension process	1. Using contextual clues, derive one or more possible interpretations of the utterance (literal and/or metaphorical) by: • deriving system embodied in metaphorical vehicle • deriving syllogism(s) used to connect system invoked literally with entities being conceived metaphorically • use syllogism(s) to infer properties attributed to metaphor subject 2. If there is a pragmatic conflict, derive another
The proposition expressed by the metaphorical utterance	Its metaphorical content
The existence of metaphorical content	Yes
The classification of metaphorical content	As the proposition expressed by the utterance
Rule for deriving metaphorical content	Reconceptualization of some or all entities in question based on category prototypically represented by the metaphor vehicle
Phenomena metaphor is like	Similes and other figures

compatible with the conventional links of our language and the taxonomy that underlies it and (2) the metaphorical vehicle serves as a prototypical exemplar of the new class. Table 1 summarizes the main features of my analysis.

2

Metaphor, Semantics, and Pragmatics

One of the primary questions of this book is how metaphor and any content it expresses fit into the framework and tools created for studying language. The study of language has traditionally been divided into the study of syntax, semantics, and pragmatics, each with its own tools and subject of study. As a result, the question of how metaphor should be studied has been considered to be the question whether metaphor is a matter of semantics or pragmatics. In this chapter I present and critique a traditional (semantic) analysis of metaphor and examine the distinction between meaning and use as the basis for the division of the study of language into syntax, semantics, and pragmatics.

A Traditional Analysis of Metaphor: Max Black

According to Max Black, a metaphorical utterance such as (4) on our list ("Steve is a sheep dog") is made up of a principal subject (Steve), a subsidiary subject (the sheep dog), and a "system of associated commonplaces" (the properties of sheep dogs that help us select the properties to attribute to Steve).[1] Given these components, Black describes the process of comprehending a metaphor as the process of applying a system of associated commonplaces of the subsidiary subject (commonly referred to as the metaphor vehicle) to the principal subject such that certain features of

[1]Max Black, "Metaphor," in *Philosophical Perspectives on Metaphor*, ed. Mark Johnson (Minneapolis: University of Minnesota Press, 1981), pp. 63–82. This system is thought to include not only the essential features of the object but also (or only) features that are habitually associated with the object by a linguistic community or subculture.

the subject are selected, emphasized, suppressed, and organized.[2] For Black, the process of comprehending a metaphor is comparable to the process of looking at one thing, through something else:

> Suppose I look at the night sky through a piece of heavily smoked glass on which certain lines have been left clear. Then I shall see only the stars that can be made to lie on the lines previously prepared upon the screen, and the stars I do see will be seen as organized by the screen's structure.[3]

That is, Black claims that in processing the metaphor "Steve is a sheep dog," we look at Steve (the stars visible in the night sky) *through* a sheep dog (the piece of smoked glass). In the process, certain features of Steve are suppressed (the stars that are behind the smoked section of glass) and other features are emphasized (the stars that shine through the lines in the glass). Since the pattern in the glass is determined by the features of a sheep dog (both its essential features and the characteristics we associate with it), in processing the metaphor we have the impression of seeing Steve through the sheep dog and the view we get of him is organized according to these features.

In a more formal and systematic description of his account of metaphor, Black says: "To call a sentence an instance of metaphor is to say something about its *meaning*, not about its orthography, its phonetic pattern, or its grammatical form."[4] Furthermore, "in the simplest formulation, when we use a metaphor we have two thoughts of different things active together and supported by a single word, or phrase, whose meaning is the result of their interaction."[5] This particular aspect of Black's theory of metaphor causes it to be classified as an *interaction theory of metaphor* in that it sees the metaphorical meaning of a metaphor as resulting from the interaction between the meanings of the principal and subsidiary subjects.[6]

Most important, since Black appeals to the notion of metaphorical

[2] Ibid., p. 78.

[3] Ibid., p. 75.

[4] Ibid., p. 66.

[5] Ibid., p. 78. Black borrows this formulation from I. A. Richards, *The Philosophy of Rhetoric* (Oxford: Oxford University Press, 1936), p. 93.

[6] Although interaction theory of metaphor is closely based on work by Richards, *The Philosophy of Rhetoric*, Black is the first to present an interaction theory of metaphor.

meaning in his analysis of metaphor, his account can be classified as a semantic theory of metaphor.[7] In fact, most of the theories of metaphor which are held to be traditional (for example, the theories of Henle, Black, and Goodman) are semantic theories.[8] Although the approach of individual semantic theories varies depending both upon their conception of meaning and upon how they view the relationship between literal and metaphorical *meaning*, all of them account for metaphor in terms of metaphorical meaning. In semantic theories, the term "sheep dog" in our sentence (4) is thought to take on a metaphorical meaning such that utterance an utterance of the sentence is true if and only if Steve has certain traits including being instrumental in guiding others (regardless of the fact that he lacks certain other traits of sheep dogs such as having paws and fur). That is, these theories take a semantic approach to metaphor by holding that metaphors express a metaphorical content that is different from the content expressed by a literal interpretation of the utterance. In fact, semantic theorists seem to build their theories of metaphor in an attempt to satisfy the commonsense intuition of metaphorical content and truth (my Criterion 3 in Chapter 1). In doing so, they provide arguments for the existence of a distinct metaphorical content (my Claim 2). At the same time, in accordance with the framework provided by traditional semantics, these theories account for the metaphorical *content* by appealing to metaphorical *meaning*.[9] That is, given the Fregean identification of meaning with content, if the metaphorical content of an utterance is held to be different from that of its literal interpretation, then it must also have a different (or metaphorical) meaning. As we shall see in the next chapter, it is this rigorous identification of meaning with content that ultimately dooms seman-

[7]To be fair to Black, he does acknowledge that there is a sense in which the rules of the language fail when it comes to the study of metaphor and that this aspect of metaphor seems to require a pragmatic approach (Black, "Metaphor," p. 67). However, he leaves this vague and does not say how it should be done.

[8]See, for example, Paul Henle, "Metaphor," in *Philosophical Perspectives on Metaphor*, ed. Johnson, pp. 83–104.

[9]Note that the metaphorical meaning in question varies depending on the conception of meaning held by the various theorists. For example, Goodman, who holds an extensionalist theory of meaning, explains metaphor without appealing to intension, in terms of second order meaning. See Nelson Goodman, "Metaphor as Moonlighting," in *Philosophical Perspectives on Metaphor*, ed. Johnson, pp. 221–27. More recently, Eva Kittay (*Metaphor: Its Cognitive Force and Linguistic Structure* [Oxford: Clarendon Press, 1987]) develops a theory of semantics based on semantic fields, and Black seems to assume some kind of intensional semantics.

TABLE 2
Features of the Traditional Semantic Analysis

Metaphoricity	Interaction between principal and subsidiary subject
Comprehension process	Deduction of metaphorical meaning from literal meaning through interaction between principal and subsidiary subject
The proposition expressed by the metaphorical utterance	Its metaphorical content
The existence of metaphorical content	Yes
Classification of metaphorical content	The proposition expressed by the utterance
Rule for deriving metaphorical content	Interaction between meanings of terms referring to the principal and subsidiary subject
Phenomena metaphor is like	Similes and other figures

tic theories of metaphor.[10] Table 2 summarizes the features of this type of traditional (i.e. semantic) analysis of metaphor.

Critique of Black

On an intuitive level, Black's analysis seems to describe metaphors and their comprehension accurately, and the analogy he draws between the processing of metaphors and the process of perception seems to be apt. That is, in understanding an utterance of (4), it *does* seem as though we see Steve *through* a sheep dog, so that the features of sheep dogs are used to organize Steve's features. Thus this analysis seems to account both for the changed view of Steve we acquire as a result of the metaphor and for the fact that some of the features of sheep dogs seem to guide us as we attempt to choose among features to assign to him. It also accounts for the intuition most of us have that metaphors express something that is judged true or false independently of the proposition expressed by a literal interpretation of the utterance. That is, semantic theories of metaphor account for the notion of a distinct metaphorical content (my Criterion 3), specifically, by introducing the notion of metaphorical meaning. Because meta-

[10]Note that my analysis of metaphor avoids this difficulty by following in Stern's footsteps and adopting Kaplan's distinction between meaning and content. See David Kaplan, "Names and Demonstratives," in *The Philosophy of Language*, ed. A. P. Martinich, 2nd ed. (New York: Oxford University Press, 1990), p. 316–29, p. 324.

phor is so prevalent and because the intuition of metaphorical content is such a powerful one, Occam's razor would seem to dictate that a distinct metaphorical content exists (my Claim 2). Thus, being able to satisfy the intuition of metaphorical content is a powerful argument for Black's theory and for other semantic theories of metaphor.

However, despite the advantages of Black's theory, it also suffers from major deficiencies, most of which are shared by other semantic theories of metaphor. In fact, the shortcomings of semantic theories of metaphor lead Davidson, Searle, Fogelin, and others to produce nonsemantic or pragmatic theories of metaphor, as we shall see in Chapters 3–6.

One difficulty with Black's analysis is that his description of how metaphors are comprehended is itself metaphorical. That is, Black employs terms used to describe vision (a physical process) in describing the comprehension of a metaphor despite the fact that comprehension cannot be identified with visual perception (in that it does not have all the properties that characterize visual perception). Since the description Black gives is metaphorical, which properties of visual perception can truly be assigned to the process of comprehending a metaphor is not made explicit or specified by the rules of the language (as is the case in literal utterances). This can be seen when metaphors are contrasted with literal utterances. For example, consider the utterance "That is a bulldozer," uttered while pointing to a bulldozer in a field. When given a sentence of this form (i.e. A is a B), it is generally safe to infer that any properties B has, A also has. In other words, if (1) A is a B and (2) B is X, Y, and Z, we can infer that (3) A is X, Y, and Z. However, this general rule does not seem to hold in the case of metaphorical utterances. That is, we can think of any number of properties of sheep dogs that Steve does not have. Moreover, we do not believe that the speaker is asserting those properties and we tend to discard them as irrelevant to the metaphor early in our processing of it. Since Black's description of how metaphors are processed is itself metaphorical, he leaves us with the task of determining what he is actually predicating of metaphors. Although some properties can be discarded easily, others are more difficult. For example, it is clear that Black is *not* saying that in processing metaphors light must hit the object of our perception and enter our eyes through the cornea. However, it is less clear whether he is asserting that some people need a remedial mechanism (akin to glasses) to grasp metaphors and that one's psychological distance from the metaphor directly affects one's ability to grasp a metaphor.[11]

[11]It could be argued that in the example I give here, I do not distinguish between

A further difficulty with the metaphoricity of Black's analysis of meta-phor is that putting an abstract process such as language comprehension in terms of the more concrete and intuitively appealing process of percep-tion (which we believe, perhaps erroneously, that we understand) gives Black's description an appeal which may tend to mask a lack of attention to detail, and this leads us to the next complaint.

Black's description of how semantic notions such as that of meaning function in this process is quite vague, despite his claim that metaphoricity is a matter of meaning. Since comprehension depends upon the semantic notions of: meaning, the proposition expressed, and truth conditions, not to address how these notions interact would clearly be remiss.

These inadequacies of Black's analysis are typical of semantic theories of metaphor. Theories that explain metaphor in terms of metaphorical meaning have the difficulty of explaining how this meaning fits in with the notion of literal meaning, both in terms of what characteristics it shares with literal meaning and in terms of how the metaphorical meaning inter-acts with literal meaning in the comprehension of an utterance. One pos-sible way of addressing these issues is to claim that the metaphorical meaning of a metaphor is like literal meaning in that (1) it is the property of words and (2) it is just another meaning of a given expression. Given these premises, a theory would say that "being pushy" is just another meaning of the term "sheep dog." This approach, which treats terms that are used metaphorically as ambiguous, with the so-called metaphorical meaning as one of the meanings of the term, has many difficulties and is one of the approaches Davidson considers and rejects, as we shall see in Chapter 3. Another way of handling the dilemma is to claim that, in cer-tain contexts, there is a change in meaning of at least some of the terms in-volved in the metaphor. If we accept that the meaning of the sentence is dependent only upon the meanings of the individual terms, the principle of composition would indicate that the meanings of the term used meta-phorically shift. For example, in the metaphorical utterance (5), we could

------

the propositions that are part of the proposition expressed (comprehended by the competent speaker) and the propositions that are implicatures of the utterance (the propositions Davidson claims metaphors make us think of). This distinction leads to two different ways of describing a conversant's understanding of an utterance, *suffi-cient* or *replete*. Conversants are thought to have *sufficient* comprehension if and only if they comprehend the propositions expressed by an utterance (i.e. what a competent speaker of the language comprehends). Conversants may be described as having a *re-plete* comprehension if they go beyond what is expressed by the utterance to derive all the inferences from the utterance the speaker intends them to derive.

say that the term "bulldozer" changes its meaning so that it no longer refers to types of landmoving equipment and now refers to types of personalities. Because these theories claim that the meaning of a given term shifts in the context, such theories are often called *meaning-shift* theories of metaphor (a term coined by Fogelin). Black seems to identify himself as belonging to this class: the selection, emphasis, suppression, and organization of the features of the principal subject via the features of the subsidiary subject "involves shifts in meaning of words belonging to the same system as the metaphorical expression."[12] That is, Black seems to believe the meanings of the metaphorical vehicle shift in being applied to the metaphorical or primary subject.

That Black explains metaphor in terms of meaning (whether we call this meaning "metaphorical" or not) is significant not only because it identifies his theory as a semantic theory of metaphor, but also because, in explaining in terms of meaning, he appeals to a distinction of great importance in the study of language, the distinction between meaning and use.

The Distinction Between Meaning and Use

The distinction between meaning and use is significant in that it both seems to play an important role in communication and has traditionally been used to distinguish between two branches of the study of language: semantics and pragmatics. Given the role of the distinction between meaning and use in delineating semantics and pragmatics, to debate whether metaphor is a matter of meaning has been to debate whether it should be analyzed in terms of semantic or pragmatic tools. However, this issue has important implications. In fact, the question whether something is a matter of meaning (and thus of semantics) has come to be interpreted as a question whether the phenomenon at issue is (1) amenable to systematic study and (2) central to the study of language. That is, in culling out issues relevant to the study of semantics, theorists hoped both to restrict the fundamental study of language to those phenomena considered to be more amenable to systematic study and to relegate to the sidelines matters that did not fit into the framework developed from this study. The reason philosophers and linguists have attached importance to careful delineation of meaning from use can be seen most prominently in the works of Donald Davidson: "Literal meaning and literal truth conditions can be assigned to words and sentences apart from particular contexts of use. This

[12]Black, "Metaphor," p. 78.

is why adverting to them has genuine explanatory power."[13] In other words, the preference semanticists have for using the distinction between meaning and use to separate out linguistic types as their object of study is based, ultimately, on their explanatory power, their ability to explain certain regularities of use of the language, owing to their context independence.

Davidson's account of the distinction between meaning and use (and thus between what is said and how what is said is used)[14] rests on a notion of first and secondary meaning he develops in "A Nice Derangement of Epitaphs."[15] Davidson explains the notion of first meaning by appealing to an example of an utterance which, like most utterances, carries with it a string of intentions. For example, given a situation in which a patient says "It's cold in here" in order to get the nurse to turn up the heat, there is a chain of intentions as follows: the patient uttered the words "It's too cold in here" in order (1) that the nurse would understand by this utterance that the patient thought it was too cold in the room in order (2) that the nurse would take remedial action (preferably that of turning up the heat). In Davidson's conception, the first item in the string corresponds to the *first meaning* while the others are *secondary meanings*. According to Davidson, the first meaning is what the interpreter must understand in order to understand what was said. In addition, the first meaning corresponds to what is ordinarily called literal meaning, which, unlike secondary intentions, is independent of context in that it can be assigned to the sentence regardless of the speaker's specific communicative intention or the particular context of the utterance (such as whether the thermostat can be controlled by the nurse and/or the patient).

The need for something like first meaning or literal meaning associated with sentence types can been seen most clearly by considering what it would be like if we did not have that notion of meaning. Suppose, instead, that we attempted to explain each utterance as a token of language. Without the notion of meaning, considered to be relatively context-independent and the property of linguistic types, we would have no background

[13]Donald Davidson, "What Metaphors Mean," in *The Philosophy of Language*, ed. Martinich, pp. 430–41, p. 431.

[14]Note that if one assumes the Fregean belief that meaning determines what is said (i.e. the proposition expressed by an utterance), one can identify these two distinctions.

[15]Donald Davidson, "A Nice Derangement of Epitaphs," in *Truth and Interpretation: Perspectives on the Philosophy of Donald Davidson*, ed. Ernest Le Pore (Oxford: Basil Blackwell, 1986), pp. 433–46.

information to allow us to decipher the utterance. In addition, the distinction between meaning and use is also necessary for the preservation of the role of linguistic competence in a theory of language. That is, if there is no clear distinction between what is said (through the utterance as an instance of language) and the effect or use of the utterance, then the ability to distinguish the role of linguistic competence from other types of competence and the explanatory power of linguistic types is lost.

Intuitive Basis

The distinction between meaning and use is not merely the invention of Semanticists but also seems to have a basis in commonsense intuitions about communication. Suppose that a frustrated husband were to say to his wife, "I'm going to call John; I can *talk* to John." A likely response by the wife, "Are you saying you can't talk to me?" is a response not only to what was said (the proposition expressed by the utterance), but to other factors (in this case, to what was implied by the utterance, given such things as tone of voice and a history of previous conversations). Personal conversations of this sort often include questions regarding what the speaker meant or intended by saying such a thing. That is, an interpreter's response to any utterance is not just to the proposition expressed but also to the fact that the speaker chose to say what was said (and to any implication of this). In other words, although a simplified view of language tends to associate one message or proposition with one utterance, there is often more than one proposition associated with a particular utterance (Davidson's secondary meanings and Grice's implicatures). In addition, while the proposition that seems to represent what was said through the utterance seems to be closely tied to the meanings of the terms, as logical semanticians desire, propositions that are implied by the utterance seem much more loosely associated with it. Furthermore, a speaker is held responsible not just for what was said but also for what was implied or otherwise communicated by what was said and for having initiated the speech act. As a result, a complete account of a linguistic interaction or explanation of the behavior of participants must analyze the utterance as an action and not just as a code to be interpreted for its message. Just as in Davidson's view, in addition to the question of what was meant or said, there exists a whole realm of how the utterance was used, which seems to include many factors, as well as additional propositional content.

The difference between what is said and what an utterance is used to do, as well as the variety of propositions that can be associated through

implicature with an utterance, can also be seen in the case of what are
sometimes called indirect speech acts. For example, consider the sentence
"It's too cold in here," uttered by a bedridden patient to a nurse who is
standing near the heater. Given a specification of the context of utterance
that includes the place of utterance (due to the indexical element in
"here"), the sentence expresses a proposition whose truth value can be determined by determining the temperature of the room and its suitability
for humans. Moreover, the grammatical form of the utterance indicates
that its illocutionary force is that of an assertion. That is, it appears that
the utterance consists merely of the expression of the speaker's opinion.
However, when uttered under the conditions described, the interpreter of
the utterance would, most likely, respond as if to a request, either by honoring it by closing the window or by refusing to honor it (saying something to the effect of "The heat can't be turned up any more"). The interpreter might also respond by bringing the speaker a blanket. The myriad
possible responses to the utterance make it clear that the response is not
merely to what has been said (which remains constant) but rather to a
combination of the information expressed and other information available to the interpreter. That is, the behavior of the interpreter cannot be
explained solely in terms of the proposition literally expressed or the truth
value of such a proposition. What is needed in order to explain their behavior is either an understanding of why someone might make such a
statement (an ability to infer the aim of the speaker) or an awareness of the
role such an utterance plays according to cultural convention, together
with a desire on the part of the interpreter to be cooperative. Yet, according to Davidson and most semanticists (with the exception of Grice and
Strawson), none of these factors should have any role in an understanding
of what is said, the proposition expressed by an utterance. Instead, the
only factors that should enter into the understanding of the proposition
expressed should be (1) linguistic competence (syntactic and semantic)
and (2) (possibly, given the case of indexicals) knowledge of certain contextual features needed for utterances containing indexical elements. Thus
the difference between what is said and the effect that is produced by what
is said is based upon the role that extralinguistic competence plays in interpretation.

    However, despite the general muddiness of the picture presented
above and the multiplicity of the propositions that can be associated
with an utterance, it does seem that speakers routinely distinguish something primary, something which seems strongly linked to the notion of

meaning and of linguistic competence. Suppose, for example, that in response to the wife's response the husband were to say "I didn't *say* that." Even if the wife (interpreter) in this conversation decides that the husband (speaker) uttered one proposition (that he wanted to talk to John) with the primary goal of communicating a different proposition (that she is hard to talk to), it is highly unlikely that she would claim that he actually said that he couldn't talk to her. Instead, in response to his claim that he didn't say anything about the ease of talking to her, she would probably defend her beliefs concerning his beliefs by saying, "Well, maybe that's not what you *said*, but it's what you *meant*." That is, although we hold a speaker responsible for what they imply by their utterances, it is nonetheless taken for granted by both participants that there is a fundamental difference between what is said and the ultimate force of the utterance. (The term "force" is used here to express the overall role the utterance plays in the conversation, that is, how the utterance is used.) In other words, the speaker's intentions in stating the utterance, together with circumstantial evidence that indicates that the ultimate force of the utterance is different from the overt one (expressed by what is said), are not seen as a challenge to what was said. What this example shows is that we seem to regard "what is said" as an objective thing, somehow dependent upon meaning and linguistic competence but independent of such things as the speaker's beliefs or goal, of other propositions that may be implied by the utterance, and even of the proposition they ultimately want the audience to believe.

Grice: What Is Said vs. What Is Conveyed

The distinction between what is expressed by an utterance and what the interpreter does with the utterance can be and is maintained even by philosophers of language who interpret sentence meaning in the light of the intentions of an speaker. That is, a belief in this distinction does not require taking a semantic approach to the study of meaning, since even philosophers who take an pragmatic approach to meaning maintain the distinction, although they may express it in slightly different terms. For example, H. P. Grice, who takes the base concept of a linguistic theory to be the mutual recognition of intentions to communicate and defines meaning (pragmatically) in terms of this mutual recognition, still recognizes the distinction between what an utterance expresses and what it is used to do. In fact, this distinction is fundamental to his work on conversational implicatures.[16] For Grice, the difference is explained in terms of primary vs. secondary intentions.[17] The primary intention is the communicative intention the speaker has, that is, it is the intention the speaker has to induce a belief in the audience such that for the act to be a communicative one (one in which nonnatural meaning occurs), the interpreter must recognize this intention and the act as so intended. In contrast, secondary intentions are those intentions the speaker has for making the utterance, such as a desire to get someone to do something. Yet Grice claims that these intentions are irrelevant to the *meaning* of the utterance, thus distinguishing between what an utterance says and what it is used to do.

In summary, the distinction between what words say and what they are used to do seems to play a role in communication, regardless of the semantic framework adopted. In addition, while we hold a speaker responsible for the implicatures of their utterances, as well as for what is said, the type and degree of responsibility is different in each case.

Syntax, Semantics vs. Pragmatics

Since Black explains metaphor in terms of metaphorical meaning, his theory classifies it as a matter of semantics. As we shall see in Chapters 3–6, more recent philosophers claim that metaphor is a matter neither of meaning nor of semantics, but rather one of *use*. The most common strategy of philosophers who take a nonsemantic approach to metaphor is to classify metaphor as a matter of pragmatics, that is, as a phenomenon to be explained in terms of the principles of conversation. Since the most common alternative way of classifying metaphor is as a matter of pragmatics, as a part of our deliberation on the proper classification of metaphor we must examine the boundaries between semantics and pragmatics. However, the distinction between semantics and pragmatics cannot be definitively presented because it is viewed differently by different theorists, with some theorists holding that there is no fixed distinction between the two. In addition, the study of new phenomena and the development of new approaches often provokes a shift in the distinction.

[16]H. P. Grice, "Logic and Conversation," in *Syntax and Semantics*, vol. 3, ed. Peter Cole and Jerry L. Morgan (New York: Academic Press, 1975), p. 41–58. Also in *The Philosophy of Language*, ed. Martinich, pp. 149–60.

[17]H. P. Grice, "Meaning," in *The Philosophy of Language*, ed. Martinich, pp. 77–78.

A Traditional Picture

As traditionally conceived, semantics and pragmatics are only two prongs of a three-pronged approach to the study of language which includes syntax, semantics, and pragmatics. From the perspective of some philosophers and linguists (such as Charles Morris), syntax, semantics, and pragmatics together are considered to cooperate to provide a complete account of language and of communicative competence. While the study of language can be defined in many ways, Davidson and many others consider it to be the study of successful acts of communication. A typical formal semantics would describe a communicative act briefly as follows: A speaker says something, either by making sounds that fall in certain patterns, or by placing marks with a certain shape on a page. The interpreter identifies the sounds or marks as instances (tokens) of certain types belonging to his or her language and, deciding what these tokens are intended to represent in the world, interprets the utterance. In a successful act of communication, the speaker arrives at an interpretation of the utterance that corresponds to the proposition the speaker intended to express by the utterance in question.[18]

In this description of an instance of language use, one can distinguish at least three types of relationships. First, there is a relationship among the symbols of the language as tokens of certain types. The rules governing these relationships determine that a sentence such as "John hit his head against the wall all day" is grammatical while the sentence "Hit his against all day John the" is ungrammatical. Second, there is a relationship between the symbols of the sentence type and the world. That is, there is the connection between the sentence as a string of symbols and the world that makes the sentence have meaning or content. This relationship represents the meaning or content of the sentence and is often expressed in terms of denoting and referring. Finally, there is the relationship between the symbols and the users of the language. In other words, there is the role the symbols play as a tool of communication.

According to the traditional taxonomy as outlined by Morris,[19] the studies of language, syntax, semantics, and pragmatics are distinguished from each other primarily by the aspects of language they consider rele-

---

[18]This description clearly leaves much to be desired since it omits such things as the projected attitude of the speaker toward the proposition. I will discuss these inadequacies later.

[19]Charles W. Morris, "Foundations of the Theory of Signs," in Morris, *Writings on the General Theory of Signs* (The Hague: Mouton, 1971), pp. 7–74.

vant in their study of it. Syntax is the study of the *form* of linguistic expressions and the rules that govern this form. That is, syntax studies the first of the three relationships cited above, the relationship among the symbols themselves. Thus syntax consists of the study of sentences as linguistic types, abstract entities capable of recurrence.

The second prong in the traditional study of language, semantics, consists in the study of the relationship between the symbols and the world, as characterized by terms such as meaning, denoting, and referring. Since our linguistic competence allows us to comprehend the meaning of a potentially) infinite number of sentences, our theory of meaning must be recursive. As a result, a theory of meaning is thought to include both the meanings of individual expressions and their rules of combination. In addition, to understand what an expression means we must grasp the connection with the world.[20] That is, in the case of referring terms we must apprehend their referents, and in the case of sentences we must understand their satisfaction conditions.[21] The realm of semantics is thus a study of meaning and reference (and truth conditions) such that a theory of semantics is thought to be made up of a theory of meaning and a theory of satisfaction conditions.[22]

The distinction between syntax and semantics can be seen in the example of an artificial language. In an artificial language, the syntax of the language determines what can be classified as a well-formed formula, an expression of the language. However, without the link between the language and the world provided by semantics, all expressions are meaningless. On the other hand, syntax and semantics are thought to be similar in many ways, as outlined by Davis.[23] For one thing, theorists of syntax and semantics have assumed that there is such a thing as a linguistic type and

[20]This assumes the Fregean distinction between the sense and reference and the need for an account of both in a theory of semantics, a reasonable assumption but one disputed by extensionalists such as Goodman who repudiate intensional notions such as that of sense.

[21]The satisfaction conditions of a sentence vary according to whether the sentence is declarative (truth conditions), interrogative (answer conditions), or imperative (compliance conditions).

[22]W. V. Quine proposes this division of semantics into the two disciplines of (1) reference (which involves individuals, sets of individuals, and the relations between them) and (2) sense (which involves such intensional notions as concepts of individuals, properties, and propositions. *From a Logical Point of View* (Cambridge, Mass., 1953; 2nd rev. ed. 1961).

[23]Steven Davis, "Introduction," in Davis, ed., *Pragmatics* (Oxford: Oxford University Press, 1991), pp. 3–13.

that the rules of both syntax and meaning belong to these types. That is, they have assumed that it is possible to study language (in a meaningful way) in the absence of context and, concomitantly, that it is possible to distinguish between linguistic competence and other types of competence that are involved in communication. For semanticists, this amounts to believing, as Davidson apparently does, that "literal meaning and literal truth-conditions can be assigned to words and sentences apart from particular contexts of use."[24] In this respect semanticists who are Davidsonian assume that the objects of their study are independent of specific contextual facts such as how hot it is, where the participants are located in the room, and what objects are visible to both. This is what gives literal meaning and truth conditions, in Davidson's terms "genuine explanatory power."

Another assumption shared by syntax and semantics is the assumption that what is said is independent of speaker intention; that is, it is not determined by what the speaker intends to communicate by uttering certain expressions or affected by what the speaker desires to accomplish by using the utterance. The third feature commonly thought to be shared by syntax and semantics is that they both study linguistic expressions and that the knowledge they encompass is specifically linguistic.

The third prong of the study of language, pragmatics, is traditionally defined as the study of language in relation to language users. In other words, the subject matter of pragmatics is utterances in their context of utterance, speech acts. However, as Davis points out, this view of pragmatics is too broad since it encompasses anything that includes language use, that is, practically every field of human study. For our purposes, we are interested in pragmatics as a field of study which, along with syntax and semantics, studies the knowledge a competent speaker must have in order to successfully comprehend and produce utterances. Since such acts often include the conveyance of implicatures as well as what is expressed directly, pragmatics must account for what makes this possible. Inasmuch as pragmatics studies the communicative act in its entirety, it takes the broadest perspective of language. While syntax and semantics are thought to study only the context-independent elements of utterances, the linguistic types that lay claim to a meaning that is context-independent,[25] pragmatics is

---

[24]Davidson, "What Metaphors Mean," p. 436.

[25]In the original conception of the study of language, as embodied in the work of Morris, syntax and semantics were thought to study context-independent elements of language. However, as the case of indexicals indicates, the truth conditions of at least some utterances (namely those containing indexical elements) are dependent upon

thought to include such context-dependent features as the extralinguistic purpose of the communicative act, aspects of the context such as the objects visible to the participants, and the body language of the speaker. As a result, the competence that constitutes pragmatic knowledge goes beyond what it specifically linguistic.

Critique and Recent Developments

The apparent clarity of the delineation described by the framework above is easily challenged. One of the primary problems for this view of semantics and pragmatics concerns the practice of distinguishing between semantics and pragmatics based on the topic of study, where the phenomena they study are considered to be different entities within the same classificatory scheme. Combined with the Fregean requirement that semantics study only entities which are context-independent, it leads to a division between semantics and pragmatics that is untenable. Consider, for example, the case of utterances containing indexical elements. In the Fregean view, the proposition expressed by an utterance constitutes its sense (i.e. the meaning of the utterance), so that it falls completely within the realm of semantics and should be as context-independent as meaning. However, in the case of utterances containing indexical expressions, the proposition expressed is clearly context-dependent and thus seems to require more than semantic competence. At the same time, the existence of metaphorical content confirms the suspicion raised by an examination of indexicals that the proposition expressed is not the property of sentence types. This leads to the desire to relegate the class of expressions containing indexicals or figurative language to the field of pragmatics, so that semantics studies utterances without indexical elements and pragmatics studies utterances containing indexicals. However, the size of the class of utterances containing indexical elements, together with the continual emergence of other types of utterances whose proposition expressed is context-dependent, makes this solution improbable at best.[26]

Another difficulty with this view of semantics and pragmatics stems from the fact that even those phenomena considered to be context-independent enough to be studied by semantics turn out to be more context-dependent than previously thought. As Recanati points out, semantics and pragmatics cannot be distinguished by virtue of the fact that the

---

specific features of the context. However, this context dependence is still different from the pragmatic dependence upon the user.

[26]Yehoshua Bar-Hillel, "Indexical Expressions," *Mind* 63 (1954): 359–79.

former studies the proposition expressed (i.e. the designata of the sentence), since the proposition expressed by many nonindexical utterances is often dependent upon such pragmatic issues as matters of relevance.[27]

One way of defending the distinction between semantics and pragmatics based on topic of study is to specify that although semantics and pragmatics study the same phenomena, these phenomena are distinguished according to level, so that the same basic phenomena are studied from different perspectives. Given the latter, more recent view, while semantics and pragmatics may overlap in the phenomenon they study, their approach differs according to how they view this phenomenon, what factors or aspects of it they consider relevant.[28] For example, while both may study a successful utterance of a particular sentence, the pragmatist would study the utterance as a speech act while the semanticist would study it as an instance of a particular sentence type.[29] That is, while semantics is thought to study the knowledge that accounts for the proposition expressed by the utterance, as determined by factors that are supposedly independent of context, pragmatics studies the way what is said is used as a tool to accomplish a particular goal. In contrast to semantics, pragmatics studies utterances as a subset of the set of purposive human action.

Another problem with the traditional framework is the modular view it assumes of language processing. On the one hand, the traditional view seems to assume that in comprehending an utterance, the audience processes it first syntactically, then semantically, then pragmatically, in such a way that the result of each of the previous step is then used in the next. However, even in the better-understood processes of language processing, this model does not seem to work. For example, in attempting to identify any given sound (such as an "ei") the audience must use contextual and nonlinguistic information to understand what it is intended to represent (e.g. the word "I" or the word "eye"). In addition, the traditional view contains another form of modularity in that its model seems to assume that even in contexts in which more than one sentence is uttered, each sentence is processed fully and what is said is comprehended in isolation from

[27]François Recanati, "The Pragmatics of What Is Said," *Mind and Language* 4 (1989). Cited from *Pragmatics*, ed. Davis, pp. 97–120.

[28]If semantics and pragmatics include different features of utterances in their studies of them, does this mean that they study different phenomena? Or would we say that they study the same phenomena but from different perspectives?

[29]John Austin introduces the notion of a speech act, and his work (e.g., "Performative Utterances," in *The Philosophy of Language*, ed. Martinich, pp. 105–14") is used as a foundation for modern speech act theory such as that of Searle.

other utterances. Yet even in nonfigurative or nonindexical utterances this is clearly not the case. Consider, for example, the following exchange:

Inquisitive stranger: Where did you live?
Newcomer: In Glen Ellyn, near Chicago.
Inquisitive stranger: I hate living in cities.
Newcomer: Actually, Glen Ellyn is no where near being a city. We had horses living across the street from us.

What this example shows is that what was said by any given sentence is not necessarily fixed or completely interpreted by any given utterance (such as the Newcomer's response). In fact, assuming that each sentence is processed to completion (enough to manifest truth conditions) assumes hindsight or an omnipotent view. The traditional view seems to imply that comprehension of a conversation is created by decoding each utterance in such a way as to produce a fully interpreted proposition, and building a picture from the resulting propositions. Instead, it seems that comprehension of any given utterance is woven together throughout a conversational exchange. In other words, the process of language interpretation seems neither linear nor modular in that the audience begins with the presumption of the relevance of all the speaker's utterances and must continually return to this so-called pragmatic fact, by seeking other information from the context or asking follow-up questions as they process any given utterance.

While the traditional view suffers from numerous problems, it may be possible to revise it in such a way as to preserve the fields of syntax, semantics, and pragmatics by revising the way they are thought to interact. However, such a revision would have to begin with the assumptions that the traditional view makes concerning the language process, such as the assumption that linguistic acts can be fruitfully analyzed in the absence of specific contextual information, the assumption that utterances are processed in a linear fashion, and the assumption that the syntactic, semantic and pragmatic processes can be studied as separate modules. As Fauconnier points out,[30] having assumed a view of language processing that includes these and other assumptions, the tools the traditional view has derived reflect these biases, which can lead to what can only be described as a vicious circle. For example, the demand of context dependence has re-

---

[30]Gilles Fauconnier, *Mental Spaces* (Cambridge: Cambridge University Press, 1994). Fauconnier also presents a cognitive semantics which accommodates the non-linearity and nonmodularity we have pointed out by accounting for language processing using mental spaces.

sulted in a model of language processing that pushes more and more phenomena out of the realm of semantics. As result, one must consider even those tools such as the notion of meaning, the notion of the proposition expressed, the notion of conversational implicature, the notion of speaker intention, and the distinction between meaning and use as suspect. Our view of language processing does just that, pointing out that conceptualization underlies even such supposedly context-independent notions as the proposition expressed by a literal utterance. Current research reflects a trend toward taking semantics as a subset of pragmatics. However, some of these approaches seem to abandon the notion of the meaning and the distinction between meaning and use altogether. For example, Sperber and Wilson believe that any attempt to separate language from its use as a tool to accomplish certain goals is fruitless. Their approach considers pragmatics as the only approach to language, and semantics as subsidiary to it, a branch which cannot provide anything of value on its own. They also abandon the distinction between the metaphorical and the literal, analyzing the metaphorical as a form of loose talk. What we need instead is a view of language processing that preserves the notion of meaning and linguistic competence and a distinction between semantic matters (concerning reference and meaning) and pragmatic matters (concerning speaker intention). It is possible that the work of Fauconnier and other cognitive semanticists can meet these requirements, honoring the distinctions and notions we hold critical and filling in the details concerning language processing, embracing both literal and metaphorical language within the same framework.[31]

Summary

In summary, students of language interested in studying metaphor face the challenge of analyzing metaphor in a way that accommodates the underlying assumptions of a theory of meaning and a view of language and communication (Criterion 10). Given this system of classification, the question whether the study of metaphor properly belongs to semantics or to pragmatics becomes the question whether what is metaphorical can be captured in isolation from aspects of the linguistic act typically regarded as pragmatics and whether these factors are indeed pragmatic. As we shall see in the remainder of this book, metaphor seems to have both semantic and pragmatic aspects. On the one hand, a metaphorical utterance seems

[31]For more details, see Chapter 6.

to express a special or metaphorical content different from what it expresses when taken literally (according to the rules of the language), a content for which the speaker is held responsible (Criterion 3). In addition, the same metaphor is often used to communicate the same idea, something which encourages the belief that what metaphor communicates is, like literal meaning, attached to linguistic types and, therefore, is a matter of semantics. Consider the utterance "Ms. Williams is a bottomless pit when it comes to assignments." In this example it seems that one is able to distinguish what is metaphorical and what is not simply by virtue of linguistic features of the utterance, without having to appeal to such contextual features as beliefs of the speaker or hearer. However, metaphor also possesses features which make it appear to be pragmatic rather than semantic. That is, as we shall see in Chapter 3, both the identification and the interpretation of metaphors are often (if not always) dependent upon features of context thought to be irrelevant to semantics. In addition, the knowledge needed to understand a metaphor seems to go beyond linguistic competence, as evidenced by the fact that someone who is linguistically competent but lacks real world knowledge (and an ability to reconceptualize an entity in terms of the role it plays in a certain system) would consistently misunderstand metaphorical utterances. Finally, as Davidson points out, metaphors often seem to be used, not so much to convey a particular proposition that might just as well have been expressed in some other way, as to provoke an awareness of similarity or a change of perspective. In fact, it would seem futile to attempt to analyze metaphor within a formal semantics, as traditionally conceived.

Our concern here is not to classify metaphor as a matter of semantics or pragmatics but rather to present an analysis of it that accommodates both its aspects that would traditionally be considered semantic (the existence of metaphorical content and truth and relative independence of the speaker's intention in expressing the utterance) and the aspects that would be traditionally considered outside the realm of semantics (such as metaphor's context dependence, lack of conventionality, and requirement of pragmatic reasoning). As a result, when considering other theories of metaphor in the following chapters, we are mostly concerned with what each philosopher's classification of metaphor as semantic or pragmatic has to say about metaphor. At the same time, we hold that the study of metaphor provides yet another argument against the traditional view of the study of language that clearly distinguishes between the semantic and the pragmatic and attempts to study issues of meaning and what is said in isolation from contextual information. For our purposes here, I wish to formulate a view of metaphor that integrates its semantic and pragmatic elements within the study of language while preserving the distinctions we hold dear (the distinction between meaning and use, meaning and content, and what was said vs. what was implied). In doing so I have challenged the traditional conception of the relationship between semantics and pragmatics without providing a clear view to replace it. However, in casting doubt on certain assumptions (such as the notion of the context independence of the proposition expressed) and in embracing others (such as the distinction between meaning and use), I have also provided guidelines for form such a view should take. At the same time, I have established further criteria for an analysis of metaphor: the intuition for metaphorical content and truth (Criterion 3) and the need for consistency with the framework provided by semantics and pragmatics (Criterion 10).

3

A Critique of Metaphor
as Meaning

Davidson is one of the first philosophers to come out strongly against a tradition of semantic theories of metaphor, claiming that "metaphors mean what the words, in their most literal interpretation, mean, and nothing more."[1] That is, according to Davidson, metaphorical utterances do *not* express any message or content (in our terms, the proposition expressed) other than that provided by a literal interpretation (this goes against our Claims 2 and 3 in Chapter 1). Thus when the woman says, "Steve is a sheep dog," the proposition expressed by the utterance assigns Steve to the canine species. Neither, in Davidson's mind, do metaphors do have a special or metaphorical meaning (this supports our Claim 1). That is, the meaning of the word "sheep dog" in the utterance is precisely the same as it would be in an utterance in which the name "Steve" actually did refer to a sheep dog and the speaker was making a remark about the type of dog Steve was. In contrast, Davidson asserts that metaphor is a matter of use. In making the claim that metaphor does not have a metaphorical meaning but rather is a matter of use, he employs two fundamental distinctions. The first is between meaning (a semantic notion) and use (a pragmatic notion, involving language as a tool used to carry out certain actions). The second distinction, which is based upon the first, is between phenomena determined by semantic factors such as meaning, that is, at the level of semantics, and phenomena determined by pragmatic factors, that is, at the level of the user. The latter distinction is critical to determining whether metaphor can be studied within the realm of semantics or whether, because it only appears at the level of the user, that is, at the level

---

[1]Donald Davidson, "What Metaphors Mean," in *The Philosophy of Language*, 2nd edition, ed. A. P. Martinich (Oxford: Oxford University Press, 1991), p. 430.

of the speech act, it can only be studied at the level of pragmatics. In other words, Davidson's claim is that metaphors are not determined by semantic factors, such as meaning, and thus do not belong in the study of semantics (this goes against our Claim 4).

In making these claims, Davidson rejects such traditional theories of metaphor as that of Black, Beardsley, and Goodman which explain metaphorical content in terms of metaphorical meaning.[2] Davidson argues against the notion of metaphorical meaning and against semantic theories of metaphor in three main steps: (1) by showing that the literal meaning of a metaphor needs to be active in order for it to be metaphorical (defeating, in the process, the view of metaphor as an extension of the literal meaning); (2) by criticizing existing semantic theories of metaphor (specifically, those that explain metaphor in terms of metaphorical meaning); and (3) by arguing directly against the notion of metaphorical meaning (see pp. 75–96 below).

A Critique of Semantic Theories of Metaphor

Dependence of Metaphoricity on the Literal

The intuition upon which Davidson bases his analysis of metaphorical utterances is his conception of metaphoricity, that which allows us to distinguish between what is metaphorical and what is literal. For example, the absence of metaphoricity is required to make the judgment that a particular utterance is no longer metaphorical, but rather has become "dead" (Davidson's terminology) or "frozen" (Black's terminology). In describing metaphoricity Davidson says: "When the metaphor ('burned up') was active, we would have pictured fire in the eyes or smoke coming out of the ears."[3] In other words, in Davidson's analysis, what makes a metaphor alive metaphorically (the essence of metaphoricity) is an evocation derived from the literal or ordinary meanings of the terms. According to this criterion, the fact that an utterance of the phrase "burned up" no longer evokes such a picture is an indication that it is no longer an active metaphor. That is, since this phrase no longer has metaphoricity, it is no longer

[2]Max Black, "Metaphor," in *Models and Metaphor* (Ithaca: Cornell University Press, 1954), pp. 41–60; Monroe Beardsley, "The Metaphorical Twist," *Philosophy and Phenomenological Research*, 22 (1962): 293–307; Nelson Goodman, "Metaphor as Moonlighting?," in *On Metaphor*, edited by Sheldon Sacks (Chicago: University of Chicago Press, 1978–79), pp. 175–80.

[3]Donald Davidson, "What Metaphors Mean," in *The Philosophy of Language*, ed. Martinich, p. 434.

a metaphor. While the application of some terms to certain objects is metaphorical (in that they evoke images of the original meaning), others either have lost their metaphoricity (as in the case of dead metaphors), or never had it to begin with (as in the case of the literal applications of terms).

Using this intuition of metaphoricity, Davidson argues that any theory that attempts to account for metaphor by explaining it as an extension of the literal meaning of a term is inadequate in that it violates the conditions of metaphoricity. To prove this analysis, Davidson uses the example of the metaphorical utterance "the Spirit of God moved upon the face of the waters."[4] Suppose the metaphor consisted in the extension of the literal meaning of the metaphorical term (i.e. "face"). In this example, the term "face," in being applied metaphorically to describe an aspect of water (i.e. its surface), would acquire an extended meaning that includes it. For Davidson, this seems to mean that the term "face" would acquire an additional member in its extension, water. If this were the case, that is, if water were something in the extension of the word "face," the metaphorical term would quite literally apply in the given situation. However, if this were the case, that is, if waters do have faces (given the extension of the meaning of "face"), then understanding the metaphor would be identical with understanding the literal meaning of the term. Yet, in Davidson's view, it is precisely the fact that what we come to believe in comprehending the metaphor is *not* a part of the meaning of the terms (together with the fact that metaphors cause us to notice likenesses) that makes a metaphor metaphorical. Thus, if we hold an analysis of metaphor as an extension of meaning, "to make a metaphor is to murder it."[5]

One might argue against Davidson that what makes a particular utterance metaphorical is the *process* of extension (stretching) itself, rather than the resulting extended meaning. However, further consideration shows that this cannot be. If what made a metaphorical utterance were the act of extension, then each metaphor could be metaphorical only once, the first time it was uttered. In other words, only novel metaphors would be metaphors. In subsequent utterances the thing to which the term was metaphorically applied would now be in the proper extension of the term. Thus the term could not be considered to be metaphorically applied. Neither, then, can metaphoricity consist merely in the extension of meaning of a term. Thus, in Davidson's words, the intuition of what constitutes

[4]Ibid., p. 434.
[5]Ibid., p. 432.

metaphoricity leads to the requirement that "an adequate account of metaphor must allow that the primary or original meaning of words remain active in their metaphorical setting."[6]

However, this requirement is not enough to show that *only* the literal meanings of the terms enter into a semantic analysis of metaphorical utterances, so to rule out the very notion of metaphorical meaning, Davidson needs to go beyond this, something he does in two ways. First, he argues for this thesis through a process of elimination, that is, by arguing against accounts of metaphor that are based on a notion of metaphorical meaning. Metaphorical utterances have either single or multiple meanings. Given that Davidson has shown that the literal meanings of the terms must be a part of the semantic analysis of metaphor, for metaphor to have a special or metaphorical meaning, it must have more than one meaning. However, if all accounts of metaphor that rely on multiple meanings are incoherent, then metaphorical utterances must have only a literal meaning.

Second, Davidson argues against the thesis of metaphorical meaning directly using arguments known as the argument from dead metaphor, the argument from simile, and the argument from nonparaphrasability. (We will examine these later in this chapter.)

Davidson: Theories of Metaphor with Multiple Meanings

Davidson first attempts to discredit the thesis of metaphorical meaning by undermining theories of metaphor that account for metaphor in terms of metaphorical meaning (i.e. theories of metaphor with multiple meanings).

METAPHOR AS AN AMBIGUOUS TERM

The first option he considers is that metaphorical utterances are simply ambiguous, having both a literal meaning and a metaphorical meaning.[7] In other words, the term "bulldozer" in the metaphorical utterance of "Margaret Thatcher is a bulldozer" would be like the term "bank" in the utterance "I went to the bank" in that it properly refers to both (1) a species of land-moving machinery and (2) a species of person. In this view, Davidson's "characteristic tension of metaphor" would result from our uncertainty concerning which meaning is intended. As Davidson con-

[6]Ibid., p. 432.
[7]Ibid., p. 432.

cludes, this account of metaphor seems clearly inadequate. One obvious flaw in this view lies in its account of the characteristic tension of metaphors as uncertainty regarding whether the literal or metaphorical meaning is intended. Experience tells us that we are rarely at a loss regarding whether something is metaphorical or not. In addition, once we have decided an utterance is metaphorical (with the removal of this uncertainty), the metaphorical tension remains. Another flaw in the view is that it contradicts our intuition about how the literal and metaphorical meanings of a metaphor interact. When Socrates describes the philosopher as the pilot of the city (seen as a ship), the literal meaning of "pilot" is used to deduce the metaphorical meaning of pilot of a city. Yet in the case of truly ambiguous terms, there is no such relation between the terms. Instead both meanings seem to be tied by convention to the term, each appropriate in a different context. In fact, one might want to claim that it is precisely the existence of the link between the literal and the metaphorical that defines metaphor, and that when this link ceases to exist (as it perhaps does in truly dead metaphors), the term ceases to be metaphorical. Thus metaphors clearly cannot be accounted for as ambiguous terms.

METAPHOR AS A NONAMBIGUOUS TERM

The second type of theory Davidson considers is one in which metaphorical utterances have multiple meanings, yet the relationship between these meanings is specified, such that the utterances are not merely ambiguous. (That is, the metaphorical meaning is given as a derivative of the literal meaning, such that the meanings are not unrelated, as in the case of ambiguous terms.) Several prominent theories that explain metaphor in terms of metaphorical meaning appear in this examination, including that of Black and Henle and the comparison view. In this type of theory Davidson includes (1) the theory that metaphors function as puns, with different meanings upon different iterations; (2) the theory that the term being metaphorically applied has two meanings in a single context, both of which are intended as part of the meaning of the utterance; (3) the theory that what makes an utterance metaphorical is its degree of novelty; (4) the theory that the figurative meaning of the metaphor is identical with the literal meaning of the corresponding simile; and (5) the view that a metaphor is an elliptical simile (the comparison view).

Metaphor as a Pun. The first analysis of metaphor that Davidson considers and rejects is the view that metaphors have two meanings which are both active in a single context in the way that both readings of puns are. However, as Davidson points out, metaphors do not seem to require reiteration (in the way that puns do) in that in processing a metaphor, "whatever meanings we assign the words they keep through every correct reading of the passage."[8] In other words, while the successful reading of a pun requires two readings or interpretations, with two distinct sets of truth or satisfaction conditions, the successful reading of a metaphor does not.

Two Meanings: One Active, One Latent. The second theory Davidson considers is one in which metaphor is considered to have both a literal and a metaphorical meaning which are connected by a rule and which take turns being latent or active depending on whether the context is literal or metaphorical.[9] According to Davidson, this theory is similar to the Fregean analysis of referring terms in sentences in modal contexts and those expressing propositional attitudes in that, in both cases, words are thought to have, in addition to their usual meaning, a different meaning which is related to the usual meaning by a rule of some sort.[10]

This theory seems to be the most plausible of the theories Davidson considers, and, possibly as a result, Davidson's critique of it is the most revealing about the underlying reasons for his resistance to the notion of metaphorical meaning.

To argue against this analysis, Davidson describes a situation in which an Earthling who has been attempting to teach a Saturnian the meaning of the word "floor" by indicating various floors and uttering the word,[11] now points to the Earth (from a spaceship) and says "Floor."[12] According to Davidson, the theory of metaphor under consideration would be un-

[8]Ibid., p. 432–33.

[9]Ibid., p. 433. Davidson seems to think this analysis corresponds to that of Henle's theory of iconic signification.

[10]In the case of referring terms in oblique contexts, Davidson specifies the rule that relates the two so that the referent of the referring term in the oblique context is the meaning of the term in ordinary contexts.

[11]To describe language learning in this way, we must assume certain things Quine has shown to be less than obvious and maybe not even reasonably assumable, especially since the two parties involved are not only from different cultures but from different races (V. W. Quine, *Word and Object* [Cambridge, Mass.: MIT Press, 1960]). That is, we must assume that we are able to indicate various objects (such as floors) to the Saturnian in such a way that the Saturnian recognizes the objects we are indicating (i.e. as opposed to floor-parts, or things that are on the floor, or a floor at a given data point in a space-time-continuum, etc.).

[12]Davidson, "What Metaphors Mean," pp. 433–34.

able to distinguish between situations in which (1) the Saturnian takes the utterance to assign the term "floor" to the Earth in such a way that one can literally say that the Earth is a floor and (2) the Saturnian understands the utterance as a metaphor.[13] Since Davidson believes these two situations are different in an important way, he cites this failure as reason to dismiss such theories of metaphor. Davidson's argument for this conclusion is as follows:

(1) This theory claims that a word has a new meaning (i.e. its metaphorical meaning) in a metaphorical context.
(2) Therefore, under this theory, the occasion of metaphor is the occasion for the learning of a new meaning.
(3) The occasion of learning a new meaning is a drill in language use (i.e. a matter of learning about language).
(4) If the application of a word to an object is a drill in language use, then it is not about the world.
(5) Metaphor is clearly about the world and not a drill in language use.
(6) Therefore, this theory is wrong about metaphor.

As we shall see, this criticism is particularly interesting because it shows that underlying Davidson's criticisms of semantic theories of metaphor are three main beliefs: (1) that metaphors are about the world in that in processing them one learns something about the world rather than about language; (2) that what is metaphorical is not conventional (and, since Davidson regards language and semantics as conventional, metaphor is independent of both); and (3) that metaphorical meaning (if it exists at all) is not tied to objects in the way that literal meanings are. In the case of literal meaning, once a term has been said to apply to an object, it belongs to that object through the rules of the language, and in seeing the term applied to that object, one acquires a new linguistic rule.

However, while this criticism is an interesting one, it relies on assumptions not spelled out and perhaps not sustainable. For one thing, premise

---

[13]Note that this passage indicates the Davidson believes there is a difference between taking a term to apply literally to an object and taking the term to apply metaphorically. This implies that he believes there is a difference between understanding the utterance "That is a floor" metaphorically and literally, which would contradict his contention that what makes an utterance metaphorical is not the meanings of the terms or what is said, but how they are used. However, this contradiction is only apparent, in that what is actually being contrasted is not a literal and a metaphorical interpretation of an utterance but rather a case of language learning and metaphor.

(1) seems to assume that for a term to have a metaphorical meaning, this meaning must be *new*. However, it is not clear what it means for the metaphorical meaning to be new. If metaphorical meanings are new in the same way that literal meanings are new (in that the metaphorical meaning of "sheep dog" in an utterance is new to someone if and only if that person has not encountered the term applied in that way), it seems that Davidson is saying metaphors are always novel. But this is clearly not the case, for not only do we reuse metaphors (such as "sun" used to indicate value), but in some cases metaphors also seem to have the same *meaning* when re-used. For example, if someone said to Romeo, in response to his claim about Juliet, "No, Celia is the sun," the term used metaphorically would have the same meaning as it did when Romeo used it. That is, we can't assume that just because a word has a metaphorical meaning in a metaphorical context, the meaning is a new one. In addition, since it is not clear what exactly it means for a metaphorical meaning to be new, it does not follow that a new metaphorical meaning is similar enough to new literal meaning to derive premise (2). That is, even in cases of novel metaphors, it is not clear that the occasion of their use is necessarily the occasion of the learning of a new meaning. This fact brings us to yet another criticism of Davidson's argument against the account of metaphor.

Premise (2) presents difficulties in that it is not at all clear that it follows from premise (1) in the way that Davidson specifies. That is, Davidson assumes that the fact that a word may have a new meaning in a metaphorical context (as "floor" may have in the case of the person speaking metaphorically to the Saturnian or "sheep dog" may have in the utterance "Steve is a sheep dog") means that the occasion is one of learning the metaphorical meaning (which may or may not be new to the participants in the conversation). However, as I will show, the occasion may instead may be one of use of the meaning rather than one of language learning, even if the metaphorical meaning *is* a new one to the audience (which is not necessary). Davidson makes several unjustified assumptions, first in deducing premise (2) from premise (1) and then in combining premise (2) with premises (3), (4), and (5). Among these are the assumptions: (A) that metaphorical meaning has to be learned before it can be used, which is necessary for deducing premise (2) from premise (1), and (B) that metaphorical meaning is learned in the way that literal meaning is learned (i.e. through ostension), which is necessary for combining premise (2) with premises (3), (4), and (5). However, neither of these assumptions is maintained by the semantic theory Davidson is examining[14] (thus the burden of proof is on Davidson) and both can be challenged.

The first assumption (A) can be challenged by our experience that novel metaphors (i.e. metaphors we have never heard before) are metaphorical. That is, novel metaphors are often used quite successfully to communicate a point or to draw one's attention to a likeness. Rumelhart's example of his child saying "Mom, my sock has a hangnail" is a good case in point.[15] While the metaphor was indubitably novel to its audience, it was clearly a situation in which it was used in order to communicate something about the world to the audience and not a drill in language. In fact it is not clear that metaphorical meaning is something that *is* learned, let alone learned through ostension, something which leads us to the second assumption.

Davidson's second assumption, (B), that metaphorical meaning is learned in the way that literal meanings are learned—through ostension—contradicts our experience with metaphorical meaning. Ostension, which draws a connection between an object and a term, such that the object is assigned to the class represented by that term, is suitable to the teaching of literal meaning, which seems to depend upon a conventional link between language and objects in the world. However, it is not clear that one can use ostension to teach metaphorical meaning, or even that metaphorical meaning is something which is taught or even learned. In fact, it is not even clear what it means to know the metaphorical meaning of a term and whether this knowledge is similar to the knowledge of a literal meaning of a term. Consider, for example, the term "sheep dog" in the metaphor "Steve is a sheep dog." To understand the metaphor—that is, to understand what is being said regarding Steve—one must know the metaphorical meaning of "sheep dog." However, to understand the metaphorical meaning of "sheep dog" one must first know the literal meaning of the term (which can be learned through ostension), yet one must also go beyond it. Knowledge of the metaphorical meaning of sheep dogs (which is clearly context-dependent) in this particular situation seems to involve seeing a sheep dog from a perspective in which certain features of sheep dogs are eliminated completely (e.g. being a member of the canine species)

[14]Since Davidson provides few details about the theory in question, it is difficult to say what assumptions it maintains. However, even given just the bare bones of a semantic theory of the type Davidson outlines we can determine that such a theory need not maintain the assumptions Davidson makes.

[15]David Rumelhart, "Some Problems with the Notion of Literal Meaning," in *Metaphor and Thought*, ed. A. Ortony (Cambridge: Cambridge University Press, 1979), pp. 78–90.

and others are modified (e.g. herding sheep becomes directing people toward a certain goal). That is, knowing this particular metaphorical meaning of "sheep dog" seems to mean knowing that a sheep dog represents (through the relation of prototypicality) a class of beings whose role is to group and move other beings in a directed way. In my analysis of metaphor, to process the metaphor is to reconceptualize sheep dogs in terms of the role they play with sheep and then to conceive of a human named Steve in terms of that role. However, knowing the metaphorical meaning of a term cannot mean that we have given up the conventional link between the term "sheep dog" and the member of the canine species that performs the herding role and therefore eliminate being a member of the canine species from the required features of a sheep dog. In other words, the metaphorical meaning of a metaphor (i.e. what we learn when we comprehend the metaphor) does not replace its literal meaning. Nor does knowing the metaphorical meaning in this situation seem to mean that given its use in another metaphorical context, that meaning must hold sway. That is, in each case we seem to need to ask what a sheep dog really is in the context, which involves a new look at the world, not the language. In addition, in each case we must use the literal meaning of the term to derive the metaphorical meaning. As a result, metaphorical meaning also cannot be a conventional or literal meaning which is additional to the original literal meaning. That is, metaphorical terms cannot be explained by ambiguity.[16]

In summary, it seems that what Davidson's counterargument has shown is that if there is such a thing as metaphorical meaning, it is not like literal meaning, in that the occasion of its use can be the occasion of its learning. In addition, it seems that metaphorical meaning is not conventional in the way that literal meaning is and, as a result, it cannot be learned through ostension, if it is learned at all. As a result, we have a new criterion to add to our list of conditions on a theory of metaphor, that is, the lack of conventionality of metaphor. (This is Criterion 12 on our list.) In addition, as Davidson says, it seems that in order to grasp the metaphorical meaning of a metaphor we are forced to see the world in a different way. Thus we must also add the fact that metaphors are about the world, rather than about language, to our list of desiderata (Criterion 13 on our list).

---

[16]A further argument against the possibility of accounting for metaphor as an ambiguous term lies in the fact that the number of metaphorical meanings any given term might have is potentially, depending on the context in which it is uttered.

Metaphor as a Novel Use. One of the easiest theories of metaphor to eliminate is that which explains metaphoricity in terms of novelty, which argues that what makes something metaphorical is merely the fact that in it some expression is applied to an object which has not been applied before.[17] This clearly contradicts our intuition that metaphors remain metaphorical for long periods of time, that the metaphoricity has less to do with novelty than with a certain relation between the actual referent of a term and its literal referent. In addition to the criticism given by Davidson, under the conception of metaphor presented there would be no way of distinguishing metaphors from category mistakes, sentences that apply a known word to an object to which it has not been applied. As a result, Chomsky's example of a nonsense sentence "Colorless green ideas sleep furiously," would be metaphorical, as would the utterance of "A whale is a mammal" to one who did not know that a whale is a mammal.

Figurative Meaning as the Literal Meaning of the Corresponding Simile. Another analysis of metaphor Davidson considers and rejects is the analysis that specifies that the figurative meaning of the metaphor is the literal meaning of the corresponding simile. Davidson summarily dismisses this (and the next analysis of metaphor) saying that this identification between metaphorical meaning and the literal meaning of a painfully trivial simile "make[s] the hidden meaning of the metaphor."[18] Since all similes, in Davidson's view, are trivially true, all metaphors would be as well. But this contradicts Davidson's belief that all metaphors are false. Thus this account of metaphorical meaning cannot be right.[19]

Davidson's belief that all similes are painfully and trivially true derives from his view of similarity, namely, his conception that any two objects are similar inasmuch as they have at least one property in common.[20] According to this view of similarity, all comparison statements (i.e. figurative

[17]Note that this does not rule out the possibility that the term is being applied to an object in an extension of the meaning, despite the fact that the audience has never seen it applied in that way before.

[18]Davidson, "What Metaphors Mean," p. 435.

[19]Note that there is a problem here even if we don't believe all metaphors to be obviously false, that is, even if we disagree with Davidson's view that the truth value of a metaphor is the truth value of its literal interpretation. For even if we hold that the truth value of a metaphor differs from that of its literal interpretation, the result that all metaphors are trivially true is clearly contradicted by examples of false metaphors, such as "My shy, quiet friend has the personality of a Doberman pincer."

[20]Fogelin cites Davidson's conception of similarity as the only thing preventing Davidson from embracing Fogelin's version of comparativism. Robert Fogelin, *Figuratively Speaking* (Yale: Yale University Press, 1988), p. 61

as well as literal) are painfully trivial in that they must all be true since, as Davidson says, "The earth is like a floor, the Assyrian did come down like a wolf on the fold, because everything is like everything."[21] Since this view of similarity (what Goodman would call the naive view) clearly contradicts what Goodman, Tversky, and indeed common sense show, Davidson's criticism cannot stand as presented. That is, since similarity is not the simplistic symmetrical relation that Davidson assumes and everything is not like everything else, Davidson cannot criticize the analysis of metaphor in terms of simile on the grounds that it would result in metaphors' being trivially true.

However, Davidson's criticism can be presented in another way. That is, whatever one's conception of similarity, if the figurative meaning of a metaphor were just the literal meaning of the corresponding simile, then most metaphors would be false (since the literal interpretation of most similes is false). Yet our intuition tells us that a utterance of "Steve is a sheep dog" is probably true, despite Steve's lack of membership in the canine species. Thus it seems that even if we give up the naive view of similarity, Davidson's criticism of this analysis of metaphorical meaning as the literal meaning of the corresponding simile can be maintained.

Metaphor as an Elliptical Simile. The final alternative Davidson considers is that of comparativism, that is, the theory that metaphor is an elliptical simile such that its literal meaning is that of its corresponding simile and its figurative meaning is the figurative meaning of its corresponding simile.[22] Davidson presents several criticisms of this analysis, among them a criticism which stems from his view of the role of the literal in the metaphorical.

> If we take the literal meaning of the metaphor to be the literal meaning of the matching simile, we deny access to what we originally took to be the literal meaning of the metaphor, and we agreed almost from the start that *this* meaning was essential to the working of the metaphor, whatever else might have to be brought in the way of a nonliteral meaning.[23]

In other words, the proposition expressed by a literal interpretation of a metaphor (e.g. "Steve is a bulldozer") is not the same as the proposition

[21] Davidson, "What Metaphors Mean," p. 435.

[22] Note that the version of comparativism that Davidson presents here is not necessarily compatible with those of other comparativists (such as Aristotle and Fogelin. For example, Davidson seems to consider comparativism to be a semantic theory of metaphor, while Fogelin argues that it is a use theory of metaphor.

[23] Davidson, "What Metaphors Mean," p. 435.

expressed by the corresponding simile ("Steve is like a bulldozer"). Yet Davidson has argued previously that the former proposition ("Steve is a bulldozer") is necessary to the utterance's being metaphorical.[24] To defend himself, the comparativist could embrace one of two options. On the one hand the comparativist could show that Davidson's argument that the literal meaning of the metaphorical utterance must be active in its processing is unfounded. On the other hand the comparativist could show that the literal meaning of the corresponding simile is enough like the literal meaning of the metaphor so that the former can evoke the appropriate images Davidson sees as necessary to metaphoricity.[25]

In conclusion, it is not clear that Davidson succeeds in ruling out the possibility of metaphorical meaning by defeating existing semantic theories. On the one hand, he handily defeats several semantic theories of metaphor, with the possible exceptions of the theory similar to the Fregean theory for oblique contexts and comparativism. However, of the theories he considers, only these two are actually held by anyone, and his criticism of them is dependent upon views that can be challenged (i.e. his view of similarity and the requirement that metaphorical meaning be similar to literal meaning in that it must be learned before it can be used). On the other hand, Davidson does *not* show that it is impossible, in principle, for there to be a semantic theory of metaphor which includes the notion of metaphorical meaning. To challenge Davidson's results, therefore, semantic theorists of metaphor need only challenge either his view of similarity (as Fogelin's theory does) or his requirements of metaphorical meaning (as Stern's and my theory of metaphor do).[26]

What rings true in Davidson's treatment of metaphor (and what we should carry with is in our remaining analysis) is that once a conventional link has been established between a metaphor and its "metaphorical meaning" such that the metaphorical phrase comes to *mean* something additional to its original meaning, the metaphor ceases to be a metaphor. For example, once "to kick the bucket" comes to mean "to die," the utterance of the former ceases to be metaphorical and becomes an idiom, a kind of instance of ambiguity. The test of metaphoricity is the degree to which the original meaning is active in the understanding of the utterance.

[24]Fogelin misunderstands what Davidson means by saying that "we deny access to what we originally took to be the literal meaning of the metaphor" and thus does not adequately address Davidson's criticism in his analysis of Davidson. Fogelin, *Figuratively Speaking*, p. 57.
[25]See Chapter 6 for other arguments against comparativism.
[26]Stern, "What Metaphors Do Not Mean."

As a result of Davidson's insights, we have added three new criteria to our list of conditions for a theory of metaphor (Criteria 11, 12, and 13).

Having concluded his criticisms of theories of metaphor based on a notion of metaphorical meaning, Davidson gives his rather sketchy arguments against the thesis of metaphorical meaning itself.

A Critique of Metaphorical Meaning

Argument from Nonparaphrasability

The first argument Davidson brings against the concept of metaphorical meaning is the argument from nonparaphrasability: "If a metaphor has a special cognitive content, why should it be so difficult or impossible to set it out?"[27] One way of spelling out the premises of this argument is as follows:

(1) Metaphorical utterances typically do not admit of paraphrasing.
(2) Any given cognitive content can be expressed in at least two different ways (i.e. it can be paraphrased).
(3) Being (easily) paraphrasable is a test of whether the cognitive content of a sentence captures its cognitive effect.[28]
(4) Therefore, the cognitive effect of a metaphorical utterance does not lie in the cognitive content of its terms.
(5) Metaphorical meaning is defined so as to capture the cognitive effect of the utterance through cognitive content.
(6) Therefore, there is no such thing as metaphorical meaning as defined.

COUNTERARGUMENT ONE

Given this interpretation of Davidson's argument, the simplest way of challenging it is to challenge the second premise, the hidden assumption that underlies Davidson's analysis. This is precisely what Goodman does: by pointing out that even literal utterances can be difficult or impossible to

---

[27]Davidson, "What Metaphors Mean," pp. 430–41, p. 438.

[28]Underlying this argument is Davidson's conception of what it means to be paraphrasable, which seems to involve not only the cognitive content of an utterance, as evidenced by its truth conditions, but also its effect, which seems to include feelings as well as thoughts we are led to contemplate. Since Davidson regards the thoughts we are led to contemplate as outside the cognitive content of the utterance, he seems to make a distinction between the cognitive content of an utterance and its cognitive effect, one which he does not justify in any detail.

paraphrase exactly, he challenges the assumption that any given cognitive content can be expressed in more than one way.[29] For Davidson to defend himself from this criticism, he would have to show that paraphrasability is essential to cognitive content, something he does not do.

COUNTERARGUMENT TWO

Another way of challenging Davidson's argument is to question the first premise, the assumption that metaphors cannot be paraphrased. However, one's view of whether or not metaphors can be paraphrased depends, among other things, on one's view of what it means to be paraphrasable, and there are at least two possible interpretations of this notion. One possible interpretation is that it asserts that metaphors have an effect (cognitive or otherwise) that cannot be duplicated by a corresponding literal utterance. According to this interpretation of paraphrasability, even if a literal expression expresses the same proposition (has the same informational or cognitive content) as the metaphorical utterance, if it does not have the same effect on the interpreter, it does not qualify as a paraphrase of it. Depending upon how broadly one interprets the term "effect," accepting this definition of paraphrasability could entail that no utterances are paraphrasable. For example, since different words carry different associations and emotional responses, if we specify that the paraphrase must duplicate these associations and responses exactly, it would be almost impossible for something to be a paraphrase. Even if we restrict the notion of effect to eliminate emotional responses, it still would seem impossible for all utterances to have paraphrases.

However, we commonly assume a less rigorous interpretation of the notion of paraphrasability, according to which what a paraphrase must capture (in order to be a paraphrase) is merely the truth conditions of the utterance.[30] According to this interpretation, we could say that metaphors are paraphrasable if and only if what they say (i.e. the propositions they express) can be expressed in some other way.

[29]Nelson Goodman, "Metaphor as Moonlighting," in *Philosophical Perspectives on Metaphor*, ed. Mark Johnson (Minneapolis: University of Minnesota Press, 1981), pp. 221–27, p. 222.

[30]Note that this type of paraphrase has its limitations, as Perry's work on indexicals has shown. That is, even though one utterance might have the same truth conditions as another (e.g. "Sandra Wallace won the Noble prize" and "I won the Noble prize") the truth conditions alone do not explain the behavior of those who comprehend the utterance. John Perry, "The Problem of the Essential Indexical," *Nous* 13, no. 1 (1979): 3–21.

Keeping in mind both interpretations of what it means to be paraphrasable, *can* metaphorical utterances be paraphrased? Some metaphors seem to be easily paraphrased. For example, instead of saying that John passed away, we can say that John died. To the degree that this utterance is metaphorical in our society (in that many of us do not regard death as a passing away into another kind of existence), this sentence alludes to death as a passage into another kind of existence in a way that referring directly (i.e. literally) to death does not. In addition, the indirectness inherent in referring to death as passing away may embody a certain kind of politeness or protocol in our society. However, since the expression "to pass away" has been used so often to convey death, the difference between using one of the terms rather than another has lessened. It seems as though the two have become almost synonymous. In addition, since philosophers of language are interested solely in cognitive effect (usually defined in terms of cognitive content expressed by the utterance), a difference residing solely in matters of social protocol does not seem to be significant. Thus it seems that at least some metaphors may be paraphrasable, under either definition of paraphrasability.

However, it may be that this particular metaphorical utterance is easily paraphrased only because, if not already a dead metaphor, it is well on its way to becoming one. In other words, since "passing away" has come to mean "dying," to substitute one for the other might more appropriately be considered a literal paraphrase of what can be considered a literal utterance. However, while dead metaphors may be easily paraphrased, they are not sufficient tests of the paraphrasability of metaphorical utterances.

Other metaphorical utterances seem more difficult to paraphrase and seem to lose more in the translation, in either interpretation of paraphrasability. For example, consider the metaphorical utterances "Juliet is the sun" or "Let us go then, you and I, when the evening is spread out against the sky like a patient etherized upon the table."[31] The fact that literary metaphors seldom wear their meaning on their sleeves but instead inspire debate and analysis which may never be completed seems to indicate that at least some metaphors are difficult, if not impossible, to paraphrase.

One source of this difficulty is that metaphors, in showing us one thing in the guise of another—in showing us the term used as a metaphor, or "vehicle"—tend to evoke the feelings one might have toward the vehicle,

---

[31]T. S. Elliot, "The Love Song of J. Alfred Prufrock," in *T. S. Eliot: Selected Poems* (London: Faber and Faber, 1954), p. 11.

as Henle points out.[32] For example, when we speak of someone passing away, rather than as dying, the use of "pass away" tends to evoke a hopeful feeling, while avoiding some of the negative feelings associated with dying. So too, when we refer to a woman as the sun we may feel toward her the kind of anticipation and affection anyone who has survived a long winter in the Midwest knows, just as considering the evening as a patient etherized upon the table may make us feel clinical and detached. Since the feeling is evoked by the identification of one thing with another, it would seem difficult for a literal paraphrase to evoke the same feeling.[33] Yet, again, for those seeking only the cognitive content of metaphor, under a less rigorous interpretation of paraphrasability, this evocation of feeling is not only not to be desired but is to be avoided.[34]

Another reason for the difficulty of paraphrasing such metaphors might be that the full expression of their meaning rarely occurs at first hearing or reading, without further interaction between speaker and interpreter. This difficulty seems to stem from at least three sources: (1) that metaphors usually express or imply an unspecified number of propositions; (2) that comprehension of all the propositions expressed by the metaphor rarely occurs in a moment or without further interaction; and (3) that which propositions are entailed by the metaphor is not explicitly specified by the metaphor. That is, it is not clear which properties of the metaphor vehicle are to be attributed to the subject of the metaphor. Regarding the first difficulty, the fact that metaphors usually express multiple propositions shows only that expressing something metaphorically rather than literally is more economical in the use of words. It does not show that there is a significant difference between what metaphorical and literal speech capture. Nor does the fact that the interpretation of many metaphors occurs in time, sometimes only with further interaction between speaker and interpreter, entail that metaphors cannot, in principle,

[32]Paul Henle, "Metaphor," in *Philosophical Perspectives on Metaphor*, ed. Johnson, pp. 83–104.

[33]One way to evoke the same feeling might be to refer to the same object in the paraphrase. The theory of metaphor that holds the figurative meaning of the metaphor to be that of the corresponding simile might accomplish this, since it would interpret "Juliet is the sun" as "Juliet is like a sun."

[34]Using David Kaplan's distinction between character and content, we could explain the difference between what we understand when we process a metaphor and its literal paraphrase by saying that while the literal paraphrase captures the content of the metaphor, it does not capture its character. This is the approach taken by Josef Stern, "What Metaphors Do Not Mean," *Midwest Studies in Philosophy* 16 (1991): 13–51.

be paraphrased. There seems to be no evidence that the metaphor expresses an infinite number of propositions. Given the more rigorous sense of paraphrasability, one can argue that a literal paraphrase would not produce the same process of discovery and thus may not be as effective an educational tool. However, from the cognitive point of view, the fact that the interpretation of metaphor requires a process does not imply that what is understood in the process is anything other than cognitive and thus expressible in a literal paraphrase.

It is the third difficulty, the fact that the metaphor usually does not specify which properties are being predicated of the metaphor subject, that seems most intractable. In some cases, contextual information is sufficient to determine what can or cannot be expressed by the metaphor. For example, when a love-stricken Romeo says to his friend, "Juliet is the sun," the fact that Romeo is in love, along with the expression of rapture on his face, indicates that the relative importance of the sun to life is relevant, and that the sun is not seen as a destructive force. However, in other cases, this does not seem to be the case. That is, if Romeo merely shows intensity which can be seen as pleasurable or painful, it is uncertain whether or not the metaphor attributes the destructive or creative qualities of the sun to Juliet. It is precisely this vagueness that makes metaphor unpopular in philosophy, since its lack of precision makes the argument within which it appears more difficult to articulate and thus to evaluate. The fact that we may *never* know which propositions are expressed may even imply that that what is expressed is not fully determined. If this were so, it would seem that to imply that some metaphors are not paraphrasable, either in the rigorous sense of the term (in which the same effect must be produced) or in the less rigorous sense (in which the same cognitive content needs to be expressed).

Yet another reason metaphors may seem difficult to paraphrase (Criterion 4) is that, along with the information they convey (the proposition they express) comes a perspective that may be as important as, if not more important than, the actual information (i.e. as captured by the proposition expressed or truth conditions of the utterance). As Black puts it, metaphorical utterances have us see one thing through or in terms of another.[35] Through this process, certain characteristics or properties of the thing viewed are emphasized, while others are de-emphasized or suppressed altogether. For example, when Socrates tells us the philosopher is the pilot

---

[35]Max Black, "Metaphor," in *Philosophical Perspectives on Metaphor*, ed. Johnson, 63–82, p. 75.

of the city, we see a philosopher as a person with navigational skills and a sense of direction rather than as a Socratic gadfly who shows us our ignorance or a person lost in obscure thoughts and discussions. In the same way, when we see Juliet as the sun, we emphasize certain properties of the sun (its centrality and importance in the universe), leave aside certain properties of the sun (such as its size and mass), and attribute the remaining properties to Juliet, with the modifications necessary to accommodate animate beings.

In the terms of my theory of metaphor, objects referred to in the metaphor (as well as others that are part of the system) are reconceptualized according to the roles they play in the system. As a result, category lines are redrawn in such a way that objects previously in categories far apart in the taxonomy are now of the same kind, while objects previously of the same kind are now far apart.[36] For example, when a metaphor has us see Juliet as the sun, we are forced to reconceptualize the sun and Juliet (in terms of the role the sun plays in a system). In the process we draw new category lines such that the property of being the center of the universe is more important (i.e. salient) than that of being animate, and thus Juliet (an animate object) is more like the sun (an inanimate object) than like a bear (another animate object). In addition, the new category lines are sufficient to override even the bonds of familial relations, so that Juliet is more like the sun than like another human being in her own family. The defining property, the property according to which the sorting takes place, is one's relative importance within one's universe. That a new schema or sorting mechanism has being introduced can be seen in the fact that the schema lingers as the background against which subsequent utterances are interpreted. After Romeo tells us that Juliet is the sun, we might easily respond that another relative is a moon that constantly tags along, and a second person is a distant planet without apparent effect and thus never noticed, a third a lost and wandering comet, a suitor who is drawn to the sun and then, in an intense rebound, is flung away from it. Or, taking the schema and using something of importance to us (rather than to Romeo) as the defining property, we might say that Juliet is not the sun, but golf is.

Thus the question whether metaphor is paraphrasable becomes the question whether this change of perspective and the creation of a new

---

[36]Goodman, "Metaphor as Moonlighting." Goodman, who maintains an extensionalist theory of meaning, describes this solely in terms of the redrawing of category lines.

schema and new categories, can be brought about by literal means. In addition, the question is raised whether this change in perspective counts as a cognitive effect and, if so, whether this cognitive effect can be brought about purely by the expression of cognitive content (the literal expression of a proposition). This question, itself, depends on one's view of the role of perspective in what is seen, whether it should be considered part of what is seen. On the one hand, since we see things from a certain perspective and do not see the perspective itself, it seems as though the two should be held apart. In the case of language, it seems that the proposition contemplated should be evaluated separately from the perspective from which it is regarded. On the other hand, in some situations, when we attempt to take the proposition in isolation from the perspective, we run into the kind of difficulties Perry discusses regarding indexicals.[37] For example, despite the fact that the proposition expressed by "You are standing in the way of the train" in a certain context may be identical with the proposition expressed by "Henry is standing in the way of the train," the two have markedly different effects on an audience.

Let us first consider how we might duplicate the effect of our sample metaphorical utterance and then consider whether our literal replacement is a paraphrase in the first (broad) or second (narrow) sense of the word. Consider the metaphorical utterance "Juliet is the sun." Romeo might have said, instead of this, "Consider the class of things that are the center of certain systems, like the sun at the center of the universe. Notice that without the sun, animate things cannot grow, reproduce, or even subsist. Notice that the day begins when the sun appears and ends when it leaves. Notice that seedlings struggle to break through the earth to find the sunlight and, when they succeed, orient their bodies so that their leaves face the sun. Notice that all planetary activity centers on the sun. For me, Juliet is in this class of things." Could such a literal paraphrase succeed and, if not, what is missing? On the surface, it does not seem as if anything is missing, especially if Romeo mentions all the properties of the sun he wishes to attribute to Juliet. As in the case of the metaphorical utterance, a new class of things is identified and Juliet is located in that class of things, together with such things as the sun. In addition, certain properties of both Juliet and the sun are emphasized, while others are left out.

Nonetheless it seems that there is a certain potential for failure in the

---

[37]John Perry, "Frege on Demonstratives," *Philosophical Review* 86, no. 4 (1977): 474–97; Perry, "The Problem of the Essential Indexical."

literal paraphrase that isn't present in the metaphorical utterance. In the case of the literal utterance it seems possible to miss the point. For example, one could fail to "add up" the various properties cited in such a way as to understand the prototype of the defined class. This failure seems to be one of failure to express the cohesiveness expressed by a metaphor, as well as the relative importance of the different properties. In the literal paraphrase it seems that one cannot judge the relative importance of the properties, their contribution to the whole.

Another potential for failure seems to lie in the ability of the paraphrase to handle new elements. In other words, it seems a vital part of metaphor that it address how previously unmentioned elements fit into the schema. For example, given the utterance "Juliet is the sun," it seems to follow easily that Romeo is a planet circling the sun, etc. However, given the literal paraphrase, it is not clear that it will result in the prompt assignment of roles within the schema that the metaphorical version clearly provides.

Yet another lack in the literal paraphrase seems to lie in its ability to rule on whether a previously unmentioned property of the object of comparison (i.e. the sun) is or is not attributable to Juliet. Given the metaphor (in context), it would seem to be fairly easy to say that the unmentioned properties of temperature and age are irrelevant, while those of an ability to show the way and provide cheer *are* relevant.

In other words, it seems that our literal paraphrase can succeed as a replacement for the metaphorical utterance only insofar as it is able to create this network of relationships, with the cohesiveness of a picture, and proper emphasis assigned to each. Pictures, or the images metaphors impart, capture and express a whole, with all the intricacies of the relationships between the various parts, in a way that seems difficult, if not impossible, to capture with a literal utterance. That is, unless the interpreter is able, via the literal paraphrase, to "get the picture," the paraphrase has failed, depending on which notion of paraphrasability is held. However, there seems to be no indication that literal language cannot be used to describe the picture (which is sufficient for our purposes if we maintain that all a paraphrase needs to do is to capture the information expressed, not necessarily from the same perspective). While there seem to be various tests of the success of the utterance (ability to handle new elements, ability to incorporate or rule out other properties associated with the metaphor vehicle, etc.), perhaps the most intuitive test is this: after hearing the literal paraphrase, does the interpreter say, "I see, Juliet is the sun?" If so, it seems that the paraphrase has succeeded. However, there are two ways of viewing the significance of this being the test. On the one hand, the fact that this is the test could been seen as illustrating the ability of the para-phrase to produce the same effect as the metaphor and thus to serve as its replacement. However, there is another way of looking at it. When the in-terpreter asks whether what is expressed is the metaphor, he could be saying not that the literal paraphrase actually captures the metaphor, but that it has given him enough clues to get it. In other words, the content of the test might actually be, "I see, what you are trying to get at is that Juliet is the sun." Given this interpretation, the response of the interpreter does not prove the adequacy of the paraphrase.

Our discussion of the problem of capturing perspective so far has ad-dressed only the first interpretation of paraphrasability, that is, the ques-tion whether the paraphrase has the same effect as the metaphor. The question remains, is the difference cognitively significant? As I have said before, this question has two parts. First, is the difference in effect between the metaphorical utterance and its literal paraphrase a cognitive one? And, second, does this difference result from the expression of different cognitive content? To answer these questions, perhaps we need to ask whether the literal paraphrase produces different knowledge than that of the metaphor. But this question would require an answer too lengthy to be addressed here.

In conclusion, Davidson's argument against the notion of metaphorical meaning based on nonparaphrasability, depends upon how one interprets the notion of paraphrasability and thus can easily be challenged. Under a broad conception of the latter, it seems quite easy to challenge the alleged nonparaphrasability of metaphor. Under a more rigorous conception of paraphrasability, we must face the question whether the unique perspec-tive acquired in processing metaphors should be considered part of its cognitive content.

Other ways of challenging Davidson's argument from nonpara-phrasability involve challenging premise (5), which defines metaphorical meaning. My analysis of metaphor does exactly this by proposing a con-ception of metaphorical meaning and content which does not require that the full metaphorical effect be captured in its content. In my analysis, what Davidson describes as the metaphorical effect results not from the content the utterance expresses (metaphorical or otherwise) but rather from the act of reconceptualization. Since this act takes place via the metaphor ve-hicle, a common result is that the audience ponders the similarities be-tween two different objects and systems, exactly as Davidson describes the process of metaphor comprehension.

Argument from Simile

The next argument Davidson brings against the notion of metaphorical meaning comes from his analysis of similes. According to Davidson:

(1) Similes, allegories, and metaphors are alike in that they bring two objects or situations into comparison with each other and make us think deep thoughts.

(2) We can account for simile and allegory without postulating a special meaning.

(3) Therefore, we should be able to account for metaphor without postulating a special, metaphorical meaning.[38]

COUNTERARGUMENT ONE

The simplest way of challenging this argument is to challenge its conclusion, Davidson's assertion that the fact that simile can be explained without appealing to figurative meaning means that metaphor can as well.[39] According to Goodman, Davidson's comparison between similes and metaphor clearly shows that the functional effect of metaphor, simile, and allegory is the same. Since these linguistic objects are functionally identical, yet remain different, metaphor cannot be accounted for or defined by appealing only to its function. Thus metaphor is not solely a matter of use.

Davidson might respond to this argument by saying that metaphor is not defined solely functionally and by providing an alternative way of differentiating between metaphor and other figures. Since Davidson does not believe that metaphors are elliptical similes, one obvious way is to appeal to the surface form of the metaphor. That is, metaphor is grammatically different from simile. Partly as a result of this, the two have differing cognitive contents and therefore different truth values.[40] Thus Davidson can say that metaphor can be distinguished from simile in that the proposition expressed by a simile actually captures the cognitive content that a metaphorical utterance brings us indirectly (i.e., not directly expressed by the meanings of the terms) to notice.

[38]Davidson, "What Metaphors Mean," p. 439.
[39]Goodman assumes this stance in "Metaphor as Moonlighting," p. 224.
[40]Davidson describes this difference as follows: "The most obvious semantic difference between simile and metaphor is that all similes are trivially true and most metaphors are false." "What Metaphors Mean," p. 437.

COUNTERARGUMENT TWO

Another way of challenging Davidson's argument is to say that in the case of simile, to which Davidson compares metaphor, there *is* something equivalent to the metaphorical meaning Davidson claims is unnecessary to the explanation of metaphor. That is, according to the analysis of some philosophers (e.g. Fogelin, Black, Stern), similes as well as metaphors have a figurative meaning which is necessary to explain their effect. This analysis is based upon a fundamental distinction between ordinary comparison statements and similes, which are considered to be figurative. Perhaps the simplest way to see this is to consider the opposing view, the view that figurative similes function as literal comparison statements. If this were true, then the statement "Steve is like a sheep dog" should have the same truth value whether it is taken literally or figuratively. Yet this is clearly not so, even if one takes a variety of different approaches to the analysis of similarity statements. In fact, the only view of similarity which supports this criticism is the naive view of similarity, which Davidson seems to hold. Under the naive view of similarity, what it takes for a comparison statement to be true is that the two objects being compared have at least one property in common.[41] Under this conception of similarity statements, all similarity statements would be true and thus there would seem to be no grounds for distinguishing between figurative and literal comparisons. However, this view of similarity is clearly inadequate, as was first indicated by Goodman.[42] For one thing, the naive view of similarity has the result that all similarity or comparison statements are trivially true and thus uninformative, and this is clearly not the case. For another thing, both the naive view of similarity and the modified view in which the objects being compared must share a certain number of properties in order to be similar conceive of similarity as a symmetrical relationship. However, as the work pioneered by Goodman and explored by many others has shown, similar-

[41]Davidson seems to hold this view of similarity, for he says, "The most obvious semantic difference between simile and metaphor is that all similes are true and most metaphors are false. The earth is like a floor, the Assyrian did come down like a wolf on the fold, because everything is like everything." Ibid., p. 437. Note that his view of similarity affects both judgments of similarity and evaluation of similarity statements, so that not only are all similarity statements true, but everything is like everything else. This is not necessary, since one might hold different standards for what makes two objects similar and what makes a statement of similarity true.

[42]Nelson Goodman, "Seven Strictures on Similarity," in Goodman, *Problems and Projects* (Indianapolis: Bobbs-Merrill, 1972), pp. 437–47. Many others have followed in Goodman's footsteps, such as Tversky, Ortony, and Fogelin.

ity is asymmetrical rather than symmetrical. As a result, the naive view of similarity cannot be sustained and Davidson's argument from simile seems to fall through.

In contrast, my analysis of metaphor, which holds that figurative content emerges from reconceptualization is able to account not only for our intuitions that something possibly true is said in cases of similes, metaphors, and allegory but also for the difference between metaphors and similes.

Argument from Dead Metaphor

The third and final direct argument Davidson gives against the possibility of metaphorical meaning derives from an examination of the process in which metaphors that are alive become dead or frozen. According to Davidson, if metaphors have a metaphorical or figurative meaning in addition to their ordinary meaning, when the metaphor becomes dead or frozen, the metaphorical meaning should become the literal meaning of the dead metaphor.[43] Since, in Davidson's view, this does not happen, there must not be a metaphorical meaning to begin with. The argument can be paraphrased as follows:

(1) The metaphor "burned up" when used to describe angry people is now dead in that it no longer evokes the vision of flames.

(2) If metaphors had metaphorical meaning, then dead metaphors should acquire that metaphorical meaning as they die, so that the literal meaning of the dead metaphor "burned up" should now include the metaphorical meaning it once had.

(3) The dead metaphor "burned up" now literally means only to be very angry.

(4) When it was alive, the metaphor "burned up" conveyed more than to be very angry so that its metaphorical meaning included more than to be very angry.

(5) Therefore, there is no such thing as metaphorical meaning.

COUNTERARGUMENT

In order to evaluate this argument, one must first consider Davidson's interpretation of what it is for a metaphor to be dead. In spelling out the argument, Davidson says that a metaphor is dead as soon as it becomes

[43]Ibid., p. 439.

part of the language. He does not explain exactly what it means to be part of the language, but he seems to mean that a term "X" is part of the language if and only if the rules of the language specify its meaning. Under this conception, the phrase "burned up" is dead in that when we say "Dad was burned up," the rules of the language produce the proposition "Dad was very angry." That is, we do not need to go beyond semantic competence to comprehend what the speaker said.

One of the simplest ways to challenge this argument is to question premise (2), Davidson's assumption that the metaphorical meaning of a metaphor should be incorporated in the meaning of the term when the metaphor dies. Before Davidson can use this as an attack on the thesis of metaphorical meaning, he should give some evidence for it. However, even if Davidson should be able to defend it, there are other weaknesses in his argument.

Another way to escape from his argument is to accept premises (1) through (3) as well as the first part of premise (4), but rejecting the second part of (4). The second part of (4) does not follow from the preceding premises but requires the assumption (A) that what is conveyed by the utterance be part of the meaning of the utterance and (B) an intensional theory of meaning. As a result, there are at least two ways of challenging it.

One approach (Goodman's) is to take an extensionalist view of meaning. Given an extensionalist view of meaning, whatever is the proper referent of the term is the meaning of that term (that is, there is no intensionalist notion that embodies the meaning of a term other than the extension itself). In one of the cases Davidson cites, to the extent that "mouth of a bottle" is a dead metaphor, the opening at the top of a bottle *is* the proper referent of the phrase "mouth of a bottle." That is, while at one time it might have been the case that only animate things had mouths, and mouths were defined as the openings through which food was taken, the term "mouth" is now ambiguous in that it can properly be used to apply either to the feeding hole of animate objects or to the openings at the tops of bottles or other such containers. Given that the opening of the bottle is now part of the extension of the term "mouth," an extensionalist can say that the metaphorical meaning of the utterance has become the literal meaning of that term. The same thing can be said about the phrase "burned up." That is, since the referent of the phrase is the same as it is in its (supposedly) dead state, the meaning must be the same. Hence the (literal) meaning of the dead metaphor *is* the metaphorical meaning of the live metaphor and hence Davidson's conclusion falls through.

Another way of accepting the first part of premise (4) while denying the second part is to challenge the assumption that all that is conveyed by a metaphor must be contained in metaphorical meaning. (My analysis of metaphor does just this by explaining the metaphoricity in terms of the process of reconceptualization.) As we saw in our discussion of the apparent nonparaphrasability of some metaphors, it seems quite reasonable to say that the truth conditions of a metaphor do not capture its entire effect. Instead, many metaphors seem to produce a change in perspective that can only be described. Yet there does not seem to be any need to require that the metaphorical meaning capture that change in perspective and retain it even after becoming part of the language. For example, when the term "hood" was alive metaphorically as applied to cars, it pointed to a likeness between a certain car part and an item worn about the face. However, now that the term has become incorporated into the language, while the connection can be dredged up, it is no longer necessary for an understanding of the utterance. That is, what once required reconceptualization to bring about the desired perspective and feature space of hoods no longer does so. As a result the previously metaphorical meaning has now become one of the literal meanings of the term "hood."

Argument from Context Dependence

Davidson rejects the notion of metaphorical meaning in part because of the reasons cited in the three arguments above, which argue directly against metaphorical meaning. Another reason for his rejection of the notion is one shared by such philosophers as Grice, Searle, Martinich, Morgan, and Fogelin, namely, the fact that metaphors seem to be context-dependent in a way unlike literal language.[44] Semanticists, whether their point of departure is the goal of accounting for linguistic competence or a belief in lexical semantics, originally conceived of their subject of inquiry as context-independent. As mentioned in Chapter 2, only something that is context-independent is thought to have the universality (or at least the systematicity) necessary (1) to be interesting to philosophy and (2) to have the potential to be explained systematically. However, metaphor and other instances of figurative speech are clearly dependent upon context in a number of ways.

[44]Davidson, "What Metaphors Mean," pp. 430–41, p. 436.

CONTEXT DEPENDENCE: DEFINITION AND TYPES

Even when we restrict the notion of context dependence to language, it still describes a wide range of phenomena. Context dependence defines a continuum, with complete dependence upon context at one extreme and complete independence of context at the other. A phenomenon is context-independent to the extent that it can be explained without reference to features of context which, since they are infinite, resist formulation. To the extent that the type and relevant conditions of context sensitivity can be incorporated into the explanation of the phenomenon, it ceases to be a problem for a theory. To take an example from physics, the dependence of acceleration on the time in which a particular distance is traversed can be taken into account in the formula. As a result, the dependence of acceleration on time is not considered to be an impediment to the systematic explanation of acceleration. When applied to meaning, we can say that meaning is independent of context to the extent that it can be assigned to linguistic expressions in the absence of knowledge of contextual features. That is, we could say that meaning is context-independent to the extent that it can be assigned to linguistic types. However, as Kittay points out, what it means for meaning to be independent of context can be interpreted in many ways. For example, it may mean:

(1) that the meaning of a word is independent of its context; or
(2) that the meaning of a sentence is independent of its context; or
(3) that features of the context figure in the meaning of a sentence in a rule-governed way, such that we may bracket these contextual features in order to consider the meaning of a sentence to be context-free.[45]

Underlying Kittay's description of three types of context dependence is the belief that, despite illusions to the contrary, the phenomena to be explained in the study of language are *all* context-sensitive to some extent. One reason for this (which is not necessarily Kittay's) is that all communication occurs in an immediate context of utterance which affects it, as well as against the backdrop of the history of a linguistic community and culture. However, this does not mean that philosophers of language cannot distinguish aspects of language that can be explained without appealing to context. It is generally accepted (for example, by Frege and Davidson) that meaning is an aspect of language which *can* be separated out in this fash-

---

[45]Eva Kittay, *Metaphor: Its Cognitive Force and Linguistic Structure* (Oxford: Clarendon Press, 1987), p. 96.

ion, an aspect such that meaning can be assigned to linguistic expressions (or types) independently of the context in which the expressions occur or the extralinguistic purpose for which the utterance is used. In addition, while meaning may be inevitably context-dependent in that it relies on the history of a linguistic community and culture and is dependent upon the meanings of other words, we may be able to separate out the specific ways in which it is dependent upon context and systematize the ways in which meaning is context-dependent. Using a similar principle, Kaplan (in the manner of possible world semantics), attempts to systematize the context dependence of indexicals by building it into his definition of their character (i.e. a function from context to content).

One way of classifying context dependence, using a taxonomy formulated by Josef Stern,[46] is to divide context dependence into presemantic, semantic, or postsemantic, according to its location in the process of comprehension.[47] *Presemantic context dependence* consists in the dependence of the linguistic unit upon the factors that shape its interpretation as a particular semantic unit. For example, upon hearing a certain sound such as "ai," speakers must use contextual features such as the context of previous sentences (linguistic context) and gestures (to their chest or eye) to determine whether the sound is a token of the semantic unit "eye" or "I" (or the beginning of yet another semantic unit such as "island" or "irony"). Once a linguistic unit has been identified as a token of a particular semantic type, its interpretation may still be dependent upon context, postsemantically so. That is, the ultimate impact of the utterance usually depends upon the extralinguistic goals of the speaker. For example, this type of context dependence is characteristic of conversational implicatures. For semanticists, what is of interest is postsemantic context dependence, since it is this type of dependence that distinguishes issues of meaning from those of use and which allows meaning to be assigned to linguistic expressions regardless of the context in which they are uttered. That is, one of the requirements Davidson has of literal (or first) meaning is that it be postsemantically context-independent. However, neither of these two

[46]Stern, "What Metaphors Do Not Mean," pp. 23, 24, and 39.

[47]Previous literature tends not to distinguish between the types of context dependence in this way. What Stern calls presemantic context dependence plays off Davidson's analysis of language but is typically ignored by semanticists. In addition, semantics has not distinguished between semantic and postsemantic context dependence but treats both as a means of distinguishing between meaning and use. As a result, for his analysis to be sound, Stern needs to justify the distinction between these.

types of context dependence just outlined successfully describes the context dependence of indexicals. For example, even though someone identifies a linguistic unit as an instance of the semantic type "I," in order to know the content of the expression, its contribution to the proposition expressed by the utterance in which it appears, the person must know who is speaking, and this knowledge is contextual rather than linguistic. However, while the knowledge is context-dependent, it is not presemantically so, since the sound has already been assigned to a linguistic type ("I"). Nor is this knowledge postsemantically context-dependent, since it does not depend upon the speaker's extralinguistic goal. Stern calls this kind of context dependence *semantic context dependence*, to be distinguished from both pre- and postsemantic context dependence. Given this framework, the question of metaphor's context dependence becomes the question whether it is presemantically, semantically, or postsemantically context-dependent.

CONTEXT DEPENDENCE OF METAPHOR

Metaphor and other instances of figurative speech are clearly dependent upon context in a number of ways, apparently even more so than ordinary (literal) language (Criterion 5 on our list of conditions). One way in which metaphor is dependent upon context lies in the fact that some metaphors cannot even be identified as such in the absence of a specification of the context of utterance. This contradicts the now defunct thesis, put forth in most detail by Monroe Beardsley,[48] that metaphors are instances of grammatical deviance and their identification criterion is precisely that grammatical deviance. Numerous counterexamples (such as "No man is an island" and "Jeremy is a butterfly"), put forth by philosophers such as Ted Cohen,[49] Joseph Stern,[50] and others, show that this is not the case. In other words, since there are (numerous) metaphorical utterances that are not grammatically deviant, grammatical deviance can neither be the criterion of identification nor the part of the definition of metaphors. As a consequence, the metaphors cited (and others like them)

[48]Monroe Beardsley, "The Metaphorical Twist," in *Philosophical Perspectives on Metaphor*, ed. Johnson, pp. 105–22.

[49]Ted Cohen, "Notes on Metaphor," *Journal of Aesthetics and Art Criticism* 34 (1976): 249–59.

[50]Josef Stern, "Metaphor and Grammatical Deviance," *Nous* 17, no. 4 (Nov. 1983): 577–99. In this essay Stern presents an argument against the thesis of grammatical deviance as expressed by Monroe Beardsley.

are context-dependent in that as semantic types, that is, without appearing in a context of utterance, they can neither be identified (an epistemological issue) nor properly defined as metaphors (a metaphysical issue).

Another way in which metaphor is clearly context-dependent is in the derivation of its interpretation. The way in which most articles and studies on metaphor proceed would seem to indicate that this is not the case, that metaphors can be assigned metaphorical interpretations in the absence of context. In fact, metaphorical utterances are typically presented for evaluation and interpretation in the absence of any identifying context. For example, in the sentences listed in Chapter 1 each sentence is given in the absence of any specification of the context in which it is uttered. Nonetheless, most competent speakers would identify (4) through (10) as metaphorical, with (3) being metaphorical in some cases and (11) being either anomalous or blatantly false.

However, this does not show that metaphors are not dependent upon context for their identification and interpretation. What it shows is merely that people are usually able to assume a standard context which is sufficient to determine metaphoricity and arrive at a viable interpretation. (In the case of commonly used metaphors, our knowledge of past interpretations guides our interpretation.) For example, consider the commonly cited metaphor "Jeremy is a wolf." Our habit of assigning proper names almost exclusively to human beings (or domesticated beasts) tells us that Jeremy is probably a human. Our past experience with the metaphorical use of "wolf" tells us that it is most likely to be used to indicate that Jeremy is either vicious or aggressively promiscuous. Knowledge of features identifiable in the immediate context of utterance—such as subject's age, the topic (e.g. male/female interaction or business strategies), the tone of the conversation (e.g. lewd, admiring, objective, horrified—are usually sufficient to determine which of two common interpretations were intended. (Note that if they were not, a question of "What do you mean?" would serve to clarify the issue.)

In contrast, consider the metaphor "The general sent a dove to greet the approaching prisoners of war." While speakers of the English language raised in the Anglo-Saxon culture would interpret this metaphor as indicating that prisoners of war were greeted peacefully, those of the Japanese culture, who see the dove as a symbol of death, would interpret it differently. In this situation, knowledge of cultural conventions is clearly a requirement for a proper interpretation of the metaphor.[51]

---

[51] This dependence upon culture can be relative to race, time, or economic or social

The diversity of ways in which context (or nonlinguistic factors) affects the interpretation of a metaphor is testified to by the extensiveness of the list of principles Searle generates in an attempt to explain the rules which he considers to guide the derivation of metaphorical content from literal content, as well as the fact that he must appeal to principles as open-ended as that consisting of "calling something to mind."[52] However, it does seem as though the types of context dependence of metaphor can be summarized, if not the actual features of context that enter into the determination of metaphorical content. That is, the identification and proper interpretation of a metaphor is dependent upon context in any number of ways, including (1) dependence upon the information provided by immediate context (linguistic and otherwise); (2) dependence upon stereotypical assumptions assigned by a linguistic community, a culture (for example, the fact that wolves are considered to be ferocious or that doves are a symbol of peace), or an individual; and (3) dependence upon pragmatic principles (such as Grice's maxims of Quantity and Quality).[53] Also, the fact that most metaphors can be identified and interpreted (to some extent) in the absence of information about the immediate context indicates that the context independence of metaphor need not rule out the possibility of a systematic explanation of metaphorical content associated with semantic types rather than semantic tokens (i.e. individual utterances).

Nor can the context dependence of metaphor be used to make a fundamental distinction between metaphorical and literal language in such a way as to remove metaphors from the realm of semantics and systematic explanations. Metaphorical utterances are clearly not the only instances of language use in which it seems that the content they express is dependent upon context. In fact, current research seems to produce more and more evidence of the context dependence of even the most flatfootedly literal language. Searle describes three different ways in which certain types

---

group. It is precisely this dependence upon cultural conventions that makes it difficult to interpret both fourteenth-century poetry, the product of our own race and in our language, or poetry of a different race. It is also what makes it difficult for minorities to perform well on generalized exams which, despite supposed objectivity, (inevitably?) slip into use of symbolic terms such as "dove" and "wolf," without regard for the fact that the interpretation of these terms is culturally relative. The contention of those who challenge the exam is that knowledge of cultural-based interpretations is neither (1) based on and thus a measure of linguistic competence nor (2) a measure of intelligence.

[52]John Searle, "Metaphor," in *The Philosophy of Language*, ed. Martinich, pp. 408–29.

[53]I challenge the latter dependence in Chapter 2.

of ordinary literal speech are context-dependent. The first type Searle describes is the now familiar phenomenon of utterances containing indexical expressions. As is now generally accepted, the meaning of an utterance containing indexicals is not sufficient to determine the proposition it expresses, and as a result semantic competence is not enough to deduce this proposition. However, despite the fact that indexical expressions are context-dependent, the features of context upon which they are dependent are such that they can be specified by a theory of meaning such as the one Kaplan provides.[54] As a consequence, although one cannot know the proposition expressed by a sentence containing indexicals without knowing certain features of context (e.g. who is speaking and who the speaker is pointing to), one can explain exactly what one would have to know in order to know the content of an expression containing an indexical (e.g. what features of the context are relevant).

However, while indexicals and metaphors are both context-dependent, it seems that they are context-dependent in different ways. One sign of this is the difference between what one knows regarding each when one is linguistically competent. Being linguistically competent in the use of an indexical gives the speaker the precise conditions of the context for locating the referent of the indexical. In contrast, it is not clear whether the same is true of metaphor. However, Searle also describes other types of literal utterances in which the context dependence of the utterance is *not* semantically realized in the utterance, such as utterances containing attributive terms (e.g. tall—which is dependent upon nonsemantic assumptions) and even some utterances with no evidence of context dependence (e.g. "The cat is on the mat"—in that what it means to be on the mat is relative to background assumptions).[55] As a result, it seems that the context dependence of metaphor is not sufficient to determine that metaphor is out of the realm of semantics.

In summary, it seems that Davidson's concern about the context dependence of metaphor is legitimate in that metaphorical meaning cannot be assigned to an utterance in the absence of a context for the utterance.

[54]David Kaplan, "Demonstratives," in *Themes from Kaplan*, ed. J. Almog, J. Perry, and H. Wettstein (Oxford: Oxford University Press, 1989), pp. 401–13.

[55]Rumelhart and Moravcsik provide other examples of the context dependence of ordinary (i.e. literal) utterances. David Rumelhart, "Some Problems with the Notion of Literal Meaning," in *Metaphor and Thought*, ed. Ortony, pp. 78–90; Julius Moravcsik, "Between Reference and Meaning," in *Midwest Studies in Philosophy* 14 (1989): 68–83.

As Morgan points out, the belief that a sentence has a metaphorical meaning seems to imply that this meaning is the property of the sentence type (as literal meaning is).[56] Yet this is something which seems not to be the case, since the metaphorical content an utterance has seems irrevocably dependent upon the linguistic context in which it is uttered and non-linguistic knowledge on the part of the interpreter. However, as Stern points out, this does not mean that there cannot be metaphorical meaning, as long as that meaning is not the actual content of a metaphor on a particular occasion of utterance but rather what links all tokens of the same metaphorical type. In other words, what is called for is some way of systematizing the contribution context makes to the determination of metaphorical content such that metaphorical meaning can have a place in semantics.[57] In addition, since metaphor is not the only linguistic phenomenon which is context-dependent in the way that metaphor is (i.e. cases of ambiguity and the examples given by Searle), metaphor's context dependence is not a reason for denying the possibility of metaphorical meaning or content.[58] By distinguishing metaphorical content from metaphorical meaning and showing its ability to account for our intuition of metaphorical truth, my analysis avoids the pitfall of the context dependence of metaphorical meaning. Furthermore, as I show in Chapter 4, the relative independence of metaphorical content of such pragmatic features as speaker intention shows metaphorical content to be within the realm of semantics, as conceived of as concerned with matter of content and truth. Yet even without these two considerations, the context dependence of metaphor cannot be used to differentiate it from literal language or to claim that it is a matter of use. Recent developments in semantics (such as the work of Fauconnier) do not require context independence of semantic phenomena *or* of semantic notions. In the model of language assumed by both my analysis and that of recent theorists of language (in which both modularity and linearity of language processing is challenged), the lines between the presemantic, semantic, and postsemantic is blurred, so that cognitive notions and pragmatic reasoning are thought to underlie the previously sacrosanct notion of reference. Thus the context dependence of metaphor doesn't challenge its status as a subject matter of semantics, but only

[56]J. L. Morgan, "Pragmatics of Metaphor," in *Metaphor and Thought*, ed. Ortony, pp. 136–47, pp. 139–40.

[57]Josef Stern and Merrie Bergmann both attempt to provide this, though in slightly different ways.

[58]I explore this further in Chapter 4.

prompts a search for a means of understanding the way semantic and pragmatic notions interact to produce understanding of both literal and metaphorical language.

Summary

Since Davidson's critique of semantic theories is so thorough, I will only briefly mention that of two other philosophers, Fogelin and Searle.

Fogelin's criticism of meaning-shift theories of metaphor is brief and to the point:

> I do not think that words can be made to change meaning in the ways that Black, Beardsley, and others suggest. When I say ironically that it is cold in here, I might mean that it is hot in here, but the word 'cold' does not thereby come to mean hot. The same is true when words are used metaphorically.[59]

While Davidson describes difficulties with the notion of metaphorical meaning itself and with semantic theories in general, Fogelin zeros in on the inherent contradiction of the notion of a meaning shift, which is one way of accommodating the notion of metaphorical meaning in a theory of metaphor. One difficulty with Fogelin's criticism is that it takes a static rather than diachronic view of language. Yet language clearly evolves over time in such a way that certain terms *do* shift in meaning and their shift seems to come about as a result of patterns of language use. This can be seen most clearly in the range of utterances between novel metaphors and metaphors which have become part of the language to the extent that they are no longer considered metaphorical. (Note that in the latter, expressions once used metaphorically can become idiomatic, so that an entire phrase or sentence acquires a meaning of its own.) For example, the meaning of the word "hood" has changed so that it now properly incorporates car parts.

However, Searle's criticism of meaning-shift theories of metaphor can resolve this issue, shoring up Fogelin's criticism to meet the diachronic view of language:

> diachronically speaking, metaphors do indeed initiate semantic changes, but to the extent that there has been a genuine change in meaning, so that a word or expression no longer means what it previously did, to precisely that extent the locution is no longer metaphorical.[60]

[59] Fogelin, *Figuratively Speaking*, p. 74.
[60] Searle, "Metaphor."

That is, even if metaphors serve as the vehicles by which terms acquire different meanings over time, to the degree that these meanings become part of the language, the terms are no longer metaphorical. Thus metaphoricity requires a lack of conventionality that literal language depends upon.

To summarize, although Davidson (with other pragmatic philosophers) sets out to show that the very notion of metaphorical meaning (along with semantic theories of metaphor based on it) is incoherent, he does not show this. What he does do is raise the important question of how to classify metaphor and metaphorical content (if you believe that there is such a thing), and provide a thorough critique of semantic theories, in the process providing several new conditions for a theory of metaphor. Specifically, he shows that the notion of metaphorical meaning employed by existing semantic theories is at odds with the conventional notion of meaning (Criterion 10 on my list). Thus he argues for my claim that there is no such thing as metaphorical meaning (Claim 1). As a result, a theory of metaphor should respect the difference between meaning and use by not arbitrarily classifying metaphor as a matter of meaning without specifying how that meaning fits into the structure provided by semantics, as many previous (i.e. traditional) theories have done. Likewise, a theory of metaphor needs to respect and perhaps account for the context dependence of metaphor (Criterion 5). At the same time, Davidson emphasizes the dependence of the metaphorical on the literal in that he shows that for a metaphorical utterance to have its characteristic tension, the ordinary meanings of the terms must be active in its comprehension (my Criterion 11). He also demonstrates the lack of conventionality of metaphor (Criterion 12) and the fact that metaphors are about the world (Criterion 13). Table 3 summarizes my evaluation of traditional semantic theories of metaphor and shows the new conditions I have added to the list of desiderata.

Davidson views his critique as conclusively paving the way for the need for a pragmatic theory of metaphor. However, despite the success of his attack on traditional semantic theories of metaphor, Davidson does *not* show that it is impossible, in principle, for there to be a semantic theory of metaphor which includes the notion of metaphorical meaning. He only shows that if one wants to give a semantic theory of metaphor, one cannot use the notion of metaphorical meaning without distinguishing it from literal meaning in such a way as to accommodate both the lack of conventionality of metaphors (Criterion 12) and their context sensitivity. As I show in Chapter 7, by distinguishing metaphorical content from metaphorical meaning and by identifying metaphoricity as a matter of recon-

TABLE 3

Evaluation of the Traditional Semantic Analysis

Metaphoricity	Fair. It seems right that metaphoricity involves looking at one thing through another. However, by treating metaphor as a matter of meaning and metaphorical meaning like literal meaning, it implies that there is no distinction between the metaphorical and the literal
Metaphor comprehension	Well, although metaphorically
The intuition of metaphorical content and truth	Well
Difficulty of specifying the satisfaction conditions of some metaphorical utterances	Not explicitly, but would seem to be tied into the fact that what can be seen cannot necessarily be put in a proposition
The context dependence of metaphor	Acknowledges but does not explain
The ubiquity of metaphor (why metaphor is used)	Poorly. Cannot explain why pointing out likenesses using literal means is any different from the use of metaphor
The relationship between metaphor and simile	Fair. Doesn't address
Treatment of different types of metaphors	Fair. Weak on common metaphors
The incorporation of metaphors into the language	Poor. Doesn't address, but there is no apparent reason why the theory couldn't explain this
Consistency with the framework of semantics	Very poor
The dependence of the metaphorical on the literal	Poor. Treats metaphorical meaning like literal meaning
Lack of conventionality of metaphor	Very poor
The fact that metaphors are about the world	Very poor

ceptualization rather than meaning (Claim 1), my analysis meets the new criteria of a theory of metaphor while accounting for the intuition of metaphorical content and truth in a way that his theory cannot. In addition, my theory accounts for metaphoricity in a way that avoids some of the weaknesses of Davidson's analysis.

As we have seen, the primary intuition underlying Davidson's analysis is that in processing a metaphor the individual who processes it derives an image (which seems to be psychological) from the literal meanings of the terms. In other words, Davidson seems to have a conception of metaphoricity as a psychological phenomenon that occurs at the level of the individual. However, this view ignores both the relative systematicity in the interpretation of metaphors that allows metaphors to be a vital part of ordinary communication and the relative dependence of the interpretation of metaphors on the influence of human experience within a community, a society, a culture and against the background of human history. By conceiving of metaphoricity in terms of reconceptualization (as my analysis does), my theory opens the door to accounting for these influences inasmuch as conceptualization occurs within and against the background of human interaction and communication. At the same time my theory of metaphor remains true to the intuition that what makes the instance of the application of a term to a certain object a metaphor does not arise from a link conventionalized in linguistic meaning, but rather from the ability of the speaker and audience to redefine how they conceive of certain objects in such a ways as to produce different features space and different truth conditions.

Davidson is not alone in his perception of the flaws in semantic theories of metaphor and in the concept of metaphorical meaning itself. In Davidson's wake several theorists hasten to provide nonsemantic theories of their own intended to be immune to the difficulties of semantic theories. Since nonsemantic theories of metaphor reject the notion of metaphorical meaning, they are not at odds with Criterion 10. However, it remains to be seen whether nonsemantic theories of metaphor are able to account for the dependence of the metaphorical on the literal (Criterion 11), and for the intuition of metaphorical content and truth (Criterion 3), while respecting the difference between meaning and use (Criterion 10). Thus I shall examine and evaluate nonsemantic theories of metaphor in the next three chapters.

4

Metaphor as Use

Metaphor and Lies

After criticizing the traditional semantic theory of metaphor, Davidson offers an analysis of metaphor as a matter of use. As a theorist who classifies metaphor as a matter of use (and thus, perhaps, a subject for pragmatics), Davidson adopts an approach similar to that of many philosophers, including Grice, Martinich, Searle, and Fogelin.[1] However, although Davidson, Searle, and Fogelin's criticisms of semantic theories of metaphor in general (and meaning-shift theories of metaphor in particular) seem very effective, the theories Davidson (and other use-based theorists) propose to account for metaphor suffer from difficulties of their own. In Chapters 4–6 I examine the classification of metaphor as a matter of use following two different approaches. On the one hand, I consider various analyses of metaphor as a phenomenon of use, considering metaphor as (1) something one thinks of when processing a metaphor (Davidson), (2) a conversational implicature (Grice and Martinich), (3) an instance of speaker meaning (Searle), and (4) a corrective judgment requested by the speaker and provided by the user (Fogelin). In the process I will show that the analyses of metaphor presented by these philosophers do not provide an account of metaphor that addresses the established criteria.

[1]Note that Davidson was the first semantic philosopher (in contrast to Grice, who analyzes meaning in terms of speaker intention) to take this approach to metaphor. Note, also, that while Davidson does not believe that metaphors have a metaphorical content, other philosophers (such as Grice and Searle) who hold pragmatic theories of metaphor do. As a result, while Davidson does not need to account for metaphorical content in his theory, theorists such as Grice, Searle, and Fogelin need to explain how such a thing as metaphorical content can fit into a theory that holds that metaphor is not a matter of meaning.

On the other hand, I also evaluate the identification of metaphor with various types of pragmatically defined phenomena, beginning with Davidson's identification of metaphor with lies and ending with Fogelin's identification of metaphor with indirect speech acts. In doing so, I show that metaphor is fundamentally different from each of these phenomena of use and that the features distinguishing it from these phenomena are precisely those which define these phenomena as phenomena of use. As a result, I intend to show metaphorical content to be the proposition expressed by the metaphorical utterance (Claims 2 and 3), and thus a fit subject matter for semantics (Claim 4).

To challenge the classification of metaphor as a matter of use, I have to show that the features distinguishing metaphor from the other phenomena of use are fundamental, while the characteristics it shares with the other phenomena of use are trivial. At the same time, I have to demonstrate the reverse regarding phenomena typically regarded as semantic. In other words, I must show that metaphor shares the fundamental characteristics of semantic phenomena, while sharing trivial or less important features with pragmatic phenomena. For example, suppose that what metaphor shares with instances of lying is the role of speaker intention. In such a case, since speaker intention is a feature which only appears when a speech act is considered an act made by a speaker with certain goals, and not at the level of semantics, which considers an utterance in isolation from the speaker, metaphor would be shown to be a pragmatic phenomenon.

In this chapter I (1) introduce the notion of metaphor as a matter of use rather than meaning, (2) examine various ways of analyzing metaphor as a matter of use, (3) present and evaluate Davidson's identification of metaphors with lies, (4) present and evaluate Davidson's causal account of metaphor, (5) establish metaphor's relative independence of speaker intention as a criteria for a theory of metaphor (Criterion 14), and in the process (6) argue for my Claims 2, 3 and 4 (i.e. that metaphorical utterances express a metaphorical content different from their literal content, that this content constitutes the proposition expressed by the utterance, and that metaphor is a semantic phenomenon).

Metaphor as a Matter of Use

While it is clear that to be a matter of use is to be beyond the realm of semantics in some way, it is less clear what it means to be a matter of use (other than to be nonsemantic). In other words, while the boundaries of what is semantic seem clear, given Davidson's assumptions,[2] being a matter of use is relatively undefined. One way to explain metaphor as a matter of use is to analyze it in the terms of a pragmatic theory of language, showing it to be based on pragmatic features. Along these lines, to be a matter of use might mean that what distinguishes an utterance as metaphorical is the purpose for which it is used (e.g. to cause one to notice a likeness), the illocutionary force of the utterance (i.e. whether it takes the form of a question or request), or any number of other things, depending on one's conception of the role of use in communication.[3]

Metaphor as Illocutionary Force

Of the possible analyses of metaphor in terms of use-based factors, the explanation of metaphoricity as a matter of illocutionary force is one of the easiest alternatives to eliminate. In Searle's theory of speech acts, illocutionary acts, which occur at the level of a speech act (characterized by a speaker, utterance, context, and an audience), are distinguished according to their illocutionary force.[4] For example, the classification of an utterance as an assertion or a request is a classification according to illocutionary force. As a result, to attempt to explain metaphoricity in terms of illocutionary force is to classify it as a speech act, a pragmatic phenomenon. However, a multitude of examples show that metaphoricity cannot be explained in this way. Consider, for instance, the following utterances:

(1) I promise to give the butterfly a talking to—*commissive*
(2) Steve is a sheepdog—*assertion*
(3) Kindly waltz yourselves out of my kitchen—*request*

Though each of these utterances is metaphorical, they are embodied in

---

[2]These assumptions include the assumption of context independence which he requires of meaning, as well as other assumptions described in the previous section. Donald Davidson, "What Metaphors Mean," in *The Philosophy of Language*, ed. A. P. Martinich, 2nd edition (New York: Oxford University Press, 1991), pp. 430–41, p. 431; "A Nice Derangement of Epitaphs," in *Truth and Interpretation: Perspectives on the Philosophy of Donald Davidson*, ed. Ernest Le Pore (Oxford: Basil Blackwell, 1986), pp. 433–46.

[3]Note that for some semanticists, any evidence of the context dependence of an expression is enough to make that expression a matter of use and thus pragmatics rather than semantics. This kind of reasoning causes Bar-Hillel to relegate indexicals to the realm of pragmatics. Yehoshua Bar-Hillel "Indexical Expressions," *Mind* 63 (1954): 359–79.

[4]John Searle, "What Is a Speech Act," in *The Philosophy of Language*, ed. Martinich, pp. 115–25.

speech acts of various types of illocutionary force. Indeed, the signs that indicate what type of illocutionary force each utterance embodies are quite independent of the metaphoricity of the utterance.[5] That is, the linguistic cues that distinguish an assertion from a question are totally independent of the metaphoricity of that utterance. As a result, metaphoricity cannot be a matter of illocutionary force, at least given this interpretation of illocutionary force.

In addition, a given metaphorical utterance can be used in a variety of ways, that is, with different types of illocutionary force. For example, an utterance of "Every hair on my body is standing at attention" can be used as an assertion (in response to the query of some medical person who is asking the effect of a certain medication). On the other hand, it can also be used as a request (when made by a person in bed to a person standing near the window with the intention of getting the speaker to close the window). As a result, it does not seem that metaphoricity can be accounted for by appealing to illocutionary force.

One might object to this argument by saying that while metaphoricity is not a matter of illocutionary force as defined, it may be the product of an additional illocutionary factor.[6] However, even if we accept this point, metaphoricity can (and will) be shown not to be a matter of illocutionary factors by virtue of the fact that all illocutionary factors are defined in relation to the speaker and the speaker's intention in making the utterance. In view of this, and given the fact that metaphoricity is relatively independent of the speaker and the speaker's intention (as we shall see in the remainder of this chapter), metaphoricity cannot be a matter of some illocutionary factor.

Other Use-Based Definitions of Metaphor

Despite the ease with which we can dismiss an analysis of metaphor in terms of illocutionary force, within the realm of use there remain a variety of ways of accounting for metaphor. Indeed, each of the philosophers cited analyzes metaphor in different ways within the realm of use. Davidson, for example, considers metaphor to be a matter of use in that he holds that metaphor occurs when language is used for a certain purpose—that is, to cause the noticing of likeness between objects typically regarded as unlike. To emphasize that it is the noticing of likeness rather than the de-

[5]As we shall see later in this chapter, the metaphoricity of an utterance is independent of speaker intention in many ways.

[6]I am indebted to Dagfinn Follesdal for this point.

ciphering of a certain kind of meaning that constitutes metaphor, Davidson compares metaphor to bumps on the head; both of them, he says, cause us to notice something as the result of a causal (rather than linguistic) process.[7] Whereas Davidson dismisses entirely the notion of cognitive or metaphorical content and holds a causal theory of metaphor, Grice, Martinich, and Searle, and Fogelin acknowledge the existence of metaphorical content as something propositional and attempt to account for it outside the realm of semantics using systematic, pragmatic principles. Grice analyzes metaphor as a conversational implicature, a phenomenon he clearly distinguishes as a matter of use rather than meaning.[8] Martinich, in his development of Grice's pragmatic theory of metaphor, also classifies metaphor as an implicature and as a case in which the speaker says one thing by what he terms *making-as-if-to-say* something else.[9] Searle's speech act theory, a modified version of the theory developed by John Austin, analyzes metaphor as a nonliteral indirect speech act (defined as a speech act in which sentence meaning and speaker meaning come apart).[10] Fogelin's theory of metaphor, which analyzes metaphor as a figurative comparison, considers metaphor to be a literal indirect speech act, and indicates that, as such, metaphor is a kind of use of language.[11]

Identification of Metaphor with Use-Based Phenomena

Another way of classifying metaphor as a matter of use is to identify it with another phenomenon considered to be a matter of use, thus showing metaphor to be determined by pragmatic factors. Indeed, each of the philosophers mentioned above does just that. To clarify what he means by saying that metaphor is a matter of use, Davidson specifically groups metaphor together with the class containing assertions, hinting, criticisms, lies, and promises. Then, within this group, he identifies metaphor with

[7]Note that for Davidson, metaphors have no special or metaphorical content. Their only content (something which drives from linguistic means) is their literal content. As a consequence, he explains the metaphorical as a matter of effect, in purely causal terms.

[8]H. P. Grice, "Logic and Conversation," in *The Philosophy of Language*, ed. Martinich, pp. 149–60.

[9]A. P. Martinich, "A Theory for Metaphor," in *Pragmatics*, ed. Steven Davis (Oxford: Oxford University Press, 1991), pp. 507–18.

[10]John Searle, "Metaphor."

[11]Robert Fogelin, *Figuratively Speaking* (New Haven: Yale University Press, 1988), p. 41.

the case of lies.[12] Grice considers metaphor to be like irony in that in both cases, the flouting of a maxim causes the audience to seek a proposition other than the one expressed by the utterance, yet one which is somehow derived from that proposition. Martinich, in the manner of Grice, considers both metaphor and irony to be cases of a making-as-if-to-say a proposition that is not the content of the illocutionary act.[13] Searle identifies metaphor with irony in that the figurative content expressed by each constitutes the speaker meaning of the utterance.[14] Fogelin identifies metaphor with indirect speech acts in that he considers both to be cases in which a primary speech act is performed by way of performing another, secondary act (the act of asserting the proposition which is false or irrelevant when taken literally).

Davidson: Metaphor and Lies

In building his case for a causal, and thus nonsemantic, analysis of metaphor, Davidson claims that metaphor is like the case of lies. Davidson defends this claim by pointing out that the same sentence type can be used to lie or not to lie, and noting that the same sentence type can also be used metaphorically or not.[15] This similarity, he claims, is sufficient to show that metaphors are like lies in being matters of use and thus outside the realm of semantics.[16] One hidden assumption in this argument is that meaning exists only at the level of sentence type. Another is that semantics is only concerned with meaning (and not, for example, with content). The result of these two assumptions is the further assumption that anything which does not occur at the level of sentence types has nothing to do with semantics.[17] Further evidence for the nonsemantic nature of metaphor and lies is the fact that semantic competence does not allow us to predict a

[12]Donald Davidson, "What Metaphors Mean," in *The Philosophy of Language*, ed. Martinich, pp. 430–41, p. 437.

[13]Martinich, "A Theory for Metaphor."

[14]Searle, "Metaphor."

[15]Davidson, "What Metaphors Mean," pp. 437–38.

[16]While Davidson does grant that there are differences between metaphors and lies, he does not consider the differences to be as important as the similarities between them. Ibid., 438.

[17]Note that if we accept these premises (that semantics studies sentence types), then we must give up to pragmatics either (1) the study of expressions containing indexicals or (2) the proposition expressed by an utterance. If we do the latter, then we can no longer identify meaning with the truth conditions of an utterance.

case either of a lie or of metaphor, even though it allows us to deduce sentence type. Davidson thus concludes that metaphors cannot be a matter of semantics, any more than lies are.

Lies: Definition

To compare metaphor with lies, we must first reach an understanding of what defines an act of lying. It is tempting to try to explain lying solely in terms of the truth value of the utterance, but a multitude of examples quickly show this analysis to be inadequate. Consider, for example, the following scenarios. Chris and Pat are discussing the sale of leaf blowers at a local store. In scenario 1, Chris, who is looking at tomorrow's date on the calendar, takes tomorrow's date for today's, deduces that the sale is over, and tells Pat "The sale is over." In scenario 2, Chris, who knows the correct date but wants Pat to pay a higher price for the leaf blower, utters the same statement.

According to the analysis of traditional semantics, the proposition expressed by the two utterances is the same, as judged by the fact that the truth conditions are identical. Thus what was said in the two cases is identical. As a consequence, the truth values of the two utterances must also be identical. In addition, if we accept that the cognitive content of an utterance is completely captured by the proposition expressed by the utterance, these utterances are cognitively equivalent. Since, from the perspective of semantics, these utterances are identical, we must turn somewhere else to account for the fact that one is a case of truth telling and another a case of lying.

Whereas semantics is concerned only with the proposition expressed, a pragmatic approach to language analyzes utterances in relation to the speaker, taking into account such things as the beliefs and intentions of the speaker. According to most pragmatic taxonomies, the scenarios would be judged similar in that in both cases the type of statement made is declarative (i.e. an assertion, according to speech act classification), with the goal of inducing the hearer to have certain beliefs. As a result, the utterances cannot be distinguished according to illocutionary force, either. The first candidate that presents itself as a means of explaining the difference between cases of lies and truth telling is the belief of the speaker. That is, in the first scenario, the speaker holds the belief he wants the speaker to have (that the sale is over), while in the case of lying the speaker does not hold this belief. However, the case of irony shows that this is not the whole story. For in cases of irony, although the speaker does not believe the proposition expressed by the utterance, we would not classify the act as a case of lying. In fact, if the audience believed the proposition expressed by the utterance (under a literal interpretation), we would say that the speaker did not succeed in being ironical. As a result, we cannot distinguish cases of lies simply by appealing to the beliefs of the speaker but must find some other factor. The contrast with irony shows that one factor that might delineate lies is the projected attitude of the speaker. One way to explain why a case of irony is not a lie, despite the fact that in both cases the speaker does not believe the proposition literally expressed by the utterance, is to say that in the case of irony, the speaker projects an attitude of disbelief. Using this approach, we could delineate lies as utterances in which the speaker does not believe the proposition expressed by the utterance and yet projects an attitude of belief in the utterance.

A more economical way of explaining what makes a lie different from irony and all other types of truth-telling utterances is to appeal to the speaker's intention in performing the utterance. In other words, we could say that what delineates a case of lying is simply the fact that in lying, the ultimate goal of the speaker is to deceive the audience, that is, to communicate to the audience a proposition the speaker believes to be false. (Note that if we accept this as an explanation, we need no longer directly appeal to the speaker's beliefs, since a speaker who intends to deceive using the utterance must not believe in the utterance.) If we accept this explanation, what differentiates a case of lying from one of truth telling (and thus what makes a lie a lie) is solely the beliefs and the intention the speaker has in making the utterance.

Given this analysis of lies, one way of explaining why Davidson identifies metaphors with lies is that he considers both to be phenomena defined in terms of the purpose for which they are used. In other words, although what makes an utterance a lie is the fact that it is used to deceive, Davidson believes that what makes an utterance metaphorical is the fact that it is intended to make someone notice a likeness between objects ordinarily considered to be different. If metaphors, like lies, were completely defined in terms of the purpose for which they are used (i.e. to cause the noticing of a likeness vs. to deceive), then their study would be completely outside of the realm of semantics and in the realm of use, to be addressed either by pragmatics or by some other science that studies the various uses of language. However, as the following arguments show, metaphor can neither be distinguished in this way nor identified with the case of lies as a phenomenon which can be distinguished according to speaker intention.

Argument Against Metaphors as Lies

ARGUMENT FROM VARIETY OF PURPOSES

For metaphor to be fundamentally comparable to instances of lying, it would need to be dependent upon the beliefs and intentions of the speaker in the same way, such that metaphoricity does not appear until these are taken into account and such that metaphors are tied to certain beliefs and purposes. However, this is not the case. The first indication that a metaphor cannot be distinguished according to the purpose for which it is used is that metaphors are used to serve a variety of purposes. In some cases metaphors seem to be used as Davidson says they are, that is, to cause us to notice a likeness between objects. For example, the point of uttering the metaphor "Your temple is your daily life" might be to cause the audience to notice similarities between temples and what goes on in them and what occurs (or should occur) in one's daily life.

However, there are many other cases of metaphorical utterances in which the purpose of the utterance is other than the one cited above. For example, consider the utterance of "Mom, my sock has a hangnail," when uttered by Rumelhart's son to his mother. Note that in this case the purpose of the utterance might be to inform the mother of a particular condition of a sock. On the other hand, the purpose might be get the mother to fix the sock. In either case, the purpose is not to cause the audience to notice the likeness between hangnails and the protuberance of material from the side of the sock, for whatever likenesses there are are trivial. Instead, the purpose of using the metaphor is as a pointer to a feature of an object that is not named. Using the name of a similar object allows the audience (1) to locate the object and (2) to infer properties that would not be readily deduced from a new name (i.e. hangnails are usually regarded as undesirable and needing to be dealt with). In addition, without even knowing the specific purpose of this utterance, we can tell that the utterance is metaphorical. As a result, it does not make sense to say that what distinguishes metaphorical utterances from other nonmetaphorical utterances is the purpose for which they are used. Thus metaphors are different from lies in that they cannot be identified by the purpose for which they are used.

Argument from Metaphorical Lies

Another argument which indicates that metaphors are fundamentally different from lies is based upon cases in which an utterance is both metaphorical and a lie.[18] Consider, for example, the case of a dog breeder who, anxious to sell a troublesome dog to a hesitant customer, says fervently to a customer, "She's a lamb." Now consider the steps someone must take in order to determine the truth of the utterance. An utterance is only a lie if (1) the speaker does not believe the proposition expressed and (2) the speaker portrays an attitude of belief in the proposition; or (3) the speaker utters the proposition with the intention of deceiving the listener. As a result, to determine whether the utterance is a lie, the listener clearly must look for clues to the speaker's beliefs, attitudes, and intentions. (It is precisely this reliance on specific knowledge of the speaker that causes lies to be classified not as a matter of semantics but as a matter of pragmatics.) Suppose that we choose the first definition of lies (the first two conditions) and, with this in mind, provide a list of the speaker's beliefs (e.g. that the dog is grouchy, seems to want to attack at random, and has bitten the last would-be customer viciously). Given that the speaker voices the utterance fervently (rather than sarcastically or with disbelief), it should seem that the audience would be able to deduce that the speaker is lying. In fact, given such knowledge, most people *would* deduce that the speaker is lying. However, suppose now that the audience is so literal-minded as to be computerlike. That is, suppose the audience, while in possession of perfect linguistic competence, is sorely lacking in pragmatic knowledge, cultural knowledge, and other types of real-world knowledge. In such a case, it seems that the audience would be quite unable to deduce that the speaker is lying, despite its knowledge of beliefs and attitude on the speaker's part which entail that the utterance is a lie.[19] To find out what has gone wrong—that is, why our criteria for evaluating whether an utterance is a lie seem inadequate—we need only substitute a nonmetaphorical version of the same lie. Suppose that the dog breeder said instead the dog was gentle and did not bite. In this case even a literal-minded audience would know that the speaker was lying. What this shows is that although the list of criteria is correct, it assumes that the speaker knows the content of the utterance (i.e. the proposition it expresses). In other words, when given an utterance that is both metaphorical and a lie, we cannot evaluate it as a lie before deciphering it as a metaphor (i.e. deducing its metaphorical con-

[18]The general strategy used in this argument in this section was suggested to me by Josef Stern in a conversation about the differences between metaphor and irony.

[19]Another alternative would be that the audience would decide that the speaker was indeed lying, but for the simple reason that dogs are not members of the class of lambs.

tent). What this situation implies is that the content of a metaphorical utterance is *not* the proposition expressed by the literal meaning of the utterance but rather its metaphorical content (Claims 2 and 3).

One way of escaping this dilemma might be to take the second definition of what makes a lie (i.e. speaker intention to deceive), so that the literal-minded audience knows only that the speaker intends to lie. However, this alternative provides no escape. For in such a case, while the audience would decide that the speaker was indeed lying, it would be for the misguided reason that dogs are not members of the class of lambs. As a result, although the audience would deduce correctly that the utterance is a lie, it would not know what it have been lied to about (i.e. the dog's personality, rather than the dog's classification within the standard taxonomy). To know this, it must first be able to interpret the metaphorical content of the utterance.

One thing this argument shows is that the conditions for something to be a lie are quite different from those required for it to be metaphorical. That is, whereas being a lie requires an (extralinguistic) intention on the part of the speaker to communicate a proposition the speaker believes is false, this condition is not a prerequisite of an utterance's being metaphorical. In addition, this argument shows that before processing an utterance as a lie, one must process it as a metaphor and deduce its metaphorical content. That is, in order to take the utterance of "She's a lamb" as a lie, one must first interpret it metaphorically to determine what proposition is proffered (and for which the speaker is held accountable). Only after this is done can the listener determine whether the proposition is true or false and, if false, whether the speaker believes the proposition expressed. The fact that one must deduce the metaphorical content before determining whether the utterance is a lie and in what the deception consists implies not only (1) that the essential features of metaphors and lies are different but also (2) that the content of a metaphorical utterance is not its literal content but rather its metaphorical content. The latter result follows from the fact that to recognize the falsity of a literal utterance, one must deduce its literal content, and to recognize the falsity of a metaphorical statement, one must deduce its metaphorical content.

In summary, what these examples and arguments show is that, in contrast to Davidson's classification, metaphors cannot be identified with instances of lying. Instead, metaphorical utterances and lies are fundamentally different in that whereas instances of lies are so only by virtue of the speaker's intention in using the utterance in order to deceive the audience, metaphoricity is completely independent of what the speaker intends to accomplish by expressing a certain proposition (via the metaphorical utterance). At the same time, the last argument seems to make a strong case that, if one accepts the intuitions of the ordinary speaker about what makes an utterance a lie, the metaphorical content rather than its literal content is the actual content of a metaphorical utterance.

Relative Independence of Speaker Intention

The argument above shows that the metaphoricity of an utterance does not depend on what the speaker is trying to accomplish using the utterance. Although this does not show that metaphor is not a pragmatic phenomenon, defined by pragmatic features, it does, by showing that metaphoricity is not dependent on the speaker's intention in the way lies are, eliminate one of the grounds for classifying metaphor as a matter of use. In addition, being independent of what the speaker intends to accomplish using the metaphor is only one way metaphor is independent of speaker intention. That is, we can show that the metaphoricity of an utterance is also independent of (1) the speaker's intention to speak metaphorically and (2) the proposition the speaker intends to communicate.

On the one hand, it is possible for a speaker's utterance to be metaphorical (or to have a metaphorical interpretation that is probable) even though the speaker did not so intend it. Consider, for example, a situation in which someone, in describing a man they know to a friend over the telephone, says, "He lives without a doorbell or any windows"—sentence (3) in Chapter 1. Given that the description of the person so far has implied that the person is reclusive, and given that the speaker in question tends to speak metaphorically, the interpreter of this utterance takes it to mean that the person is closed to possible interaction with others. Suppose, however, that the speaker was actually attempting to speak literally, that is, that they were attempting to convey the proposition that the man lives in a physical structure without a doorbell or windows. In this situation, we could say that the speaker said something metaphorically without intending it. (Note that in this analysis, this use of the term "say" does not require or imply that the speaker intended to say what is said (or even that they intend to say anything). In this example the speaker not only fails to speak literally but also fails to communicate the desired proposition (i.e. the utterance displays a combination of the two conditions). However, it is also possible for someone to attempt to speak metaphorically and fail, yet still communicate the proposition they want to communicate. For example, consider a situation in which someone says, "That machine's [pointing to an airplane] wing is red," not knowing that the item in question is properly within the range of the term "wing." In this case the speaker would convey the proposition they intended, yet they would not be speaking metaphorically, despite their belief that they are.

It is also possible for a speaker to attempt to speak metaphorically and either to succeed completely or to some degree or to fail completely. The results of such attempts might be regarded, to the degree that they produce metaphorical utterances, as good metaphors, bad metaphors, or anomalous utterances. For example, a metaphor which seems to draw numerous connections between the realms of two different objects might be deemed a "good" metaphor.[20] On the other hand, we might say that an utterance of sentence (11) produces a metaphor that is so bad as to be an anomalous statement rather than a metaphor, in that a viable metaphorical interpretation cannot be found.[21]

Another way metaphoricity is independent of speaker intention concerns the proposition the speaker intends to convey. That is, a speaker might attempt to speak metaphorically and succeed, and yet fail to convey the proposition they had intended to convey. In such cases, although the speaker succeeds in speaking metaphorically, the proposition conveyed is not the desired proposition, owing either to a misunderstanding of what certain objects represent in a culture or to a failure to provide enough information to help the interpreter select the desired metaphorical interpretation. For example, someone who says in a letter (without providing further detail), "Gerald is a real wolf," with the intention of conveying that the person is ferocious, may communicate, given a certain audience, that the person is aggressively promiscuous.

What these examples show is that in metaphorical utterances, as in other utterances, a speaker sets out with the intention of achieving a goal by communicating certain propositions and a certain attitude (e.g. one of belief) toward that proposition. However, the speaker's ability to communicate that proposition is limited by their mastery of the language; their awareness of the audience's linguistic, cultural, and personal background; their ability to determine what information needs to be communicated in order to express the desired proposition with the appropriate attitude; and

---

[20]The metaphor here is judged to be good in terms of an aspect of metaphor Fogelin calls "richness of comparison" and considers to be one of two factors according to which the quality of a metaphor is measured. Fogelin, *Figuratively Speaking*, p. 99.

[21]That is, we cannot find an ad hoc category of which the metaphor vehicle is a prototypical representative.

their ability to bring all these factors together to achieve their goals. At the same time, since what is said is the result of contextual information available to all parties, the speaker is responsible for proper use of this, as well as for linguistic competence. For example, if the speaker says something about "that woman" while looking directly at a woman in a group, what is said will be considered to be about the woman the speaker is looking at. In other words, successful communication depends upon more than linguistic competence (or the mere intention to communicate), even in literal language use, and the speaker is held responsible for these factors as well. Thus metaphorical utterances (and their metaphoricity) cannot be held to be dependent on speaker intention any more than literal utterances (my Criterion 14). Rather, the metaphoricity of an utterance and the successful utterance of a metaphor depend upon the speaker's enabling the audience to reconceptualize the entities involved appropriately so as to derive the proposition the speaker wishes to convey.

Davidson's Account of Metaphor

After attempting to draw a parallel between the case of metaphors and lies, Davidson proposes an account of metaphor which, by his own admission, is only a sketch of a theory.[22] However, despite the sketchiness of his presentation, Davidson's theory is distinguishable as a use-based theory of metaphor, one which analyzes metaphor as a nonsemantic phenomenon and which explains the process of its comprehension without appealing to the notion of metaphorical meaning.

While there are as many use-based or nonsemantic theories of metaphor as there are aspects of use related to language, Davidson's approach is unique in that he chooses to explain metaphor using a *causal* theory. That is, Davidson is adamantly opposed to explaining the comprehension of metaphor (which tends to make up the bulk of any theory of metaphor) as a cognitive process, in which one either decodes a message thought to be embodied in the meanings of the terms (as semantic theories do) or derives the implicatures of the utterance as a speech act (as Grice does). Davidson's opposition to this approach can be seen in the following:

> The central error about metaphor is most easily attacked when it takes the form of a theory of metaphorical meaning, but behind that theory, and statable independently, is the thesis that associated with metaphor is a cogni-

22Davidson, "What Metaphors Mean," p. 431.

tive content that its author wishes to convey and that the interpreter must grasp if he is to get the message. This theory is false, whether or not we call the purported cognitive content a meaning.[23]

In this passage Davidson distinguishes his views on metaphor not only from semantic theories of metaphor but also from any theories which hold that metaphors have a cognitive content necessary to their comprehension (my Claim 2), whether these theories identify that content as the proposition expressed by the utterance (as semantic theories of metaphor do) or a propositions associated with the utterance by pragmatic means (as pragmatic theories do). As a result, this particular criticism of Davidson's applies equally well to the theories of Grice, Martinich, Searle, and Fogelin, in that each of these writers acknowledges a metaphorical content despite the fact that each also professes to have a nonsemantic (specifically, pragmatic) theories of metaphor. Most nonsemantic theories of metaphor (such as those of Grice et al.) can be classified as pragmatic theories in that they attempt to account for metaphor using pragmatic principles of conversation. However, Davidson sees communication as a subset of the set of rational acts and does not believe either (1) that it is possible or worthwhile to distinguish communicative acts from other rational acts or (2) that rational acts conform to a set of principles that can be specified (as opposed to general rules of thumb).

In opposition to what he calls a cognitive approach, Davidson says that metaphor brings about its effect the same way a bump on the head does.[24] What makes a particular bump on the head metaphorical is its effect, the fact that it makes us notice a likeness between two objects typically considered to be unlike. Metaphorical utterances differ from other statements that induce us to note likenesses in that "ordinary similarity depends on groupings established by the ordinary meanings of words."[25] According to Davidson, it is the fact that similarity usually parallels word meaning (i.e. objects with the same name are similar to each other) that causes us to infer that the metaphorical is a matter of meaning. However, in Davidson's view, this inference is false, for the metaphorical is a matter neither of meaning nor of language but rather one of effect. Using terminology borrowed from Austin's speech act theory, Davidson's claim can be trans-

[23]Ibid., p. 440.
[24]Ibid., p. 439.
[25]Ibid., p. 431. My analysis describes this same phenomenon by saying that in literal language, the conceptualization involved is embodied in the standardized taxonomy and metaphysics and is captured by the rules of the language (i.e. the meanings of the terms).

TABLE 4

Features of Davidson's Analysis

Metaphoricity	A matter of use. The noticing of likeness caused by deriving literal content
Comprehension process	1. Derive the literal content 2. Note the similarities
The proposition expressed by the metaphorical utterance	Its literal content (first meaning)
The existence of metaphorical content	Claims there is none
The classification of metaphorical content	Doesn't believe there is metaphorical content
Rule for deriving metaphorical content	Similarity
Phenomena metaphor is like	Lies

lated into a statement that metaphoricity is a matter of illocutionary force.[26] Table 4 presents a summary of the features of Davidson's analysis.

Critique of Davidson's Analysis

One of the major discrepancies between Davidson's account of metaphor and the intuitions of the ordinary speaker is his claim that the truth conditions (or content) and thus the truth value of a metaphorical utterance are none other than those of the literal interpretation of the utterance. In other words, given that the literal interpretation of the utterance "Her words barked at me, but did not bite" is false, since only certain types of animals—not words—bark), then the metaphorical utterance must also be false.[27] Davidson is led to make this claim on ac-

[26]That Davidson identifies metaphors with lies confirms this analysis that he is classifying metaphor as a matter of perlocutionary force. I explore this later in this chapter.

[27]Davidson, "What Metaphors Mean," p. 436. Davidson qualifies this notion as follows "This is not to deny that there is such a thing as metaphorical truth, only to deny it of sentences." The implication here is that in the normal course of things, that is, in cases of literal utterances, truth *is* the property of sentences. What does it mean to say that there may be such a thing as metaphorical truth, although it could not be the property of sentences? One answer seems to be that if there is such a thing as metaphorical truth, it may be the same kind of truth but it does not appear in a theory of language in the same way. That is, it is not related to the meanings of sentences or to what is said in the utterance. This position would leave Davidson open to developing a theory of metaphorical truth along the lines of Grice and Fogelin. That is, what would be considered metaphorically true would be some proposition conjured

count of (1) his belief that what any utterance says, be it metaphorical or not (i.e. the proposition it expresses) is precisely what the utterance says according to the rules of the language, and (2) the fact that he equates the proposition expressed by the sentences with the truth conditions of those sentences.

Objection One

Davidson's claim goes against our intuitions in at least two ways. For one thing, the behavior of most ordinary speakers of the language seems to indicate that the truth value of a metaphorical utterance is quite different from that of the proposition expressed according to the ordinary (i.e. literal) meanings of the terms. That is, when sentences are uttered that are blatantly false when taken literally, yet true if taken metaphorically, speakers of the language react to those expressions as though something true has been said.[28]

At first glance it seems as though the challenge to Davidson's analysis which is posed by our intuitions is based upon the opposition between the truth values of the utterance taken literally and those of the utterance taken metaphorically. In fact, this is the analysis of the situation Fogelin gives in describing the conflict between our intuitions and Davidson's analysis. Fogelin believes that the inherent difficulty of the Davidsonian analysis (in addition to the fact that he only *sketches* a causal explanation of metaphorical force and does not develop it fully) is that it does not provide a candidate for the metaphorical truth of an utterance which is literally false.[29]

However, an examination of other types of metaphorical utterances in which the truth value of the utterance taken metaphorically is identical with that of the utterance taken literally shows that the difference between the truth values of the metaphorical utterance taken literally versus what it seems to have when taken metaphorically is only a manifestation of the

---

by the interpreter as a consequence of what the metaphor causally led him to notice. For example, after hearing the metaphorical utterance that the philosopher is pilot of the city, an interpreter might entertain the proposition that the philosopher leads the people of the city.

[28]Note that Davidson denies that there is any metaphorical content. As a result, he is against any approach to metaphor which claims that metaphorical utterances have both a literal and a metaphorical interpretation.

[29]Fogelin, *Figuratively Speaking*, p. 75.

problem. Ted Cohen's example of "No man is an island" is a case in point.[30] For despite the fact that the truth value of a metaphorical utterance may be the same taken literally or metaphorically, the interpreter's response to the utterance cannot be taken as a response to the literal interpretation of the utterance, since it would be inappropriate when taken as such. For example, given an utterance of the metaphor "No man is an island," an audience would probably comment on how people are affected by and affect the world around them, a response inappropriate to a literal interpretation of that utterance. In other words, the interpreter's response to the utterance seems to reflect a different *propositional content* than the one the utterance would have if interpreted literally, and not just a different truth value, which is an argument against Davidson's main claim and for Claim 2 of my theory of metaphor.

Objection Two

Our intuition that metaphors have a different propositional content than the one produced by the rules of the language is reflected in another conflict between the Davidsonian analysis and our intuitions regarding metaphorical utterances. According to Davidson, understanding a metaphorical utterance consists in grasping the proposition literally expressed by that utterance. And yet if someone were to react to the utterance as though they took the utterance literally, we would say they had failed to understand the utterance. In other words, grasping the metaphorical content (which differs from the literal) seems to be one of the requirements for comprehending a metaphorical utterance, and not just for the success of a communicative act. This difference can be seen by comparing the audience's reaction to an utterance whose purpose they did not understand versus a metaphorical utterance whose metaphorical interpretation they failed to grasp. In the former case the audience would probably respond by asking what the person was trying to *do*, whereas in the latter they would react by asking what the person was trying to *say*. But this is an argument for Claim 3 of my analysis of metaphor, the claim that metaphorical content is the proposition expressed by the utterance.[31]

---

[30]Ted Cohen, "Figurative Speech and Figurative Acts," *Journal of Philosophy* 72 (1975): 669–84.

[31]As we shall see later, the *kind* of failure that can occur when processing a metaphorical utterance is indicative of the kind of phenomenon metaphor is.

Objection Three

Another difficulty with Davidson's account, as Stern indicates,[32] is that while Davidson emphasizes the dependence of the metaphorical on the literal, it is not clear that his causal theory (as presented in "What Metaphors Mean") accounts for this dependence. In Davidson's account, it seems that metaphor does its work simply by juxtaposing two objects via the referents of the terms literally assigned to them, in such a way that there is no cognitive connection between the metaphorical effect and the literal. However, as Stern points out, this has the result that

> while Davidson claims that the metaphorical depends on the literal, much of what is usually included in our notion of the literal meaning of a sentence does no work in and is even excluded from, Davidson's account of this dependence relation.[33]

As a result, we are limited in our ability to use the literal meaning of the metaphor in the explanation of its effects.

Suppose, as Davidson does, that metaphor consists entirely of the use of metaphorical utterances to bring our attention to the similarities between objects or ideas. That is, according to Davidson, the utterance "Margaret Thatcher is a bulldozer" is metaphorical only in that it is used to draw our attention to similarities between the referent of the subject (person) and the referent of the predicate (bulldozer). Since, in Davidson's view, the metaphorical effect of noticing similarities is brought about by the opposition between the two objects that cannot be identified, it should not matter whether the subject and object are reversed or whether the predicates are different. However, "A bulldozer is Margaret Thatcher" is clearly different from the original metaphor and both are different from "Margaret Thatcher climbed into the bulldozer." That is, it seems as though Davidson's causal theory fails to account for the dependence of the metaphorical on the literal, which is one of the criteria for a theory of

[32]Josef Stern, "What Metaphors Do Not Mean," *Midwest Studies in Philosophy* 16 (1991): 13–51, pp. 27–38.

[33]Ibid., p. 30. Note that the criticism Stern levels against Davidson is the same criticism Davidson brings to bear against the theory of metaphor as an elliptical simile, namely that it violates the requirement that the literal meaning of the terms be active in the processing of a metaphor. To decide whether Davidson's theory is inconsistent (or Stern's interpretation is misguided), we would have to determine whether Davidson's view of causation really requires that the literal meanings of the term only be active as terms which pick out objects in the world. In this case, Stern's interpretation and criticism of Davidson would be correct. In addition, if Davidson's criticism of comparativism is correct, it would also apply to his own theory.

metaphor which causes him to reject several semantic theories of metaphor (Criterion 11 on my list).

Response to Objections

Despite the apparent discrepancy between the behavior of ordinary participants and the claim that the propositional content of metaphors is that of their literal interpretation, Davidson believes that these two are reconcilable. One response to the first criticism of Davidson (Objection 1) is to take Searle's pragmatic approach that what appears to us as a special or metaphorical content is an instance of speaker meaning rather than one of sentence meaning.[34] In other words, we could explain our intuitions that the person in question failed to understand the utterance by saying that while they understood what was *said* in the utterance, they failed to understand what was *meant* by the speaker. However, although this may seem a viable option (one accounts for our intuitions of metaphorical content without requiring that the expression have a different meaning), it is not a move supported by Davidson, as he indicates when he says: "Nor does its maker say anything, in using the metaphor, beyond the literal."[35] Davidson's criticism of Searle's account is two-fold. For one thing, unlike Searle, Davidson does not believe that the metaphorical should bear the name of meaning, whatever the kind of meaning intended. As Josef Stern argues,[36] Davidson's disagreement with Searle is not merely terminological, that is, based on a disagreement on what to name various types of entities. Instead, what is at stake is what can properly be called meaning in a theory of semantics. Since, in Davidson's view, meaning is something independent of such things as speaker's intentions, it simply cannot be said that what a speaker intends to communicate with an utterance is the *meaning* of that utterance, even if one qualifies the description by calling the meaning in question *speaker* meaning. In addition, unlike Searle, Davidson does not believe that metaphors have a special content which must be deduced in order for the audience to successfully grasp them.[37]

Davidson would most likely take another tactic in order to defend his analysis against the first criticism. That is, he would explain that the apparent discrepancy between the behavior of ordinary participants on the one hand and the claim that the propositional content of metaphors is that

[34]Searle, "Metaphor." I explore this analysis further in Chapter 2.
[35]Davidson, "What Metaphors Mean," p. 431.
[36]Stern, "What Metaphors Do Not Mean," p. 16.
[37]Davidson, "What Metaphors Mean," p. 440.

of their literal content on the other as resulting from the assumption that the behavior of speakers is a reaction solely to the proposition expressed by the utterance. This assumption is indeed mistaken since, as Davidson points out, the behavior of interpreters is typically a reaction not only to the proposition expressed through the utterance in a context and its truth value but also to the *effect* of that utterance. This effect may be partially due to a number of factors, including the conventional role such an utterance might play in a culture, other information known to the participants, and the beliefs and desires of the participants. In other words, Davidson would explain the discrepancy between the proposition expressed and the behavior of the participants in terms of the distinction between what is said, and how what is said is *used*. As discussed in Chapter 2, we typically (1) regard "what is said" as an objective thing, independent of such things as speaker intention and (2) include factors in addition to the proposition expressed by an utterance when attempting to account for the behavior of the participants. As a result, the discrepancy between the behavior of the participants and the literal content of an utterance is not sufficient to claim a metaphorical content which is the proposition expressed by the metaphor. Thus Davidson's analysis would be seem to be safe from the first criticism.

Davidson might respond to the second criticism (Objection 2) by claiming that the commonsense view of what it means to understand an utterance involves grasping not only the proposition it expresses (with its concomitant truth conditions) but also what the speaker intends the audience to notice. If we accept this, we can only say that someone understands an utterance if they derive the effect the speaker ultimately intends to achieve, as well as the proposition expressed. For example, in processing an utterance of "It is very cold in here," if the audience does not close the window, we might hold that they missed the point and thus failed to understand the utterance. Davidson might claim, in parallel, that in order to understand the metaphor "Juliet is the sun," one would need to grasp the likeness the speaker intended the audience to notice in order to understand the utterance. However, the two cases are clearly different. For while the bedridden speaker might claim that the audience missed the point or failed to be cooperative if they did not close the window, the speaker cannot say that the audience misjudged the truth conditions of the utterance or misunderstood what was said. However, in the case of metaphor, this is precisely what seems to be happening. In other words, while the argument that the comprehension of an utterance includes the comprehension of the speaker's intentions might allow Davidson to escape the first criticism, it does not address the second criticism, which is based on the intuition of a distinct metaphorical content.

In conclusion, it seems that Davidson's account suffers from major flaws in that he is unable to account for our intuition of metaphorical content and truth (Criterion 3). Nor, if Stern is right, does Davidson actually account for the dependence of the metaphorical on the literal (Criterion 11), despite his claims to the contrary. That is, Davidson's causal explanation fails to account for the dependent relationship between the literal and the metaphorical in such a way as to account for its systematicity. Davidson rejects the notion of metaphorical meaning precisely because he seeks the explanatory power of semantics. Yet in denying the role of types in metaphor, he robs metaphor of this systematicity, as well as fails to account for the knowledge speakers of the language seem to need in order to properly process the language, the ability to distinguish and interpret metaphorical utterances.

Another consequence of Davidson's position on metaphor is a rift between the common understanding and use of the terms "meaning" and "truth" on the one hand and the semantic understanding and use of these same terms on the other. That is, when we observe the behavior of participants in speech acts, we cannot help but see that they judge the truth of a metaphorical utterance not according to a literal interpretation of the utterance, but rather according to a metaphorical interpretation. In other words, not until a metaphor has been understood metaphorically (other than literally) does the interpreter evaluate the utterance. If the speaker were to take the utterance literally and evaluate it as such, they would be judged not merely as uncooperative (as someone is judged when they take a euphemism literally), but as having missed the point. Yet Davidson tells us that although there may be such a thing as metaphorical truth, it is not something that belongs to sentences (or sentences in a context).

Table 5 summarizes our evaluation of Davidson's analysis of metaphor.

Summary

Because a causal theory of metaphor is not the only possible use-based account of metaphor, showing Davidson's account to be inadequate does not show that all use-based theories of metaphor are inadequate. Nor does it establish metaphorical content as the proposition expressed by a metaphorical utterance, rather than one pragmatically associated with it. In fact, Davidson's adamant opposition to the notion that there is a cognitive

TABLE 5

Evaluation of Davidson's Analysis

Metaphoricity	Well. It seems right that the metaphoricity of the utterance depends upon the literal. However, Davidson cannot account for the figurativeness of similes or the falseness of some similes
Metaphor comprehension	Fair
The intuition of metaphorical content and truth	Poorly. Cannot account for this
Difficulty of specifying the satisfaction conditions of some metaphorical utterances	Well. Designs account to meet this condition
The context dependence of metaphor	Acknowledges but does not explain
The ubiquity of metaphor (why metaphor is used)	Poorly. Cannot explain why pointing out likenesses using literal means is any different than the use of metaphor
The relationship between metaphor and simile	Fair. Doesn't account for the figurativeness of similes or the falseness of some similes
Treatment of different types of metaphors	Weak on common metaphors
The incorporation of metaphors into the language	Does not account for
Consistency with the framework of semantics	Designs his account to meet this condition
The dependence of the metaphorical on the literal	Debatable[38]
The lack of conventionality of metaphor	Well. Came up with this condition
The fact that metaphors are about the world	Well. Came up with this condition
The relative independence of speaker intention	Poorly

content associated with metaphor which one must grasp in order to understand the metaphorical utterance distinguishes his theory from most (if not all) use-based theories (as well as from semantic theories), placing it in a class of its own. However, since nonsemantic theories of metaphor do

---

[38]In some respects Davidson handles this condition quite well in that he claims that the content of the metaphor is its literal content and this literal content generates the image that constitutes metaphoricity. Yet Josef Stern points out that Davidson's analysis is weak in that all that is required for Davidson's analysis is the literal meanings of the principle and subsidiary subject. That is, the analysis has no way of distinguishing between metaphors and similes. I address this point elsewhere. For more on the topic, see Stern, "What Metaphors Do Not Mean."

not have access to the notion of metaphorical meaning, it is particularly difficult for them to provide an account of metaphorical content, something semantic accounts easily do.[39] To do so, without running afoul of the condition of being consistent with the tools of semantics and pragmatics (Criterion 10 on our list), such theories must either give up the assumption that the proposition expressed by an utterance its meaning[40] or they must argue that metaphorical content is not, in fact, the proposition expressed by the metaphorical utterance but merely a proposition pragmatically associated with it. As a result, the next step is to consider whether use-based theories of metaphor which acknowledge a cognitive content associated with metaphor and necessary to its processing fare any better than Davidson's causal theory.

In the meantime, I have established metaphor's relative independence of speaker intention as a criterion for a theory of metaphor (Criterion 14). I have also defended my claim that metaphor expresses a metaphorical content that is different from the content it expresses under a literal interpretation (Claim 2). Lastly, I have begun to establish that metaphorical content is the proposition expressed by the utterance, rather than something pragmatically associated with it (Claim 3), which would establish metaphor as a semantic phenomenon (Claim 4).

[39]Fogelin describes this as the main "dilemma" for theories of use.

[40]Note that this assumption is based on Fregean semantics and seems impossible to give up.

5

Metaphor as Use

Metaphor and Irony

Identification of Metaphor and Irony

Within the species of nonliteral language, metaphor and irony tend to be grouped together. Metaphor and irony are commonly considered to be similar in that in both, as they are traditionally conceived, what the speaker means (i.e. wants to say) is considered to be something *other* than what is said (as opposed to something *in addition* to what is said, as is thought to be the case in indirect speech acts). For example, if Liz responds to a question about how she is doing with "Just wonderfully," spoken *ironically* (as identified by conventional clues such as the tone of voice and obvious conflict between speaker's beliefs and literal sentence content) common sense says that what she means (i.e. the speaker meaning) is that she is not doing well at all, in opposition to what is actually said (the proposition literally expressed). In the same way, when Romeo says that Juliet is the sun, it is thought that what he means (that Juliet is beyond compare) is different from what is said (that Juliet is a gaseous blob at the center of our universe).

Grice: Metaphor as a Conversational Implicature

Grice was the first to argue for an identification between metaphor and irony in that (1) he classifies both of them as cases of conversational implicatures and (2) he considers the figurative content of each to consist of the implied propositional content.[1] In the Gricean framework, the proposi-

---

[1]H. P. Grice, "Logic and Conversation," in *The Philosophy of Language*, 2nd edition, ed. A. P. Martinich (Oxford: Oxford University Press, 1990), pp. 149–60, p. 156. More specifically, he classifies them both as cases in which the first maxim of

tional content associated with an utterance can be classified into (1) *explicatures* (what is said) and (2) *implicatures* (what is implied). Although he does not define it precisely, Grice associates the former with the conventional meaning of the utterance,[2] that is, the proposition the hearer would derive given knowledge of the language and the belief that the speaker is speaking literally. In contrast, propositional content that is associated with the utterance but is not part of what is said is considered an implicature, something which is implied by what is said in that it is required to make sense of what is said. Grice further classifies implicatures into two types (1) *conventional implicatures* (which follow from what was said regardless of the context of utterance) and (2) *conversational implicatures* (which are dependent on the context of utterance). Examples of the former would include the implicature that John has two children that follows from the utterance that John has three children. Examples of the latter include the implicature that Chris wants to go swimming that follows from the announcement (in certain contexts) that she remembered to bring her swimsuit. The difference between the two is that conversational implicatures are highly context-dependent and thus must be considered pragmatically rather than semantically determined.[3] In all species of implicatures, since implicatures are needed in order to make sense of utterances (which is what makes them implicatures), it is first necessary to determine what was said.

The second component of Grice's analysis of metaphor and irony is based upon his conception of communication. In the Gricean view, cooperative discourse (i.e. language use) is governed by conversational maxims in accordance with the Cooperative Principle: "Make your conversational contribution such as is required, at the stage at which it occurs, by the accepted purpose or direction of the talk exchange in which you are engaged."[4] That is, in order to be cooperative, participants in discourse are bound to follow certain maxims, including the maxims of Quality, Quantity, Relation, and Manner. For example, a cooperative speaker (one who

---

Quality is violated and he considers the figurative content of both to be derived in some way from that of the proposition expressed.

[2]Ibid., p. 151.

[3]Grice does not use this terminology, but his analysis of conversational implicatures is based upon interpretation by the audience of what the speaker's intends to communicate in coordination with observation of principles of communication, all pragmatic notions. Since what is implied is clearly distinct from what is said (p. 150), Grice considers conversational implicatures to be clearly not a part of meaning and thus outside the realm of semantics.

[4]Ibid., pp. 151–52.

is obeying the cooperative principle) will observe the first maxim of Quality by saying only that which he knows to be true.[5]

The fact that being cooperative requires following these maxims allows hearers, in cases of cooperative endeavors, to use the flouting of the maxims to determine that what the speaker intended to convey by an utterance is *not* the conventional meaning of the utterance, provoking a search for the intended speaker meaning.[6] In other words, according to Grice, the flouting of conversational maxims is used to provoke the derivation of implicatures which are not part of what is said (via conventional meaning) but which allow the speaker to make sense of what is said. Flouting a maxim is different from the two other possible ways of failing to follow a maxim in that (1) its obviousness to both parties keeps it from being a case of simply not following a maxim (as in the case of lying) and (2) the fact that the speaker is speaking and does not state an intention not to be cooperative keeps it from being a case in which the speaker opts out of following the maxim.[7] For example, if someone utters "What lovely weather" in weather that clearly is not lovely, the obviousness of the disparity between the truth of matter and the proposition expressed by the utterance keeps the utterance from being a case of lying (the truth is too obvious). At the same time, the speaker has not announced or given any indication of an intention to cease to be cooperative (for example, a prisoner under torture might speak nonsense in order to avoid giving out information). As a result, Grice would classify the utterance as one in which one of the maxims of Quality has been flouted (maxim of truthfulness). In such cases, the audience must conclude that the speaker intentionally violated the maxim yet is still intending to be informative, and so their task is to derive the intended speaker meaning.[8]

[5]Ibid., p. 153.

[6]Ibid., p. 156. Grice does not define the term "intended speaker meaning" or make it a core term as Searle does. However, he explains that what he means by it is whatever proposition the speaker wants to get across.

[7]Although Grice cites four ways of failing to follow a maxim, including a description of conflicting maxims as one of these, the latter is actually a reason to fail to follow a maxim, rather than a way failing to follow a maxim. Martinich mentions this is his introduction to *The Philosophy of Language* and in his work "A "Theory for Metaphor," in *Pragmatics*, ed. Steven Davis (Oxford: Oxford University Press, 1991), pp. 507–18.

[8]Note that this lays the foundation for the subsequent development of reinterpretation theories of metaphor, that is, theories that see metaphor comprehension as a reinterpretation of an expression whose literal interpretation proves faulty in one way or another. Searle's theory is the most notable example: he develops Grice's and Austin's principles into a theory of speech acts and places metaphor and irony with the

Given this framework, Grice classifies metaphor and irony as implicatures because he sees them as instances in which what is expressed cannot possibly be what is intended by the speaker. That is, they are cases in which the intended speaker meaning is not the conventional meaning but rather one derived via the conversational maxims and, owing to their pragmatic nature, implicatures, rather than part of what is said. In addition, because the propositional content associated with metaphor and irony is highly context-dependent, Grice classifies them as instances of conversational implicatures rather than conventional implicatures. Yet these conversational implicatures are different from the example of a conversational implicature in which Chris announces she remembered to bring her swimsuit as a way to convey her desire to go swimming. The difference lies in the fact that in the example cited the implicature is a consequence of the proposition expressed, and both are considered to be part of what is expressed by the use of the utterance. In contrast, in the cases in which a maxim is flouted, the proposition literally expressed is jettisoned completely and does not constitute any part of the intended speaker meaning.[9] As a consequence, given a proposition that is blatantly inappropriate and unintended, the audience is put in the position of having to derive a speaker meaning other than the one overtly expressed and yet, in some unspecified way, related to it.

For Grice, both metaphor and irony (as conversational implicatures), result from the flouting of the first maxim of Quality, that of not saying what one believes to be false.[10] In addition, both metaphor and irony have a propositional content which differs and must be derived from the proposition expressed. According to Grice, the way in which speaker meaning is derived in cases in which the sentence meaning is blatantly false is by using the proposition literally expressed to derive a related proposition (presumably one that makes sense in the context, although Grice does not specify this.) To give a complete account of these phenomena, therefore, Grice

---

class of indirect speech acts, those in which what the speaker intends is other than the proposition literally expressed. See John Searle, "Indirect Speech Acts," *The Philosophy of Language*, ed. Martinich, pp. 161–75. Such theories tend to fall into one of two camps depending on whether they hold that what prompts the reinterpretation is falsity (a semantic property) or lack of conformity to pragmatic principles (a pragmatic property).

[9] As we will consider later, this difference can be used to criticize the Gricean analysis.

[10] Note that since not all metaphors are literally false (e.g. no man is an island), this analysis is incorrect. However, Grice could easily accommodate such metaphors by classifying them instead as cases in which the maxim of Relation is violated.

TABLE 6

Features of Grice's Analysis

Metaphoricity	Unclear. Perhaps in terms of similarity or pragmatic deviance
Comprehension process	1. Derive the literal content 2. Note pragmatic conflict 3. Derive speaker meaning using similarity
The proposition expressed by the metaphorical utterance	Its sentence meaning
The existence of metaphorical content and truth	Yes
The classification of metaphorical content	Conversational implicature
Rule for deriving metaphorical content	None given. Perhaps uses similarity
Phenomena metaphor is like	Irony and other conversational implicatures

must specify how the proposition representing speaker meaning is to be derived. In the case of irony, Grice specifies that the proposition thought to express speaker meaning consists of the contradictory of the proposition expressed. Thus, in the case of an utterance of "John is a fine friend" in a context in which the utterance is blatantly false, the listener takes the contradictory of the proposition, deducing that John is not a fine friend. (In contrast, Searle advocates taking the opposite of the proposition, producing the stronger proposition "John is a terrible friend" as the intended speaker meaning.[11])

In the case of metaphor, however, Grice does not have available a simple rule such as taking the contradictory of the proposition. Instead his only guide for the formation of the implied proposition is that the hearer should make sense of it in the context, perhaps by using the similarity relation (e.g., sheepdogs are like managers).[12] Table 6 summarizes the features of Grice's analysis.

Objection to Grice

While Grice's conception of metaphor and irony is intuitively appealing in that it accounts for both these figures of speech (and others, as well) by relying on basic pragmatic principles, it is subject to various criticisms. One obvious difficulty is the sketchiness of Grice's account. Although he

[11]John Searle, "Indirect Speech Acts."
[12]Grice, "Logic and Conversation," p. 156.

provides a means for deriving speaker meaning in the case of irony, he does not provide a comparable rule for metaphor, even though he maintains that, given the cooperative nature of the endeavor, it should be something the listener is capable of deriving from what was said.

In defense of Grice, we could take his theory as a sketch (as he intended it) and evaluate the subsequent developments of his theory rather than his own limited sketch. As a theory which classifies metaphor as a matter of pragmatics, Grice's approach is similar to that of many philosophers, including Davidson.[13] However, as was discussed in Chapter 4, given that Davidson's causal account of metaphor is noncognitive in that he rules out the possibility of metaphorical content, we cannot turn to Davidson to fill in Grice's gaps.

However, Searle and Martinich (and Fogelin) provide elaborations of Grice which are consistent with the identification of metaphorical meaning with speaker meaning. As a consequence, they are faced with the task of explaining how the relevant speaker meaning is derived from the metaphorical utterance by the listener.[14] At the same time, since these philosophers, in the manner of Grice, hold the content of the utterance (the

[13]Fogelin would classify both of these theories as literalist theories of metaphor. Literalist theories—in opposition to meaning-shift theories, which hold that the metaphorical force of a metaphor is a matter of meaning—hold that metaphorical utterances mean what they say under a literal interpretation.

[14]While this may sound like a psychological issue, it need not be interpreted in this way. What is sought is not a description of specific techniques used by speakers which depend upon such features of context as their assumptions, desires, intentions, and so forth, but rather an algorithm that relates sentence meaning (as determined by the rules of the language) and the derived interpretation. In other words, what is sought is the equivalent of the rules of the language that allow the derivation of sentence meaning from word meaning and, supposedly, the derivation of the proposition expressed from sentence meaning. (Note that the picture underlying this description is one in which word meaning, together with the rules of the language is used to derive sentence meaning, which is used in the complete absence of context to derive the proposition expressed [what is judged as true or false].) On the basis of indexicals, this picture has been revised by Kaplan and other in such a way that sentence meaning does not provide propositional content in the absence of context but instead merely constrains the derivation of the proposition expressed so that determinate and specifiable features of context influence the proposition expressed by a given sentence. For example, the interpretation of the indexical "I" requires an identification of the speaker. Even given Kaplan's revisions, such that determinate and specifiable features of context influence the proposition expressed in a way controlled by rules of the language, this kind of semantics is currently challenged by pragmatists such as Sperber and Wilson, Carston, and Recanati. See, for example, François Recanati, "The Pragmatics of What Is Said," in *Pragmatics*, ed. S. Davis (Oxford: Oxford University Press, 1991), pp. 97–120.

proposition expressed) to be that provided by a literal interpretation via the sentence meaning, they provide "reinterpretation" theories of metaphor, that is, an approach to the processing of metaphors that maintains that the metaphorical content of an utterance is derived by first deriving the literal or conventional meaning, noticing a conflict between that content and the conventions of conversation, and then deriving an alternative, figurative content.

Martinich on Metaphor and Irony

Martinich presents his theory of metaphor as simply picking up where Grice left off.[15] Using Grice's terminology and classification of metaphor as a conversational implicature, he fills in the gap left by Grice by providing a method of deducing metaphorical content consistent with Grice's framework. For Martinich, the debate over whether metaphorical content is an explicature or an implicature can be resolved by appealing to his distinction between saying and what he calls *making-as-if-to-say*. According to Martinich, a speech act can be classified as one of making-as-if-to-say (rather than one of saying) if the speaker is using the utterance to convey something other than the proposition that is expressed by the sentence (as deduced using conventional, i.e. literal, means). The example that Martinich sees as epitomizing this class of speech acts is that of irony. That is, Martinich considers a case of irony to be a situation in which the speaker utters a sentence in order to convey a proposition other than the one expressed by the sentence he utters.[16]

Metaphor as Conversational Implicature

FIRST ARGUMENT

Martinich provides two arguments in defense of Grice's classification of metaphor as a conversational implicature. Martinich's first argument, which uses his distinction between saying and making-as-if-to-say, is

---

[15]Martinich, "A Theory for Metaphor."

[16]Note that Martinich's distinction between saying and making-as-if-to-say provides a vehicle for distinguishing between different types of conversational implicatures, specifically between those in which the proposition that is ultimately conveyed follows from the proposition literally expressed and those in which the proposition conveyed is incompatible with and takes the place of the proposition literally expressed. As a consequence, Martinich provides a possible solution to the criticism of Grice posed by Sperber and Wilson. Dan Sperber and Deirdre Wilson, "Irony and the Use-Mention Distinction," in *Pragmatics*, ed. Davis, pp. 550–63.

based upon the claim that the literal interpretation of utterances is usually false.[17] Since most would agree that the speaker of the metaphor "Steve is a sheepdog" aims at the truth, it would be wrong (according to Martinich) to say that the speaker is asserting a proposition expressed by a literal interpretation of the sentence. As a consequence, it seems reasonable to say that the speaker only makes-as-if-to-say the sentence the speaker utters (or the content expressed by it). In Martinich's terms, the speaker *says* one thing by *making-as-if-to-say* another. That is, by making-as-if-to-say something which the audience finds to be false (or irrelevant, in the case of nonstandard metaphors), the speaker says something else, through implication.

A hidden assumption in this argument is that any given sentence in a context can have only one possible content, that expressed under a literal interpretation of the sentence in that context. This assumption is inevitable for those who hold (1) that the content of a sentence is determined solely by its meaning and (2) that the meaning of an expression does not shift in a metaphorical context (i.e. meaning is independent of context). While these assumptions can be convincingly challenged, the first constitutes the backbone of traditional Fregean semantics and the second is the main reason given by philosophers such as Fogelin and Davidson for rejecting semantic theories of metaphor (such as that of Black[18]). However, even if one accepts these assumptions, a more penetrating criticism can be made. While this argument shows (given the aforementioned assumptions), that what is said in the case of a metaphor is the literal content of the utterance, all it shows is that what the speaker intends to convey cannot be the proposition expressed by the utterance. This argument does not show that what the speaker intends to convey is an implicature of the ut-

---

[17]Note that since the literal interpretations of metaphorical utterances are not always false, this analysis cannot be complete. Martinich handles the difficulty with a division of metaphors into standard and nonstandard metaphors, such that standard metaphors are those whose literal interpretation is false. While he develops his theory based upon standard metaphors, he then extends it to account for nonstandard metaphors. In both cases, (1) the listener decides that the literal interpretation of the metaphorical is false and (2) the metaphorical is an implication which the listener derives from the context in conjunction with some sort of beliefs (i.e. cultural, communal, etc.). The only difference between the two for Martinich is that in nonstandard metaphors the audience must go through an extra step in deciding that since the utterance flouts the maxim of quantity (in that the literal interpretation is not informative), it must be intended to be taken as false. Once the proposition expressed is taken is false, then the metaphorical interpretation is generated as in standard metaphors.

[18]Max Black, "Metaphor," in *Philosophical Perspectives of Metaphor*, ed. Mark Johnson (Minneapolis: University of Minnesota Press, 1981), pp. 63–82.

terance—not in the traditional sense of implicature, in which what is implied follows from what is said. [19]

SECOND ARGUMENT

Martinich's second argument (which is similar to Grice's) is directed against Merrie Bergmann's claim that what a person communicates by certain metaphorical utterances are assertions:

> What a person asserts must be explicit and determined by the rules governing the use of the words uttered; but what a person, speaking metaphorically, means by the sentence in question is not explicit in the utterance, but implicit, and is not governed by the rules for the use of those words. [Consequently] what the speaker communicates he communicates by some kind of implication.[20]

In this passage, Martinich makes the claim that the content put forth by assertions can be none other than the proposition expressed, as determined by the rules of the language. That is, a linguistic implication of what is said (such as the implication that Marge has two children which follows from "Marge has three children") is not part of the assertion (or of what is said). As a consequence, since metaphorical content is neither explicit nor follows from the rules of the language, it cannot be the content of an assertion. Instead, it must be an implication of an assertion.

One might object to this argument by criticizing Martinich's introduction of the notion of assertion. According to the traditional use of the term, an assertion is a certain kind of speech act such that to say that the utterance of "Pierre is a butterfly" is an assertion is to contrast it with a question, or a promise. In other words, to classify an utterance as an assertion is to classify it according to illocutionary force. However, as Martinich himself points out, utterances containing metaphors can be used in speech acts of various types of illocutionary force.[21] The example Fogelin gives is one in which a Dutch uncle says, "I promise to clip the wings of the butterfly." Given the many types of speech acts containing metaphors, it seems unreasonable to ban metaphors from the class of assertions. However, it seems that Martinich can defend himself by accepting assertions as a kind of speech act, and by saying that although metaphor can be used to make assertions (even true ones), the assertions they make are not consti-

---

[19]We will pursue this criticism further after considering Martinich's second argument.
[20]Martinich, "A Theory for Metaphor," p. 509.
[21]Ibid., p. 508.

tuted by the proposition expressed by the utterances, but rather by implications of this proposition. Since his point remains intact without the use of the term assertion, it seems that such a defense is sound.

Objection to Martinich and Grice

Although Martinich is able to compensate for the sketchiness of Grice's analysis of metaphor, his development of Grice only reveals a factor which can be used to put forth a more serious criticism than the criticism of incompleteness. Martinich, in the manner of Grice before him, classifies metaphor and irony (and any resulting figurative meaning) as conversational implicatures, that is, as something which is implied by the utterance in that it is necessary to make sense of the utterance in conjunction with the context. For example, he explains the derivation of the metaphorical content of "My love is a red rose" by postulating a premise, dependent on context of "A red rose is beautiful, or sweet-smelling, or highly valued, . . . ," thus leading to the conclusion "Therefore, my love is beautiful, or . . ."[22]

However, as Sperber and Wilson point out,[23] it is not clear that metaphor and irony can be classified as conversational implicatures, given the description of conversational implicatures that Grice provides. The most obvious sign of a discrepancy lies in the examples of conversational implicatures that Grice uses to define how conversational implicatures are processed. The problem lies in the fact that in the examples that typify conversational implicatures, both the sentence meaning and the resulting conversational implicature are thought to be intended by the speaker. In contrast, in the cases of metaphor and irony, the proposition derived in order to reconcile the utterance with the principles of cooperative conversation *substitutes* for the sentence meaning of the utterance in that it is taken as what is intended by the speaker. That is, it seems that if metaphor and irony are cases of implicature, this kind of implicature is different from, and possibly inconsistent with, the notion of implicature as typically employed.

Another seeming inconsistency in Grice appears in his description of how the implicature is derived when he reaches the cases of metaphor and irony. While describing standard conversational implicatures as propositions that bring the speaker's behavior in line with the rules of cooperative

[22]Ibid., p. 511.
[23]Dan Sperber and Deirdre Wilson, "Irony and the Use-Mention Distinction," in *Pragmatics*, ed. Davis, pp. 550–63.

speech (by bringing the utterance to relevance or truth), in the case of metaphor and irony, Grice talks about the speaker saying or making-as-if-to-say something "he does not believe" (rather than something which is only apparently untrue or irrelevant). In addition, rather than showing the speaker as saying something which implies something else which justifies the utterance, Grice describes the speaker as "trying to get across some other proposition than the one he purports to be putting forward."[24]

However, it is not clear that this difference, as evidenced by Grice's examples and descriptions, is sufficient to show that metaphor and irony violate the conditions of being a conversational implicature, since the notion of implicature may already incorporate them or may be able to be stretched to incorporate them without creating an inconsistency. One place to turn in order to reach a judgment is Grice's definition of implicature:

> a man who, by (in, when) saying (or making as if to say) that p has implicated that q, may be said to have conversationally implicated that q *provided that* (1) he is to presumed to be observing the conversational maxims or at least the cooperative principle; (2) the supposition that he is aware that, or thinks that, q is required in order to make his making as if to say p (or doing so in *those* terms) consistent with this presumption; and (3) the speaker thinks (and would expect the hearer to think that the speaker thinks) that it is within the competence of the hearer to work out, or grasp intuitively that the supposition mentioned in (2) *is* required.[25]

Unfortunately, this definition does not provide a definitive judgment in that it neither establishes nor rules out metaphor and irony as cases of conversational implicature. On the one hand, metaphor and irony meet the definition of conversational implicatures in that they meet the first and third conditions. On the other hand, they seem not to meet the second condition since the proposition they derive does not justify the utterance, but instead replaces it.

To explore the ramifications of this difference, we can use Grice's description of how a conversational implicature is processed. According to the Gricean analysis, given the stimulus of an apparent violation of one of the maxims of cooperative conversation, the audience looks for a proposition which, when taken as an assumption, allows the audience to view the irrelevance, in Gricean terms, as "only apparent." For example, consider a situation in which someone, when asked by B how C likes the new job, an-

[24]Grice, "Logic and Conversation," p. 156.
[25]Ibid., p. 154.

swers as follows: "C has not yet been to prison." The apparent irrelevance of the answer forces B to search for some proposition which makes this irrelevance "only apparent." Since to make the irrelevance of an utterance only apparent can only mean to show that utterance is *not* irrelevant, then the proposition in question must modify the information the audience has so that the utterance is now relevant. In Grice's example, the audience formulates something to the effect that "C is potentially dishonest" as a proposition which would make the utterance relevant.[26] Since Grice claims that the implicature shows that the speaker is being cooperative, both what he said and what he has implied must be relevant and potentially true.[27]

Given this as a model, let us attempt to apply the Gricean analysis to the case of metaphors, specifically, to the metaphor that Grice provides, "You are the cream in my coffee."[28] According to Grice, the process begins when the audience, upon processing the sentence meaning of the utterance, realizes that the utterance seems obviously false, since people are not dairy products. The obviousness of the violation shows that the speaker is not merely failing to fulfill a maxim (e.g. by lying). In addition, the speaker has given no sign of wanting to opt out of being cooperative (e.g. by babbling in order to get rid of the audience). As a result, the audience is left with the task of finding a proposition which makes the apparent falseness of the utterance only apparent. That is, the audience must find a proposition that, if assumed true, makes the utterance possibly true.

As described above, Martinich's analysis of metaphors follows the given model and, for the given metaphor, would produce as an implicature a proposition that would make the metaphor true: "The cream in my coffee is what makes life enjoyable and worth living."[29]

There are at least two problems with the analysis given. The first concerns a discrepancy between this analysis and our intuition of metaphorical content. That is, in the example above, our intuitions tell us that its metaphorical content is, rather than the derived implicature, some propo-

[26]Note that any number of propositions might serve this purpose. For example, the proposition that C had been to jail for behavior at his last job.

[27]Note that there is no guarantee that these *are* true. However, it must not be the case that they are blatantly false, or the speaker would be in violation of the cooperative principles.

[28]Ibid., p. 156.

[29]Note that for this premise to function properly the predication must be one of definition and not just the assignment of qualities. In other words, the definition of "being the cream in one's coffee" must be "being what makes life enjoyable and worth living."

sition to the effect that "You are what makes my life enjoyable and worth living." In other words, while the implicature in question is a premise that, together with the utterance, produces something which corresponds to our intuition of the metaphorical content of the utterance, the implicature cannot be identified with the metaphorical content itself.

While this difficulty is startling, it is rather easily overcome by appealing to the distinction Carston makes between two types of conversational implicatures: implied premises and implied conclusions.[30] While the non-metaphorical utterances Grice (and Martinich) give as examples of conversational implicatures are such that the generated implicature is of the former kind, there is no reason metaphorical content could not be of the latter kind. Thus Grice and Martinich could respond to our objection by identifying metaphorical content as the implied conclusion of a conversational implicature, which would place their analysis in line with our intuition of the metaphorical content of a metaphorical utterance.

The second difficulty concerns the form of the argument and is more difficult to overcome. The reason for searching for an implicature, given Grice's analysis, is the need to show the utterance to be either relevant or possibly true. However, the implicature one arrives at in the case of a metaphor which is literally false is itself necessarily false. To see this, one need only consider the example Grice provides concerning the cream in one's coffee. According to Grice, the audience seeks an implicature that reconciles the apparent falseness of the metaphorical utterance. In the example cited, the proposition that would meet that condition is "The cream in my coffee is defined as what makes my life worth living." As a result, this proposition would seem to be the implied premise. However, this statement merely spells out the redefinition (reconceptualization) of the entities that makes the utterance metaphorical and thus false. That is, in Grice's solution to the apparent falsity of the metaphor, only pushes the metaphoricity (and thus falseness) into another proposition (the implicated premise). Given Grice's analysis, it seems that one would then have to seek yet another implicature in order to reconcile the resulting implicature with presumption that the speaker is speaking cooperatively. Yet none is forthcoming since the only way for a metaphorical utterance to be true is for its implied redefinition (or reconceptualization) of certain entities to be true. In other words, although implicatures are designed to justify a certain content, in the case of metaphor, the so-called implicature ac-

[30]Robyn Carston, "Implicature, Explicature, and Truth Theoretic Semantics," in *Pragmatics*, ed. Davis, pp. 33–51.

tually changes the content by redefining what it means to be a certain thing. Since the resulting implicature, although it seems to capture an aspect of metaphoricity, does *not* reconcile the apparent falsity of the metaphorical utterance, Grice (and Martinich) fail to provide an analysis of metaphorical content within the framework of semantics and pragmatics (thus violating Criterion 10).

One might attempt to defend Grice by appealing to the fact that the implicature in question ("The cream in my coffee is what makes life enjoyable and worth living") is a proposition which it is reasonable as well as informative to assume. Indeed, it does seem as though we assume something like this when we process a metaphor: in order to understand a metaphor, it seems we must assume (at least for the sake of understanding what is said) a proposition of the sort proposed (i.e. "The cream in my coffee is what makes life enjoyable and worth living"). However, Grice provides no means of justifying the assumption of this proposition and his classification of this proposition as an implicature clearly violates his definition of implicature.

CONCLUSION

One might defend Martinich and Grice by saying that it is possible to preserve the intuitions behind their account without classifying metaphor and irony as conversational implicatures. What is central to Grice's account is merely that metaphor and irony are cases in which the rules of conversation are used to deduce the fact that the speaker's meaning is other than the conventional sentence meaning (i.e. a maxim is flouted and the speaker's meaning must be deduced).

However, this defense does not solve the problem that, given the flawed nature of Grice's account of metaphorical content as an implicature of the literal content of the utterance, he is left completely without an account of metaphorical content. In other words, his theory provides neither (1) an account of how the interpretation of a metaphor is derived nor (2) an explanation of how the figurative interpretation is related to the proposition expressed under a literal interpretation of the utterance or to the conventional meanings of the terms or sentence nor (3) a classification of metaphorical content that is consistent with his theory of conversation (i.e. as an explicature or as an implicature. Nor does his theory provide an explanation for why one might want to use a metaphor instead of a literal expression. In fact, the only thing that Grice *does* provide is an explanation of how one determines that a given utterance is metaphorical (i.e. when

TABLE 7
Evaluation of Grice's and Martinich's Analysis

Metaphoricity	Poor. Only vaguely identifies this as related to similarity
Metaphor comprehension	Poor. As discussed, the identification of metaphor as a conversational implicature is faulty. Also, Grice does not provide a clear rule for deriving metaphorical content. Finally, as we shall see in Chapter 6, any reinterpretation theory of metaphor (such as Grice's) conflicts with psychological studies
The intuition of metaphorical content and truth	OK
Difficulty of specifying the satisfaction conditions of some metaphorical utterances	Does not address this
Context dependence of metaphor	Does not account for this
The ubiquity of metaphor (why metaphor is used)	Does not address this
Relationship between metaphor and simile	OK. Could account for similarities between them in that both are based on similarity, but lacks a means of differentiating between them
Treatment of different types of metaphors	Does not address this
The incorporation of metaphors into the language	Does not address this.[31]
Consistency with the framework of semantics and pragmatics	OK. This notion of sentence meaning is consistent with semantics, but the analysis of metaphorical content as a conversational implicature is faulty
The dependence of the metaphorical on the literal	Poor. Accounts for this in that Grice says the metaphorical meaning is derived using the sentence meaning and the principle of similarity. However, as we discussed, the analysis of metaphorical content as a conversational implicature is faulty
The lack of conventionality of metaphor	Well
The fact that metaphors are about the world	Does not address but does not contradict
Relative independence of speaker intention	Poorly

[31]It could be explained in terms of Morgan's short-circuited implicatures. We could expand Grice and Martinich's analysis to account for this feature of metaphor by employing the notion of a short-circuited implicature. According to Morgan, if certain implicatures are used enough, they become short-circuited in that the audience comes to interpret the erstwhile implicature as the actual content of the sentence uttered (e.g. "passed away" for death). Jerry L. Morgan, "Two Types of Convention in Indirect Speech Acts," 250.

the maxim of truthfulness is flouted), except that even this is not adequate, since the flouting of the maxim of truthfulness occurs in cases of both irony and metaphor. In other words, what Grice *actually* provides, within the framework of a pragmatic theory, is an account of how one recognizes that the utterer's meaning of a given utterance is other than the conventional meaning. Since the identification of metaphor is dependent upon pragmatic distinctions (with metaphor itself treated as an implicature), the implication is that metaphor is purely a pragmatic phenomenon. At the same time, Grice provides a sketch of a "reinterpretation" theory of metaphor, that is, an approach to the processing of metaphors that maintains that the metaphorical content of an utterance is derived by first deriving the literal or conventional meaning, noticing a conflict between that content and the conventions of conversation, and then deriving an alternative, figurative content. Table 7 summarizes our evaluation of Grice's and Martinich's analysis.

Searle on Irony and Metaphor

Grice and Martinich are not alone in their identification of metaphor with irony. Searle's analysis of metaphor also identifies the two in that it analyzes both as cases in which the speaker's utterance meaning "comes apart from sentence meaning."[32] Searle further extends the identification between metaphor and irony in that, within this class (which also includes indirect speech acts),[33] he deliberately distinguishes between (1) indirect speech acts (such as those epitomized by the common example of "Can you pass the salt . . ." used as a request) and (2) metaphor and irony, on the basis of his belief that the former are cases in which the sentence meaning *is* part of the speaker meaning and the latter are cases in which it is *not*.[34] That is, Searle identifies metaphor and irony in that (unlike

---

[32]Searle, "Metaphor," in *The Philosophy of Language*, ed. Martinich, pp. 408–29, p. 408.

[33]One thing that makes it difficult to evaluate Searle's analysis is that he uses the term "indirect speech act" in two different ways. In his most general use of the term, an indirect speech act is any act in which speaker utterance meaning is different from the sentence meaning (i.e. the content of a sentence given by the rules of the language in a literal interpretation). In a secondary use, Searle applies the term to a subclass of this class of utterances so that what is intended to be conveyed is both the sentence meaning and something more. At the same time, Searle explains his theory of speech acts using two different distinctions, that between the literal and the nonliteral and that between the direct and the indirect speech act. In addition, at times he seems to conflate the two.

[34]Searle, "Metaphor," p. 426.

Metaphor as Use

TABLE 8
Features of Searle's Analysis

Metaphoricity	A relationship between the speaker meaning and sentence meaning as defined by Searle's eight principles
Comprehension process	1. Derive the literal content 2. Note pragmatic conflict 3. Derive speaker meaning using the 8 principles
The proposition expressed by the metaphorical utterance	Its sentence meaning and metaphorical content. (Note the inconsistency here)
The existence of metaphorical content and truth	Yes
The classification of metaphorical content	Speaker meaning
Rule for deriving metaphorical content	The eight principles
Phenomena metaphor is like	Irony

Davidson but like Grice and Martinich) he considers them both to have a *figurative* content (metaphorical and ironical, respectively) which constitutes speaker meaning and does not include sentence meaning (although it is related to it in some way). Indeed, for Searle, as for Grice and Martinich, it seems that the only difference between metaphor and irony is that, within virtually identical processes required to process metaphorical and ironical meanings, different rules are used to deduce the figurative meaning from the sentence meaning. (In the case of irony, Searle specifies that one takes the opposite of the sentence meaning. In the case of metaphor, he provides a list of eight principles which can be used to derive the metaphorical meaning from the sentence meaning.)

Searle's approach to metaphor is also like that of Davidson, Grice, and Martinich in that it treats metaphor as a pragmatic phenomenon rather than a semantic one. For although Searle classifies metaphorical content as an instance of speaker *meaning*, his speaker meaning is not a semantic notion (as the name implies) but rather a pragmatic notion, analyzed in terms of speaker intention and dependent upon the cooperative principles of conversation.[35] To evaluate Searle's analysis, we must examine the no-

[35]Searle seems to attempt to have the best of both worlds. By classifying metaphor as *speaker's* meaning, he escapes the rigorous conditions of meaning (i.e. context independence) and is able to incorporate other propositions which seem to be associated with the utterance yet are not part of sentence meaning. On the other hand, by classifying it as speaker's *meaning*, he implies that the regularity of semantics applies

tion of speaker meaning, the class and subclasses of indirect speech acts, the classification of metaphor within this framework, and the account of the derivation of metaphorical content from sentence meaning. Table 8 summarizes the features of Searle's approach.

Objection to Searle

Searle's analysis of metaphor is appealing for many reasons. One is that it seems to account in a simple way for the intuition in cases of metaphor and irony that what a speaker means to say is not the proposition expressed by the sentence according the rules of the language. That is, Searle's analysis seems to hold that what the speaker is accountable for is not sentence meaning but speaker meaning and for presenting it in such a way as to make it possible to deduce the speaker meaning. (According to Gricean and most pragmatic theories, in making an utterance, the speaker is bound to follow the rules of cooperative conversation, i.e. to say something that is true, relevant, etc.). This fits in with our intuitions that in processing a metaphorical utterance such as "Juliet is the sun," what we hold the speaker accountable for is not the literal interpretation of the utterance, or Searle's sentence meaning, but rather the metaphorical meaning, which in Searle's theory is part of the speaker meaning (Criterion 3).

Searle's account is also appealing in that it introduces a structure which explains a number of such phenomena (metaphor, irony, indirect speech acts, etc.) using similar principles. On an intuitive level, Searle's analysis fits in with the fact that, in hearing a metaphorical utterance we do not comprehend (i.e. whose metaphorical meaning we do not grasp), we often ask for the metaphorical meaning using the question "What do you

---

to the determination of this content, thus rescuing it from Davidson's "jungle of use." In this sense, Searle's theory is similar to that of Josef Stern ("Metaphor As Demonstrative," *Journal of Philosophy*) for Stern's theory also manages to escape Davidson's criticism of meaning-shift theories of metaphor by appealing to Kaplan's distinction between meaning and content and referring to metaphorical content as *content*, thus freeing it of the need to be context-independent. At the same time, Stern uses this distinction to claim that the systematicity of semantics applies to metaphor in that he describes a rule which marches different contexts to different contents (the metaphorical character) which determines metaphorical content. However, Searle's theory is different from Stern's in that Searle sees metaphor as a matter of pragmatics rather than semantics in that it is distinction from sentence meaning. In contrast, Stern analyzes metaphor as an expression of what is said, the proposition expressed by an utterance. As a result, while Searle groups metaphor with indirect speech acts, Stern considers the latter group to be distinguished by use, and thus a side issue to the determination of metaphorical meaning.

mean?" Likewise, if someone says something seemingly without a purpose, despite its literality and the obviousness of what is said, we may ask the same question. For example, consider a situation in which, on the eve of a woman's wedding, her future mother-in-law tells her that on the day of *her* wedding, her father offered to smuggle her out of the country. Although linguistic competence together with contextual knowledge might tell the bride what was said (i.e. the proposition expressed), she would probably still wonder what the point was, what the mother-in-law meant by saying what she said. However, the very concept of speaker meaning which simplifies and unifies Searle's account produces difficulties when examined closely.

One final reason for the appeal of Searle's analysis is that it seems to address the needs of psychologists such as Rumelhart who insist that the concept they need philosophers of language to provide is a notion of conveyed meaning (rather than proposition expressed), since it is this notion that must serve as the basis for theories of language comprehension. That is, Searle's notion of speaker meaning seems to correspond to the notion of conveyed meaning that (according to Rumelhart) models of language comprehension are in need of.[36]

OBJECTION FROM OBSCURITY OF SPEAKER MEANING

One objection to Searle's account is that in classifying metaphorical content as speaker meaning, it leaves the notion of speaker meaning somewhat obscure. To explain speaker meaning, Searle contrasts it with sentence meaning as follows: "[speaker meaning is] what a speaker means by uttering words, sentences, expressions," in contrast with "what the words, sentences, and expressions mean."[37] In Searle's view of language, sentences and words "have only the meanings that they have."[38] That is, sentence and word meanings are objective in that they are independent of what the speaker intends to communicate by using them. In contrast, the speaker meaning of an utterance, while related to the sentence meaning, is dependent upon what the speaker "might utter it to mean."[39] In other words, it is dependent upon speaker intention in a way sentence meaning is not. However, as we shall see, this notion of speaker meaning not only is

[36]David E. Rumelhart, "Some Problems with Literal Meanings," in *Metaphor*, ed. A. Ortony (Cambridge: Cambridge University Press, 1979), pp. 78–90.
 [37]Searle, "Metaphor," p. 409.
 [38]Ibid.
 [39]Ibid.

vague and even inconsistent in various ways but, depending on how it is resolved, it fails to account for metaphorical meaning the way Searle specifies.

To begin with, the very use of the term "speaker meaning" is suspect, given the understanding of meaning as a timeless enduring entity which remains constant within varying contexts. Davidson describes meaning as follows: "Literal meaning and literal truth conditions can be assigned to words and sentences apart from particular contexts of use. This is why adverting to them has genuine explanatory power."[40] However, Searle can defend himself from this criticism by pointing out that the term "meaning" is also used to refer to what the speaker expresses by an utterance, the point the speaker is trying to get across (as in the use of "What do you *mean* by that, young woman?").

However, even if we accept this defense, it is unclear whether Searle uses the term "speaker meaning" in a consistent manner. One major difficulty is that speaker meaning is not a clear cut concept. Even if we limit speaker meaning to a communicative role, by defining speaker meaning as that which the speaker intends to communicate, we are still left with various ways the concept can be interpreted.[41]

One possible interpretation of speaker meaning (based on its description of what the speaker really means) is that it serves as a mirror of the speaker's beliefs. However, this interpretation of speaker meaning does not produce a consistent idea of speaker meaning, as can be seen when the test is applied to cases of lies. For example, consider a situation in which a presidential candidate lies to a reporter, saying he has never smoked marijuana. If the speaker meaning of the utterance were to consist of the speaker's beliefs, then the reporter, although he understood the sentence meaning, would not grasp the speaker meaning. In fact, for the lie to be successful, the reporter must not grasp the speaker meaning. Yet, elsewhere in his argument, Searle indicates that for an act of communication to be successful, the audience must grasp the speaker meaning. As a result, it does not seem as though speaker meaning is intended to capture the speaker's beliefs.

Suppose, instead, that speaker meaning is intended to capture the main

[40]Donald Davidson, "What Metaphors Mean," in *The Philosophy of Language*, ed. Martinich, pp. 430–41, p. 431.

[41]Note that the notion of conveyed meaning suffers from the same weakness as that of speaker meaning, and thus the works of those who use it without a definition which specifies its relation to known entities such as the proposition expressed (e.g. Rumelhart) are susceptible to the same criticism.

point of the utterance. For example, in the case of the future mother-in-law's story, Searle might say that the speaker meaning is "There is a way out of this wedding." However, this would seem to imply that all utterances have some proposition which captures the main point of the utterance, which clearly is not so. For example, the future-mother-in-law might be telling the story just to pass the time and distract the bride from the coming event. Or she may have no particular motive at all for telling the story. This conflicts with the fact that Searle seems to believe that speaker meaning determines the truth conditions of the utterance, implying that it must be propositional in nature.[42] To remedy this, Searle might specify that speaker meaning encompasses whatever propositions the speaker intends to communicate using an utterance. This view of speaker meaning would lead to difficulties with incompetent speakers or even competent speakers who lack contextual or cultural information. Finally, the speaker meaning could include both the proposition expressed by the utterance and any implicatures of it. If this were the case, since every utterance has implicatures and since speaker meaning would always be different from sentence meaning, no utterance would be literal or direct. In addition, the boundaries of speaker meaning would be unclear. Given the obscurity of the notion of speaker meaning, it is difficult to evaluate Searle's claim that metaphorical content is the speaker meaning of an utterance. However, it does seem as though, no matter what interpretation is taken, an analysis of utterances in terms of speaker meaning would result in almost all utterances being nonliteral (I explore this below).

OBJECTION FROM CONFLATION OF THE DISTINCTION
BETWEEN THE LITERAL AND THE NONLITERAL AND
THE DIRECT AND THE INDIRECT

Another problem with Searle's analysis of metaphor as a type of indirect speech act is that Searle seems to conflate two distinctions: that between the literal and the nonliteral and that between the direct and the indirect, either intentionally or unintentionally. At times Searle treats the distinction between the literal and the nonliteral as something that occurs at the level of semantics in that it concerns the relationship between a sentence type and the proposition expressed by the sentence type. For example, in discussing utterances in which speaker and sentence meaning come apart, Searle says "the meanings of the words uttered by the speaker do

---

[42]Searle, "Metaphor," p. 412.

not exactly and literally express what the speaker meant."[43] This description implies that the distinction between the literal and nonliteral concerns the relationship between the sentence meaning and a given proposition.

However, elsewhere in his argument Searle writes as though the distinction between the literal and the nonliteral were a distinction between types of speech acts. This can be seen in his definition of literal utterances as utterances in which

> A speaker says S is P and he means S is P. Thus the speaker places object S under the concept P, where P = R. Sentence meaning and utterance meaning coincide.[44]

To define literal utterances in this way implies (1) that the distinction exists at the level of speech acts, (2) that literal utterances are, in fact, direct speech acts, and (3) that nonliteral utterances are those in which speaker meaning and sentence meaning come apart. In addition, in his presentation of this definition, this kind of speech act is contrasted with speech acts in which sentence meaning and speaker meaning do not coincide, and these cases are described as indirect speech acts. As a result, it seems that Searle is also identifying nonliteral speech acts with indirect speech acts. If this is so, then what Searle is doing is accounting for the distinction between the literal and the nonliteral in terms of the distinction between the direct and indirect. This conflation on Searle's part may well be an attempt to eliminate the need for the distinction between the literal and the nonliteral by showing that it is contained in the distinction between the direct and the indirect. However, as we shall see, this classification is problematic.

ARGUMENT AGAINST CLASSIFICATION OF METAPHOR
AS AN INDIRECT SPEECH ACT

Another criticism of Searle's analysis challenges his classification of metaphor as an indirect speech act.[45] This criticism is based on Searle's definition of indirect speech acts as "cases in which one illocutionary act is performed indirectly by way of performing another."[46] In Searle's analysis, in order for an act to qualify as an indirect speech act, there must be two separate acts performed, such that each act meets the condition of

---

[43]Ibid., p. 408.
[44]Ibid., p. 427.
[45]That is, as an illocution in which speaker meaning and sentence meaning come apart.
[46]Searle, "Indirect Speech Acts," p. 161.

being a separate act, as identified by a separate illocutionary force. Searle
drives this point home as follows:

> Such cases, in which the utterance has two illocutionary forces, are to be
> sharply distinguished from the cases in which, for example, the speaker tells
> the hearer that he wants him to do something; and then the hearer does it
> because the speaker wants him to, though no request at all has been made,
> meant, or understood.[47]

In the latter case, since no separate illocutionary force is generated (i.e. as
a request), via the recognition on the part of the audience that the speaker
intends to perform a request via the audiences' recognition of that intention, the speech act is not an indirect one. That is, there must be two separate illocutionary forces in the utterance—as identified by the communication of the speaker to the audience of an intention to commit a primary
(nonliteral) act (via nonliteral means) for it to qualify as an indirect speech
act. As a result, having certain conversational implicatures is not enough
to make an utterance indirect, unless there are two illocutionary forces. In
addition, for an illocutionary act to be indirect, its primary illocutionary
act must be nonliteral rather than literal.[48] That is, the primary communicative act the speaker performs must be the act performed indirectly by
means of another.

   However, it does not seem that metaphor meets the conditions required
of indirect speech acts. The main difficulty is that the metaphoricity of an
utterance seems to be completely independent of illocutionary force. Consider, for example, an utterance of the metaphor "The philosopher is the
pilot of the city." Without knowing the intentions of the speaker or
whether the speaker communicates this intention to the hearer, we cannot
judge whether the utterance is indirect or not. However, we can tell
whether the utterance is metaphorical or not. In other words, the illocutionary force is determined by factors that are independent of the factors
that determine metaphoricity. As a result, a metaphorical utterance cannot meet Searle's condition of being an indirect speech act (unless of
course it appears within the context of and indirect speech act).

   Someone might argue that the problem with this example is that one
can determine metaphoricity with little knowledge of the circumstance,
yet all metaphors are not that way.[49] That is, one might argue that there is

---

[47]Ibid.

[48]Ibid., p. 163.

[49]That is, metaphors are dependent upon contextual knowledge for identification
and interpretation. If some metaphors appear to be context-independent, it is only be-

no difference between metaphors and indirect speech acts in that in both cases, one usually needs more information. However, the knowledge of context it takes to derive the metaphorical content is different from that required to determine directness or indirectness. For example, compare a case in which the utterance is made in response to a query concerning what philosophy students should be taught versus the case of an utterance in response to a query, made in recessionary times, concerning which professions are least important to society and thus susceptible to elimination from educational offerings. While this contextual information may be enough to affect the metaphorical content, it does not affect whether an utterance is direct or indirect, which is dependent upon illocutionary force (i.e. the intention with which the utterance is made and the communication of that intention).[50] As a result, since indirect speech acts are dependent upon illocutionary force, then the directness or indirectness of a speech act is independent of its metaphoricity.

OBJECTION FROM INSUFFICIENCY
OF THE PRINCIPLES

One of the most frequent objections to Searle's analysis of metaphorical content concerns the adequacy of his principles as a means of deriving metaphorical content.[51] That is, it is unclear whether Searle's account of metaphor really accounts for the relation of metaphoricity. This objection is based on the fact that Searle's principles, by virtue of their very comprehensiveness, are explanatorily weak. In other words, while the principles seem successful insofar as they can accommodate the metaphorical meaning of any metaphor we can think of, what one principle rules out as the metaphorical meaning of an utterance, another rules in. That is, given a particular metaphorical utterance, the principles do not even narrow the

---

cause the knowledge of context necessary to their recognition and interpretation is general enough to be a part of background knowledge.

[50]Note that Fogelin implies that context *does* determine directness or indirectness in his example of an utterance of "This hike is longer than I remembered." Robert Fogelin, *Figuratively Speaking* (Yale: Yale University Press, 1988), p. 40. However, Searle would disagree with this on the ground that for an act to be indirect, the primary act must be one of a different illocutionary force marked by the communication of intention on the part of the speaker to the audience. While a competent speaker will *use* context to communicate a certain intention, it is the intention and its recognition that determine the act, not the context.

[51]Josef Stern, "What Metaphors Do Not Mean," *Midwest Studies in Philosophy* 16 (1991): 13–52, pp. 17–18. Jerry L. Morgan, "Observations on the Pragmatics of Metaphor," in *Metaphor*, ed. Ortony, pp. 136–47, pp. 144–45.

class of possible metaphorical meanings, let alone provide the intended metaphorical meaning. As a result, we cannot say that these principles allow the speaker to derive the metaphorical meaning.

In addition, as Morgan points out,[52] the vagueness of Searle's fourth principle, which specifies that the metaphorical meaning of an utterance may be anything "called to mind" by the literal content of the utterance, casts doubt on whether Searle's principles are even a good attempt to capture metaphoricity.[53] If asked how the set of all things called to mind can be narrowed to include only those metaphorically related to the sentence meaning, Searle would probably appeal to speaker meaning. Yet this dependence on speaker intention is a further weakness in Searle's account of metaphoricity. In explaining the role of speaker intention in speaker meaning, Searle uses Chomsky's example of the meaningless utterance "Colorless green ideas sleep furiously." According to Searle, even a nonsense sentence such as this one can have a metaphorical speaker meaning if the speaker so intends.[54] However, in the absence of some perspective or context that would allow the audience to arrive at a meaningful interpretation of the utterance that stands in a metaphorical relation to the sentence meaning, such a sentence cannot be metaphorical. That is, our intuitions tell us that while speaker intention may determine what the speaker wants to communicate and, when stated, provide a clue to the intended metaphorical content of the utterance, it does not determine metaphoricity in that it alone does not make something metaphorical (Criterion 14).[55] Thus, given a nonsense sentence and no way to adjust our perception so as to perceive a metaphorical relation, we would judge that while the speaker may have intended to speak metaphorically, they failed to do so.

OBJECTION FROM INCOHERENCE OF SEMANTICS

One final criticism which can be brought against Searle stems from Davidson's warning not to mistake the proposition that an utterance makes us think about with the proposition expressed by that utterance.[56] That Searle seems to be saying a metaphorical utterance is capable of ex-

[52]Morgan, "Observations."
[53]Searle, "Metaphor," p. 424.
[54]Ibid., p. 409.
[55]For an examination of the relationship between speaker intention and metaphor, see the second half of this chapter, under "Arguments Against Metaphor as Irony."
[56]Davidson, "What Metaphors Mean," p. 438.

pressing a content which is merely "called to mind" by the sentence meaning of that utterance makes him susceptible to this criticism.

Searle might defend himself by saying that while, unlike Davidson, he does believe that metaphorical utterances have a metaphorical content beyond their literal content, he does *not* identify this metaphorical content with the sentence meaning of the utterance. In addition, since the metaphorical content is based upon speaker intention and generated by the audience to bring the utterance in line with the principles of cooperative conversation, it is clearly a matter of pragmatics rather than semantics. If Searle were able to show that the sentence meaning rather than the metaphorical content is what is expressed by the utterance, he would escape the charge of mistaking entities associated with an utterance for what is actually expressed by that utterance.

However, a number of Searle's arguments are at odds with this position that the proposition expressed by a metaphorical utterance is not the metaphorical content. For example, in order to contrast metaphorical utterances with literal utterances, Searle says that

> in the case of the metaphorical utterance, the truth conditions of the assertion are not determined by the truth conditions of the sentence and its general terms. In order to understand the metaphorical utterance, the hearer requires something more than his knowledge of the language, his awareness of the conditions of the utterance.[57]

In other words, it seems that the content of a metaphorical utterance, as corresponding to the truth conditions of the utterance, is none other than the metaphorical content of the utterance rather than the sentence meaning. However, if Searle holds this position, he must either give up the notion that semantics (via sentence meaning) determines the proposition expressed by an utterance (i.e. what is said) or give up the truth-conditional notion of speaker meaning.[58]

[57]Searle, "Metaphor," p. 412.

[58]In this regard Searle's analysis is similar to Bergmann's in that she, too, holds that the content of an assertion containing a metaphorical utterance is the metaphorical content rather than the literal content or sentence meaning of the utterance. Bergmann's and Searle's accounts are also similar in that both claim to present a pragmatic rather than semantic analysis of metaphor. See Merrie Bergmann, "Metaphor and Formal Semantic Theory," *Poetics* 8 (1979): 213–30. Also in "Metaphorical Assertions," in *Pragmatics*, ed. Davis, pp. 485–94.

SUMMARY

While Searle's analysis of metaphor is intuitively appealing, the first objection calls into question the classification of metaphorical content as speaker meaning and even the clarity of the concept of speaker meaning. The second objection argues that Searle conflates two separate distinctions, that between the literal and the nonliteral and that between the direct and the indirect, most likely in an attempt to account for the former in terms of the latter. The third objection challenges the identification of

TABLE 9

Evaluation of Searle's Analysis

Metaphoricity	Poor. The principles are too weak
Comprehension process	OK. Suffers from weakness of principles
Difficulty of specifying the satisfaction conditions of some metaphorical utterances	Well. Based on the diversity of the principles and difficulty of choosing between them
The relationship between metaphor and simile	Does not address
Treatment of different types of metaphors	Weak on common metaphors and on what unifies all metaphors
The ubiquity of metaphor (why metaphor is used)	Does not account for
The incorporation of metaphors into the language	Does not account for
The dependence of the metaphorical on the literal	Does not account for it but is not incompatible with it
The context dependence of metaphor	Acknowledges but does not explain or distinguish metaphorical context dependence from the literal context dependence he describes
Consistency with the framework of semantics	Poor. Alternately identifies the truth conditions of a metaphorical utterance with its literal and its figurative meaning
Consistency with the framework of pragmatics	OK. Notion of speaker meaning is somewhat obscure
The fact that metaphors are about the world	Does not account for this but is compatible with it
The lack of conventionality of metaphor	Well
The intuition of metaphorical content and truth	Fair. Identifies metaphorical content as speaker meaning, which poses problems with semantics
Independence of speaker aim and intention	Poor

metaphor as an indirect speech act within Searle's framework in that it makes the claim that unlike most indirect speech acts of the kind Searle describes, metaphorical utterances generally include only one illocutionary act. The fourth objection is that Searle's principles do not successfully provide a means of deriving metaphorical content from sentence meaning. Nor, given their vagueness, do they seem to capture the nature of metaphoricity, since they allow almost anything to be the metaphorical meaning of an utterance. The fifth and final objection calls into question Searle's conception of semantics. In the next section we will see that Searle's identification between metaphor and irony is also problematic, as we examine the relationship between the speaker and a metaphorical or ironical utterance. Table 9 summarizes our evaluation of Searle's analysis of metaphor.

Arguments Against Metaphor as Irony

One apparently superficial distinction between metaphor and irony is that whereas we can almost always detect whether or not an utterance is metaphorical in the absence of a specified context, it seems impossible to tell whether or not an utterance is ironical in the same absence of context. Consider, for example, the utterance of "She is the center of our home; we rotate around her." Without knowing the context in which the metaphor was uttered, even though we can come up with a context in which the utterance could be literally true (for example, a dance is being performed in a home such that each dancer rotates around the person in the center), most people would predict that the utterance is metaphorical, and would stand a good chance of being correct. This is true of most metaphors, a fact that once provided support for the now defunct thesis that metaphors are instances of grammatical deviance.[59] (As mentioned before, these examples do not in fact show that metaphors are independent of context, either for identification or for interpretation. They simply show that cul-

---

[59]For arguments against the thesis that metaphors are grammatically (and thus semantically) deviant, see Josef Stern, "Metaphor and Grammatical Deviance," *Nous* 17, no. 4 (Nov. 1983): 577–99. Counterexamples to this thesis are also cited by Ted Cohen in "Figurative Speech and Figurative Acts," *Journal of Philosophy* 72 (1975): 669–84, and "Notes on Metaphor," *Journal of Aesthetics and Art Criticism* 34 (1976), 249–59. For arguments in support of this thesis, see Monroe Beardsley, "The Metaphorical Twist," *Philosophy and Phenomenological Research* 22 (1962): 293–307, "Metaphor and Falsity," *The Journal of Aesthetics and Art Criticism* 35 (1976): 218–22, and "Metaphorical Senses," *Nous* 12 (1978): 3–16.

tural and real-world knowledge allow us to infer a probable context against which we can determine whether or not an utterance is metaphorical and what a likely or unlikely interpretation would be.)

However, while cultural and real-world knowledge seems to provide us with a background that allows us to identify (and perhaps interpret) most metaphorical utterances without knowing the details of the actual context, the same stockpile of knowledge does *not* seem to be able to help us with ironical utterances in the same way. For example, consider Grice's example of an ironical utterance: "X is a fine friend."[60] In the absence of context we would be quite unable to determine whether or not the utterance is ironical; only on learning that the person in question has performed a terrible misdeed do we suspect that the utterance is ironical. In other words, while both metaphor and irony seem to depend upon context, they do not seem to do so in the same way. To understand the difference, it seems we must understand what is lacking in the generic knowledge of background that allows us to determine the metaphoricity of many utterances yet does not allow us to determine the irony of even one ironic utterance.

Irony and the Speaker

DISCREPANCY BETWEEN PROPOSITION EXPRESSED AND THE FACTS

In the case just cited, it seems to be the information that the so-called friend has committed a terrible deed that allows us to determine that the utterance is ironic. This hypothesis is supported by the fact that most authors, when citing cases of irony, identify their examples of irony by describing some discrepancy between the facts and the proposition expressed. However, a further examination shows that this discrepancy is not the whole story, as supported by the following counter example.

SPEAKER'S KNOWLEDGE OF DISCREPANCY

Suppose we know that the friend in question has indeed committed a misdeed, and yet we also know that the speaker cannot know this. In such a situation, in the absence of any information showing that the speaker knows of some other offense against him, we would not judge the utter-

---

[60]H. P. Grice, "Logic and Conversation," in *Syntax and Semantics*, vol. 3, ed. Peter Cole and Jerry L. Morgan (New York: Academic Press, 1975), pp. 41–58.

ance to be ironical.[61] In other words, it does not seem to be the misdeed (or the discrepancy between the friend's actions and the statement concerning his character) that makes the utterance ironical. If our knowledge of the misdeed allows us to suspect that the utterance is ironical, it is only because this knowledge makes us suspect that the speaker also knows of the misdeed. That is, it seems to be the speaker's knowledge of the deed that is significant. However, this is not the whole story either.

SPEAKER'S BELIEF IN THE PROPOSITION

Suppose that although the speaker knows of the misdeed, either (1) she has decided that the friend in question performed the deed with the best of intentions or (2) she has forgiven the friend. In this situation, we might decide the utterance is not ironical. Thus being ironical is not based solely on the speaker's knowledge of conflicting facts. Instead, whether or not the utterance actually *is* ironical seems to depend on whether the utterance is genuinely intended by the speaker, rather than on the deeds the friend in question performed and whether the speaker knows of the deeds. In other words, it seems to be the relationship between the speaker and the utterance that makes an utterance ironical, a relationship that is not determined solely by knowledge but, in some as yet unspecified way, by attitude as well. One possibility is that what makes an utterance ironical is the fact that the speaker does not believe in the proposition expressed. That is, in the case just described, the utterance would *not* be ironical since the speaker genuinely believed the proposition expressed. To test this assumption, let us consider the following situation.

Suppose that the speaker in question is involved in a plot with the person of whom she is speaking to convince mutual friends that they are enemies (perhaps to cast aside suspicion that they are in fact lovers). X's misdeed has actually been part of his efforts to make mutual friends believe he and the speaker are at odds with each other. To do her part in convincing their friends of the enmity, the speaker has two choices: (1) she can say, with overt sincerity, that X and she are enemies, or (2) she can say ironically that X is a fine friend. If she succeeds in projecting an attitude of en-

---

[61]Note that we might think, in this case, that it is ironical that the speaker believes his friend to be a fine one when, in fact, he is a traitor. However, in this case what is ironical is not the utterance, but the situation, caused in some way by the discrepancy between the speaker's beliefs regarding his relationship with a certain person and the actual state of the relationship.

mity toward X, either will accomplish her purpose.[62] That the speaker can successfully use an ironic utterance to convince her audience of her attitude toward a certain state of affairs (or person, in this case, X), despite the fact that she does in fact believe the proposition that X is a fine friend, shows that it cannot be the lack of belief in the proposition expressed that makes it ironical.

SPEAKER'S OVERTLY EXPRESSED ATTITUDE

To confirm this conclusion and to further explore the exact nature of the relationship between the speaker's attitude and the proposition literally expressed in an ironical utterance, let us consider one last case. Suppose that the speaker not only knows of the friend's misdeed but has decided, partly on the basis of this information, that the so-called friend is actually an enemy. However, the speaker does not want to reveal that she considers the person in question to be an enemy (perhaps to protect herself from being suspected of committing a crime she is currently planning against the friend). Thus she utters the sentence in question *as if she genuinely means it*, that is, as if she intends the proposition it literally expresses, despite the fact that she actually thinks of the person in question as an enemy. In addition, when her audience asks if she means what she says, she replies, in conformity with her feigned attitude of friendship toward the friend in question, that she does.

It seems that there are at least two ways of analyzing this situation. In one analysis the speaker is speaking ironically in saying "X is a fine friend," but then is lying when she says she genuinely believes the proposition (in order to affirm the truth of the proposition literally expressed). Another possible analysis is that the speaker is lying in the original utterance and then lying again. No matter how we analyze this situation and classify the two acts, it clarifies the role of belief in the proposition expressed. That is, since a belief in the proposition expressed does not determine whether the person is lying or speaking ironically, this belief cannot be what identifies a case of irony.

The difference between the two possible analyses is to be found in the difference between lying and irony. It is tempting to explain the difference between an utterance's being a case of irony and its being a case of lying by appealing to speaker intention. In other words, since lying requires that the speaker's intention be to deceive, and irony does not, it seems that the

---

[62]Fogelin would argue that the ironic utterance might be more successful in conveying rancor since it forces the audience to deduce the intended proposition.

intention to deceive would be sufficient to identify a case of lying as opposed to one of irony. However, this analysis is not correct, as the previous example shows. Since it is possible to use irony to lie to someone (that is, to have them believe a proposition considered to be false by the speaker), it is possible that someone can intend to deceive someone and yet be speaking ironically.

Consider the different success conditions of the two types of utterances. A case of lying is successful only if the speaker does *not* convey that they do not believe the proposition expressed by a literal interpretation of the utterance. In contrast, a case of irony is successful if and only if the speaker (1) conveys that they do not believe the proposition expressed by a literal interpretation of the utterance and (2) conveys this in such a way that the audience knows that they intend that their attitude be known. (Note that if the latter condition is not met, the audience might think the speaker is lying or hiding the truth.) While the success conditions of an utterance do not determine a type of utterance (that is, we may call a lie a lie even though it is not successful in deceiving the audience), they *do* point to the relevant features of the utterance. In other words, the difference between the success conditions of lying and those of irony shows that it is not the belief in the proposition that determines whether or not an utterance is ironical. Instead what is relevant is the speaker's projected attitude toward the proposition. If the speaker is speaking ironically, then they will express an attitude of disbelief in the proposition (either through body language or other contextual means), even if the overall purpose of the utterance is to deceive the audience. In other words, given the case above, in deciding whether the first utterance is a case of lying or irony, we would have to examine the projected attitude of the speaker toward the utterance. In this case, since the person uttered the sentence as if they genuinely believed it, it seems that the second analysis is correct. In other words, it would seem that the utterance is a case of lying rather than one of irony.

CONCLUSION

What these examples show is that in order for an utterance to be ironical, its content must be related to the speaker's overtly expressed attitude in a certain way.[63] In other words, in order for an utterance to be ironical,

---

[63]This analysis is similar to both Fogelin's and Grice's analysis in that the intention which is critical to the identification of the utterance as a figure (in Fogelin's analysis) or a case of flouting a maxim (in Grice's analysis) is the overt one. Fogelin, *Figuratively Speaking*; Grice, "Logic and Conversation."

the speaker must project an attitude of disbelief in the proposition.[64] In addition, the fact that someone can use a case of irony to convey disbelief in a proposition in which they actually believe indicates that whether or not they actually believe the proposition is irrelevant to the utterance's being a case of irony.

This dependence of irony on the overtly expressed attitude of the speaker would account for the fact that our generic background knowledge does not suffice to determine whether or not an utterance is an instance of irony when given out of context. For a given speaker's attitude cannot possibly be a part of the generic background knowledge we have as members of a linguistic and cultural community. While the generic knowledge that allows us to predict (with great reliability) that an utterance is metaphorical may provide us, given some contextual information, with clues that allow us to infer when an utterance might be ironical (when the proposition literally expressed seems to be at odds with the speaker's beliefs as indicated by body language), it does not determine when an utterance is ironical. In other words, not only does the nature of irony require that the participant have specific contextual information in order to recognize it as an instance of irony (an epistemological issue), but whether or not the utterance is a case of irony depends upon the speaker's overtly expressed intentions with regard to this particular utterance (a metaphysical issue). (A further consequence is that since irony is so dependent upon a nonsemantic feature [the speaker's overtly expressed attitude], it clearly falls into the realm of pragmatics rather than semantics.)[65]

---

[64]Note that this analysis accounts for a phenomenon (commented on by Fogelin), that the propositions ultimately conveyed by a case of irony cannot easily be accounted for by a rule of transformation, either by Grice's rule of taking the contrary or Searle's rule of taking the opposite. As Fogelin points out (*Figuratively Speaking*, pp. 9–12), a director's ironic statement of "I see you have your lines down pat" to an actor can express a wide range of propositions. Fogelin accounts for this by appealing to the diverse effects of context. According to this account, the variety of propositions would seem to suggest that these propositions are not the content of what is said but are hypotheses the listeners make concerning the speaker's true beliefs. Since the propositions are not linguist implications of the proposition expressed but are instead implications (in a nonlinguistic sense) of the fact that the speaker has portrayed disbelief in a certain attitude, there is no need for a single rule to describe their content. That the emotional intensity the speaker conveys affects the contents of the propositions the listener derives confirms that irony is an expression of the speaker's attitude toward a proposition rather than the production of a particular proposition (either the contrary or the contradictory).

[65]In "Irony and the Use-Mention Distinction," Sperber and Wilson present and defend the view that irony is a case of a "mention" of a sentence rather than an actual

What we have uncovered provides support for Avishai Margalit's observation that it seems utterly impossible for someone to say something ironically without intending to do so.[66] That is, if a person intends to express the proposition as if it is sincerely meant and if the person genuinely believes the proposition, then the utterance is not ironical, no matter what the other circumstances may be.[67] Since the speaker's attitude regarding the utterance is critical, the absence of the specified attitude would cause the utterance not to be ironical.

Since metaphors can be identified as such in the absence of this kind of knowledge of speaker attitude, it would seem that speaker attitude does not play a role in their individuation. If so, this would provide specific grounds both for distinguishing between metaphor and irony as phenomena and for arguing that metaphor should not be classified as a matter of pragmatics (Claim 4). However, to confirm this, we have to examine the role of the speaker's intention, beliefs, and attitudes in metaphor.

Metaphor and the Speaker

As we have seen, it seems impossible for an utterance to be ironical if the speaker projects an attitude of sincere belief in the proposition the literal interpretation of the utterance indicates. That is, the presence of a speaker and the speaker's attitude toward the proposition is critical to an utterance's being ironical. However, this does not seem to apply in the case of metaphorical utterances.

One might object to a distinction between metaphor and irony based on speaker attitude by pointing out that the first instinct of most people when presented with a metaphorical utterance is often to ask for the speaker's intention, apparently in the same way that someone checks to see if an utterance is ironical (Do you really mean this?). This fact suggests that metaphor is related to the speaker in the same way that irony is. Yet, as we shall see in the following example, this notion does not stand up to scrutiny. While people might ask about speaker intention, this is only be-

---

case of use. In this case, what makes an utterance ironic is the speaker's portrayed attitude toward the utterance, which is one of parody. In other words, what makes an utterance ironic is both the speaker's intention and the speaker's projected attitude toward the utterance, both matters of use rather than of semantics.

[66]Avishai Margalit, "Animism Animated," *Journal of Philosophy and Judaism* 1, no. 1 (1990): 41–49, p. 41.

[67]Note that as our last example showed, irony is dependent either on the speaker's overtly expressed attitude of disbelief alone or on that attitude combined with a genuine disbelief in the proposition.

cause the speaker's intended utterance meaning provides a clue to the proper interpretation of the utterance, a way of choosing between different possible interpretations. However, this does not mean that the speaker's overtly expressed attitude toward the proposition determines whether or not it is metaphorical. In other words, while, in the case of irony, the speaker's overt intention toward the proposition expressed *determines* whether or not the utterance is ironical (in the sense that the speaker's attitude is the final word), this is not so in the case of metaphor. One could say that while speaker intention does play a role in the production and processing of metaphors, the role it plays is similar to the role it plays in literal speech. In other words, if the speaker is competent, then speaker intention is an indication of the content of the sentence. However, speaker intention does not determine the content of an utterance, be it an instance of literal or nonliteral language. Whatever determines the content of an utterance seems to involve the rules of the language, in conjunction with certain contextual features and the possibility of reconceptualizing the entities' reference in the utterance, all of which are independent of the speaker's specific intentions. But this is an argument for metaphor's being a matter for semantics rather than pragmatics (Claim 4).

ARGUMENT FROM ABSENT SPEAKER

To compare metaphor and irony, let us consider the following example. Suppose that the utterance "X is a fine friend" were broadcast over a loudspeaker, complete with such clues as a sarcastic tone that are conventionally used to advertise that a given utterance is ironical. What would the audience learn from the utterance? Given the clues in question, most audiences would suspect that the utterance is ironic. As a consequence, they would probably infer that the person in question did not believe the proposition expressed under a literal interpretation of the utterance. However, suppose that they were then informed that *no one* issued the sentence that was broadcast; that the sentence was the result of the interaction of various circuits. To say the utterance is ironical would no longer seem possible, a fact in accordance with our analysis that being ironical requires a certain attitude and goal on the part of the speaker. If there is no speaker, no one to feel and express an attitude toward the utterance, then it seems impossible to say that the utterance is ironical. In other words, while we use external clues (such as a sarcastic tone of voice) to detect that an utterance may be ironical, these do not determine that something is ironical. What determines it is the attitude of the speaker toward the proposition expressed.

Now suppose that the sentence "The philosopher is the pilot of the city" is broadcast under similar conditions, and consider possible reactions by the audience. Someone (a child) who does not know what a philosopher is and is willing to entertain the idea that a city is (literally) a boat might take the sentence to say that a philosopher's job is to get up each morning and, taking the wheel of the city, guide the city to another location. Someone else might understand the predicate in a similar way and, knowing what a philosopher does, decide that the utterance is false. Yet another might not know what a philosopher does and yet, on the ground that it is impossible to steer a city, also take the utterance as false. (All of these people would be taking the utterance literally.) In contrast, someone less literal-minded might take the utterance to express the proposition that the philosopher should be the president of the country or part of its legislative branch. Still another might think that what is said is that the philosopher guides the country by teaching its people. These latter people would be taking the utterance metaphorically (although they differ in the specific interpretation of the metaphor).

Now suppose that these people were told that no one uttered the broadcast words, that the utterance was randomly generated. In such a case, the audience could not speculate on the intention of the speaker or the speaker's attitude toward the utterance. Indeed, one would probably say that this case would not even constitute a speech act. Certainly, without a speaker, there could be no conversational implicature, no indirect speech act, and no instance of irony. In addition, the audience could no longer use the intention of the speaker as one of the many clues to the proper interpretation of the utterance, nor could they say that any particular interpretation was intended or even that anything was really said (in the sense of "say" distinguished by Martinich such that a parrot says nothing[68]). However, this does not mean that the possible metaphorical interpretations the audience derived would cease to be either metaphorical or possible interpretations, only that it could not be said that a speaker intended any particular one of them. In other words, while the absence of a speaker who consciously intends the utterance eliminates the possibility of

[68]See Martinich, "A Theory for Metaphor." What is critical to this sense of "say" is that the utterance have illocutionary force. For an utterance to have this force, there must be a speaker who intends to utter the proposition expressed.

irony, in that such a situation would be missing critical pragmatic elements, it does not rule out metaphor in the same way. Not only does this argue against an identification of metaphor with irony, but it also argues in favor of keeping metaphor within the realm of semantics vs. pragmatics (Claim 4).

ARGUMENT FROM CHILDREN

While the speaker's intention and attitude (1) are factors which aid the listener in figuring out which is the appropriate interpretation of the sentence and (2) contribute to the speaker's intended meaning, they do not, in and of themselves, determine that an utterance or interpretation of an utterance is metaphorical. One can see this in the case of children. In the process of acquiring a language, children utter sentences which seem to be metaphorical. That is, while the utterances successfully make their point, the proposition expressed by a literal interpretation of the utterance is different from the point that is made, although the latter is systematically related to it in a way that makes it possible to decipher it. For example, consider the case of a child who says, "Mom, my sock has a hangnail," *without* knowing that hangnails are such that socks cannot literally be said to have them. In such a case it would be wrong to say that the child has mastered the use of metaphor, for the child is simply making a category mistake. However, the fact that the child does not know that the proposition they intend to express is only metaphorically related to the sentence they utter (rather than literally related) does not mean that the proposition that must be understood for the listener to understand the utterance is not metaphorical. Nor, if the situation is reversed and it is the competent speaker who produces the metaphor and the child who errs in such a way as to understand the intended content as the literal interpretation, does this mean that the intended content is not metaphorical. In other words, it seems it is the proposition itself that is metaphorically related to the sentence, something which is a factor of the meaning of the sentence, along with other factors such as presuppositions one might associate with the referents of the terms.

In other words, for someone to understand an utterance metaphorically, the proposition they believe the utterance to express must be related to the proposition expressed by a literal interpretation of the utterance in a certain way. What this seems to show is that metaphoricity consists in a certain relationship between the proposition literally expressed and that taken as the proposition expressed in that context, rather than in a certain relationship between the speaker or speaker intention and the proposition expressed by the utterance. But this is an argument for my analysis as the result of reconceptualization (Claim 5).

ARGUMENT FROM BODY LANGUAGE

Another clue that irony is fundamentally different from metaphor based on its relationship with the attitude of the speaker can be seen in the way body language is used to supplement the utterance. Consider, for example, situations in which someone who is presented with an utterance that is ironical or metaphorical does not know the language in which the utterance is expressed. If someone does not know the language used in an utterance, it is clearly impossible for them to deduce the proposition expressed or determine that the utterance is metaphorical. As a consequence, they cannot determine the metaphorical content of the utterance. However, in certain conversational settings, even without knowing the language spoken, it is conceivable that one could deduce, from the person's facial expression and tone of voice, that the utterance is ironic. That is, in determining whether or not an utterance is ironic, it seems as though the clues that are appealed to are those that indicate the speaker's attitude toward the proposition expressed by the utterance. At the same time, it seems that a metaphorical utterance is (1) more dependent upon the conventional meaning of the utterance, as supported by linguistic competence than an ironical utterance, (2) completely independent of the attitude of the speaker, as expressed by body language, and (3) dependent on the ability to reconceptualize entities referred to in the utterance.

Consider also examples in which body language is not available to the listener, as when an utterance occurs in print. In such cases, if an utterance is intended ironically, it is common to say so explicitly (e.g. "She said X ironically"). In cases where it is not explicitly mentioned that the utterance is intended ironically, other means are used to describe the speaker's attitude toward the utterance, either directly (e.g. "Dorothy, who hated her stepmother with a passion, as known to everyone in the group, stated 'I love Melody dearly' with a malevolent smile that clearly bespoke the lie in her words") or by more indirect means (e.g. Fogelin's example: the admiral, upon seeing two of his ships blown out the water, said "Good show"). In the latter case, while the speaker's intention or attitude is not spoken of directly, one can infer these from the situation as described, as well as from the fact that the example is presented within a discussion of ironical utterances.[69] In other words, since the ironic quality of an utterance is dependent upon the attitude of the speaker toward the proposition expressed, for a listener to deduce that an utterance is ironical, they must deduce that attitude on the part of the speaker, either through body language or, when that is not available, through other clues.

ARGUMENT FROM MULTIPLE USES

One final source of criticism one can bring against the identification of irony with metaphor comes from utterances that are both ironical and metaphorical, especially those occurring in settings where the only clues to the speaker's attitude are indirect (e.g. the speaker's attitude is not mentioned and body language is not available to the reader).[70] For example, consider an utterance of "You are my banana" which appears in a text. Suppose you wanted to know whether the utterance is ironical or not, in the absence of any clues regarding the speaker's attitude. The first step would be to produce a metaphorical interpretation of the utterance. For example, in a given culture, being a banana might represent someone who acts in a serious way. Given this as a possible metaphorical interpretation, it would then be possible to determine whether or not the utterance is ironical by using contextual clues to deduce the speaker's actual beliefs concerning the speaker and comparing the two (for example, in the case of an utterance directed at someone the speaker believes is not serious enough, the utterance would seem ironical). Without having an explicit description of the speaker's attitude, and without an interpretation of what it means to be a banana, the reader would clearly be incapable of deducing that the utterance is ironical. In other words, whenever an utterance is both metaphorical and ironical, before the reader can determine whether the utterance is ironical, they must first derive a metaphorical in-

[69]Note that in such a case, it is still possible that the utterance may not, in fact, be ironical, since the circumstances described do not make the utterance ironical (something only the speaker's attitude regarding the utterance can do) but only give a clue to the speaker's attitude. In the case described, it may be that the admiral did intend the utterance sincerely, in recognition of the progress the ships were able to make before being sunk. Or the admiral may have been a traitor who slipped up by cheering for his own side in front of other officers.

[70]The strategy for the argument in this section was suggested to me in a conversation with Josef Stern.

terpretation.[71] The inviolability of this condition, reminiscent of the fact that we cannot determine whether an utterance is true or false or a lie before determining the proposition expressed, seems to call for an explanation. If metaphor were a matter of use, in the way that a lie or a promise is a matter of use, then does not seem as though it should be necessary to derive the metaphorical interpretation prior to analyzing the utterance as a speech act. The need for an explanation becomes even more certain as we contrast the case of metaphorical utterances with that of other utterances which are considered to be instances of use.

Consider, for example, an utterance that is both a promise and a lie, categories which are considered to be pragmatic rather than semantic since each is determined by the speaker's beliefs and intentions rather than by what is said. Given an utterance that is both a promise and a lie, a speaker is quite able to determine whether the utterance is a lie or a promise independently. In other words, one does not have to determine the falsity of the utterance before recognizing it as a promise, since what makes the utterance a promise is the role that certain linguistic structures play in a culture when uttered. Nor does one have to recognize the utterance as a promise before recognizing it as a lie, since what makes an utterance a lie is the intention to deceive.

What these examples show is that processing a metaphor seems to be connected with the production of what is said (a semantic issue) in a way that irony, lies, and promises are not. One explanation that accommodates both this insight and the picture of irony derived from the examples presented is that the reason the metaphorical interpretation must be derived before we can determine whether an utterance is ironical is that metaphorical interpretation is necessary to derive the content of the utterance, a factor which is necessary to the processing of any kind of use, be it a lie, a promise, or some other kind of use. In other words, the assumption that the metaphorical content (rather than the literal content) is the actual content of a metaphor accounts for (1) the difference between metaphor and irony and (2) the fact that one must deduce metaphorical content before determining pragmatic factors such as whether the utterance is a lie or an instance of irony.

---

[71]This is also true in other cases where different types of utterances are used in different ways. For example, in cases where a metaphor is used to lie, to say something profound, or to make fun of someone, before the use to which the metaphor is put to can be deduced, the metaphorical interpretation must be derived.

Summary

In conclusion, the identification between metaphor and irony is not sustainable in the light of the different relationship each has with speaker intention and attitude. As we established in Chapter 4, while speaker intention can be used as a clue to the proper interpretation of metaphor, it does not determine that an utterance is metaphorical.

The arguments from Absent Speaker, Body, Children, Language, and Multiple Use all challenge the identification of metaphor with irony that has been made by many pragmatic theories of metaphor (Fogelin calls these theories literalist theories). In addition, our critique of Grice and Martinich's accounts of metaphor challenge the analysis of metaphor as a conversational implicature, and our critique of Searle's account challenges the classification of metaphor as an instance of speaker meaning. Furthermore, the fact that one must deduce the metaphorical content of a metaphor prior to determining such other pragmatic factors as whether the utterance is a lie, is an argument that metaphorical content plays the role of the proposition expressed by the metaphorical utterance (Claim 3 on my list). This result would indicate that metaphor is a semantic rather than pragmatic phenomenon (my Claim 4). However, to conclusively challenge the notion of metaphor as a matter of use, we also have to examine Fogelin's account of metaphor, which analyzes metaphorical content as the result of a cognitive process undertaken by the speaker in response to the falsity or irrelevance of metaphor.[72]

---

[72]This position is in opposition to that of Davidson, who in analyzing what we call metaphorical content as an effect of processing and rejecting the literal proposition, provides a causal rather than cognitive account of metaphor.

6

Metaphor as Use

Metaphor and Indirect Speech Acts

Having argued for the other major claims of my analysis, I next present arguments for the analysis of metaphorical content in terms of reconceptualization over other means of accounting for metaphorical content. In this chapter I evaluate the most plausible alternative (and pragmatic) account of metaphorical content (that of Fogelin) and then present additional arguments for my account of metaphor in terms of reconceptualization.

Fogelin's Analysis of Metaphor

One final way of classifying metaphor as a matter of use is to identify it with indirect speech acts, as Fogelin does.[1] Fogelin, like other pragmatic theorists, responds to the truth in Davidson's criticism of semantic theories of metaphor by rejecting the notion of metaphorical meaning.[2] Since, like Davidson and most theorists of traditional semantics, Fogelin identifies the meaning of an utterance with its truth conditions, he goes on to reject the notion that a metaphorical utterance expresses a proposition other than the one it literally expresses, that is; he rejects the notion of a metaphorical utterance's having figurative truth conditions. However, since he acknowledges the validity of the intuition of metaphorical content and truth (Criterion 3), he is put in the position of having to present a pragmatic analysis that accommodates this intuition. Briefly stated, the solution Fogelin presents to this dilemma is to say that, in addition to the

[1]Robert Fogelin, *Figuratively Speaking* (Yale: Yale University Press, 1988).
[2]Ibid., p. 74.

proposition they express directly, metaphorical utterances also convey a figurative proposition which is pragmatically associated with them. Specifically, he proposes a classification of metaphorical utterances as indirect speech acts, with metaphorical content being the literal indirect content of the indirect speech act. In other words, while Fogelin acknowledges a metaphorical content (he calls this a figurative meaning), he accounts for this content through pragmatic analysis, as something derived by the audience in accordance with the principles of cooperative conversation, in the manner of Grice, Martinich, and Searle. However, in contrast to this group, Fogelin identifies metaphors as literal indirect speech acts and classifies metaphorical content as their indirect content.[3]

As Fogelin points out, two different distinctions are involved in such a classification: the distinction between literal and nonliteral language and the distinction between direct and indirect speech acts. According to Searle,[4] the latter distinction is determined by the speaker's intention to use an utterance such that the main point or force of the utterance (Searle's speaker meaning) is not captured by the content of the utterance (Searle's sentence meaning) but instead is an implicature of it. For example, given a situation in which someone at a dinner party asks someone if they can pass the salt, the force of the utterance is a request that the salt be passed rather than a question concerning the abilities of the person in question to pass the salt. Since the distinction between direct and indirect speech acts depends upon the illocutionary force of the utterance and thus upon the intention of the speaker, it is one that exists only at a pragmatic level and does not affect the proposition expressed by the utterance. Thus Fogelin's treatment of metaphor and metaphorical content is ultimately pragmatic. Furthermore, in keeping with the traditional notion of indirect speech acts, as articulated by Searle, in classifying metaphor as an indirect speech act Fogelin holds that *both* the literal content and the derived metaphorical content are intended by the speaker, that is, are part of what the speaker intends to convey.

It is more difficult to characterize the distinction between the literal and the nonliteral (Fogelin identifies this with the figurative). Fogelin initially describes this distinction as a way of "taking" an utterance, that is, as a

---

[3]Ibid., p. 41.

[4]Fogelin's position on this is the same as that of John Searle, who specifies the distinction in "Indirect Speech Acts," in *The Philosophy of Language*, 2nd edition, ed. A. P. Martinich (Oxford: Oxford University Press, 1990), pp. 161–75.

matter of "whether the speaker intends his utterance to be taken literally or non literally."[5] This description implies that figurativeness (or literality) is a way of interpreting an utterance, implying that it is a matter of what proposition (or content) is associated with the utterance, possibly a semantic notion. Accordingly, Fogelin speaks of a metaphorical content as being the intended message of the metaphor rather than its literal content. However, he also later denies that there is any such thing as a figurative meaning: "Speakers speak figuratively, but words do not have figurative meaning."[6] To resolve this apparent conflict, Fogelin does not appeal to a distinction between meaning and content (which my analysis distinguishes and his identifies); rather, he introduces the notion that an utterance might express the same proposition whether interpreted literally or figuratively but might have a different truth value depending on a shift in the criteria of evaluation or feature space. That is, according to Fogelin, the so-called metaphorical content of a metaphor is none other than the literal content of its counterpart simile, as judged via a shifted view of the context producing a different feature space. Thus the figurativeness of metaphor resides safely in the pragmatic realm, in something the audience does after deriving the literal meaning by performing the desired shift in feature space, in accordance with the maxims of cooperative conversation. In this view, the distinction between the literal and the nonliteral depends upon whether a corrective judgment is needed to determine what the speaker intended to say.

Fogelin's analysis of metaphor has three major components: (1) his comparativist belief that metaphors are elliptical similes, (2) his adoption of Grice's framework in his analysis of figurative speech acts such that certain propositions associated with an utterance are analyzed as propositions pragmatically associated with an utterance and derived by the participants in keeping with the maxims of cooperative conversation, and (3) his conception of the processing of the truth conditions of comparison statements, based upon Tversky's account of similarity.[7]

---

[5]Fogelin, *Figuratively Speaking*, p. 39.
[6] Ibid., p. 96.
[7]Amos Tversky, "Features of Similarity," *Psychological Review* 84 (1977): 327–52.

Fogelin as a Comparativist

As a comparativist, Fogelin adopts the conception of metaphor as an elliptical simile that is often attributed to Aristotle.[8] However, in response to substantial criticisms of comparativism from Davidson, Black, and others, Fogelin clarifies what he considers to be the comparativist thesis. In Fogelin's interpretation, comparativism consists of the following two claims, the conflation of which (he holds) has been the basis of most of the criticisms levied against comparativism:

> I. The *literal* meaning of a metaphor of the form 'A is a ø' is the same as the *literal* meaning of the counterpart simile of the form 'A is like a ø.'
> II. The *figurative* meaning of a metaphor of the form 'A is a ø' is the same as the *figurative* meaning of the counterpart simile of the form 'A is like a ø.'[9]

In other words, the literal meaning of the metaphor "Steve is a sheepdog" is that of "Steve is like a sheepdog" and its figurative meaning is the figurative meaning of "Steve is like a sheepdog." One notable feature of this analysis is that Fogelin, unlike Davidson, acknowledges the existence of a figurative or metaphorical content (i.e. figurative meaning). Another is that Fogelin gives a partial rule for deriving metaphorical content, specifically by deriving the content of the concomitant simile. One final notable feature is that Fogelin specifies that metaphors (and similes) have two meanings: one literal and one figurative. This fact seems at odds with semantics in that traditional semantics specifies that any given utterance has only one meaning, its literal meaning. In addition, by specifying that metaphors have a metaphorical meaning, it seems as though Fogelin opens his theory to Davidson's critique of semantic theories of metaphor and the notion of metaphorical meaning. However, while Fogelin holds that metaphors express a metaphorical meaning, he does not view this meaning as a kind of literal meaning of the sort specified by semantics. Fogelin later emphasizes that while he may speak of metaphorical meaning, he does not believe in a distinct metaphorical meaning.[10] Instead, what Fogelin speaks of as metaphorical meaning may be better represented as metaphorical truth value. That is, as we shall see in our critique, Fogelin attempts to specify the existence of a distinct metaphorical truth value without introducing a distinct metaphorical meaning or even a set of truth

---

[8]Aristotle, *Rhetoric*, 1406b–1410b.
[9]Fogelin, *Figuratively Speaking*, p. 29.
[10]Ibid., p. 96.

conditions. In theoretical terms, as a pragmatic theory of metaphor that wants to acknowledge metaphorical content, Fogelin's account searches for a way of classifying what appears to be metaphorical content (resulting in a metaphorical truth value) in keeping with traditional semantics. As we shall see in the next section, Fogelin's vehicle of choice results from his partial adoption of Grice's framework in analyzing figurative speech acts in such a way that certain propositions associated with an utterance are analyzed as propositions pragmatically associated with an utterance and derived by the participants in keeping with the maxims of cooperative conversation.

The Figurative as the Result of Corrective Judgments

The second major component of Fogelin's analysis of metaphor is his partial adoption of Grice's framework in his analysis of figurative speech acts. Since Fogelin dismisses the notion that a metaphorical utterance has a metaphorical meaning, he also dismisses the classification of metaphorical content as the proposition expressed.[11] Nonetheless, since he agrees with the intuition that metaphorical utterances invoke the evaluation of truth conditions that are not those of its literal interpretation, he is forced to come up with some way of classifying metaphorical content which acknowledges it and yet does not challenge the classification of the proposition expressed by the metaphorical utterance as its literal content. To do this, in analyzing the figurative and, specifically, the metaphorical, Fogelin appeals to one of the basic concepts of speech act theory, indirect content, itself derived from Grice's notion of conversational implicature.

Fogelin's analysis of metaphor is part of his more comprehensive analysis of figurative speech acts, which he divides into the class of *figurative comparisons* (such as similes and metaphors) and the class of *figurative predications* (such as irony, hyperbole, and meiosis). According to Fogelin, what these classes share, what makes them both instances of figurative speech, is the fact that, in both cases, in order to grasp the proposition the speaker intends to convey (not the proposition expressed but the figurative meaning), one must perform a corrective judgment in interpreting them, such that "the parties engaged mutually understand that a corrective judgment is being invoked."[12] The corrective judgment in question produces a proposition other than the one expressed by the utterance. For

[11]Ibid., p. 29.
[12]Ibid., pp. 16, 30.

example, in processing the ironical utterance of "She is my very best friend," the audience must process the utterance according to the rules of the language in order to decipher what is being said, then perform a corrective judgment on the proposition expressed in order to deduce the proposition the speaker is actually intending to express (and for which we hold him accountable). Although Fogelin's analysis thus includes a figurative or ironic content which is different from the literal content (i.e., the content derived according to the rules of the language), unlike a semantic theorist of figurative language, he classifies this figurative proposition as indirect content.

For Fogelin, the difference between the two classes of figurative acts lies in the fact that whereas in figurative predications the corrective judgment changes the meaning (or content) of the utterance,[13] in figurative comparisons the corrective judgment does not affect the content. Instead, Fogelin claims that in the case of figurative comparisons the corrective judgment in question affects the *context*.[14] Fogelin's description of the corrective judgment performed in figurative comparisons is confusing in that it is not clear what exactly the context is (i.e., is it a matter of who is speaking, what time of day it is, how hot it is, how far away the objects of discussion are?). In addition, given various interpretations of what Fogelin means by context, his description also seems wrong in that it is not possible to change the context or the items within it. However, what Fogelin seems to mean by this, given his subsequent description of the difference between literal and figurative comparisons, is that in processing figurative comparisons, conversants alter their view in such a way that the features of the entities referenced that are taken as salient are not those normally considered to be salient. (Note the similarities to my analysis of metaphor.) For example, in processing the metaphorical utterance "Margaret Thatcher is a bulldozer," the audience selects a new feature space according to the features that are relevant in the context *before* evaluating its truth. In Fogelin's view, given a figurative feature space, it is possible to say that while the content of the metaphorical utterance is its literal content, it has different truth or satisfaction conditions from those it would have if taken literally. That is, while the content of the metaphorical utterance "Steve is a

---

[13]Why doesn't Fogelin's analysis of figurative predications suffer from the same problem as that of semantic analyses of metaphors? In other words, if the corrective judgment alters the content of an ironical statement, isn't Fogelin forced to say that the meaning is also changed?

[14]Fogelin, *Figuratively Speaking*, p. 88.

sheepdog" is its literal content, given the feature space specified by the taxonomy underlying literal language use, its truth value in a given context is different than it would be if taken literally.[15] As a result, his theory is able to escape the dilemma plaguing pragmatic theories of metaphor, namely that of accounting for metaphorical content and truth without acknowledging metaphorical meaning. Yet this analysis presents certain problems for semantics, as we shall see later.

The Content of Comparison Statements

The third feature of Fogelin's analysis is his conception of the truth conditions or content of comparison statements. Fogelin's claim that the metaphorical content of an utterance is its indirect content stems from his classification of comparison statements as being "factually lean or content-hungry."[16] According to Fogelin, comparison statements are content-hungry in that the only information they convey is the fact that two objects bear similarity to each other. Although people often use comparison statements to convey more than the proposition that two objects are alike, that is, as a means of attributing properties to the subject of the comparison statement, this is not part of the content they express. Instead, Fogelin views the weighing of features (as well as the selection of the relevant feature space) as part of the process of evaluation, rather than part of the comprehension of the actual content. He thus classifies the attribution of properties to the subject (such as the assignment of pushiness to Steve) as indirect content. Given this classification, while the corrective judgment that accompanies the processing of a metaphorical utterance does not produce a distinct figurative content (only a different truth value), the attribution of properties we ordinarily consider to be a part of metaphorical content is, in Fogelin's conception, the indirect content of the utterance.

The leanness that Fogelin sees in the content of comparison statements emerges as a way of defending his analysis against Davidson's criticism. That is, as we noted before, in attempting to account for the intuition of metaphorical truth without appealing to the notion of metaphorical meaning, Fogelin claims that the meaning of figurative utterances is the same as that of a literal interpretation, while the truth value is different.

---

[15]Another way of looking at this is to say that Fogelin interprets the process of "taking" an utterance literally or figuratively as a matter of what feature space one selects in evaluating the truth of the utterance.

[16]Fogelin, *Figuratively Speaking*, p. 78.

TABLE 10
Features of Fogelin's Analysis

Metaphoricity	Shifted view of context resulting from selection of different aspects of the context as relevant
Comprehension process	1. Derive the literal content. (Steve is a sheepdog) 2. Note pragmatic conflict 3. Derive the relevant simile. (Steve is like a sheepdog) 4. Note pragmatic conflict 5. Change view of context to modify truth conditions. (Steve is like a pushy person) 6. Derive indirect content. Steve is pushy
The proposition expressed by the metaphorical utterance	The literal meaning of the concomitant (figurative) simile
The existence of metaphorical content	Believes that what passes as metaphorical content (meaning) is actually the literal meaning but with altered truth conditions
The classification of metaphorical content	Indirect content of concomitant simile
Rule for deriving metaphorical content	Derive literal content and truth conditions. Then, shift view of context, what is relevant to judging the truth of the utterance
Phenomena metaphor is like	Indirect speech acts and similes

To do this, Fogelin requires that the possession of certain properties that influence the truth value of the utterance *not* be part of the content. Table 10 summarizes Fogelin's analysis of metaphor.

Critique of Fogelin

Several of the basic intuitions underlying Fogelin's analysis are compelling. Fogelin's basic premise is that in processing any comparison statement (metaphorical or literal), we assume a frame of reference (or perspective of the context) according to which certain features of the objects in question are deemed salient and thus relevant to the judgment (i.e. part of the feature space). Underlying this premise are (1) an understanding of the salience and selection of features as relevant to the processing of metaphors, (2) an awareness that this is the basis for figurativeness and metaphoricity, and (3) an acknowledgment that context plays a role in the selection of features. All of these features (which my analysis embodies) give Fogelin's analysis certain advantages over the other pragmatic theories of metaphor. In particular, acknowledging the role of feature salience and selection in the processing of similarity judgments and metaphors allows his account of metaphor to go beyond that of Davidson by allowing a metaphorical content without abandoning traditional constraints on the notion of meaning. Fogelin is also able to explain the similarity between metaphor and simile, account for the nonreversibility of metaphors, and account for our intuition that what is different in the metaphorical interpretation of a term such as "bulldozer" is the features to which one attends. However, despite the similarities between our analyses, there are several serious differences, specifically our explanation of how feature selection occurs (in my analysis, via reconceptualization in terms of role), the classification of metaphorical content (i.e. as the proposition expressed via indirect content of the counterpart simile), how metaphorical content is generated (i.e. as a corrective judgment applied to the content of an elliptical simile vs. a judgment via reconceptualization), how metaphors are processed (i.e. whether they require a reinterpretation model of comprehension), and whether they see similarity (or conceptualization) as the basis for understanding figurative language. As we shall see, these differences provide arguments against Fogelin's analysis and for an analysis in terms of reconceptualization.

Objections to Fogelin's Analysis

The awkwardness of Fogelin's apparatus (in classifying metaphor as an indirect speech act and identifying metaphorical content as the indirect content of an elliptical simile) leads to several specific arguments against his analysis of metaphor. Given that my analysis in terms of reconceptualization shares the strengths of Fogelin's analysis, while avoiding its major weaknesses (via the vehicle of reconceptualization in terms of role and the distinction between meaning and content), showing the inadequacy of Fogelin's analysis indirectly argues for my analysis in terms of reconceptualization (Claim 5).

FROM TERMINOLOGY (INDIRECT SPEECH)

One initial criticism that can be brought against Fogelin is based upon the fact that his conception of indirect speech acts is vague and inconsistent. In addition, it often conflicts with Searle's model of indirect speech acts and, as a result, it suffers from difficulties that Searle's analysis avoids. In his analysis of indirect speech acts, Searle takes great pains to point out that it is (1) the speaker's intention to use an utterance in a certain way (that is, with a certain illocutionary force different from the one indicated by grammatical cues), together with (2) the communication of that intention, that makes a certain speech act indirect. In the case of statements used to make requests,

> the utterance is made as a request; that is, the speaker intends to produce in the hearer the knowledge that a request has been made to him, and he intends to produce this knowledge by means of getting the hearer to recognize his intention to produce it.[17]

In Searle's definition, without the speaker's intention and his communication of that intention to the audience, a speech act is not indirect, even if it carries certain conversational implicatures the understanding of which are critical for us to say that the audience is being cooperative. Take, for example, a case where Sally tells Harry she is starving. Even if Sally declares herself to be starving in the hope that Harry, upon hearing her utterance, will offer to take her out to dinner, and even if Harry complies, unless Sally intends this to happen as the result of a request and unless Harry recognizes the utterance as a request, the speech act is not indirect. That is, it is the *way* the utterance is used, its type as a communicative tool, that determines whether a speech act is indirect rather than the fact that the audience can infer one proposition from another.[18]

In contrast, Fogelin's definition of indirect speech acts seems weaker in that he indicates that a context of utterance (i.e. state of affairs independent of speaker intention and its communication) is enough to make a speech act indirect. For example, when considering an utterance of "This hike is longer than I remember," he claims that what would make it indirect would be "the context," that is, whether the hiker was tired or not.[19] Unless the term "context" refers to the speaker's intention as evidenced by the context, this clearly contradicts Searle, who would say that while the speaker might *use* the context to communicate his intention to the audience, it is the communication of the intention that makes the act indirect, rather than the context itself. Fogelin also blurs the line between direct and indirect speech acts by weakening the concept of indirect speech, in

---

[17]Searle, "Indirect Speech Acts," p. 161.

[18]There seems to be a range of ways of classifying propositions associated with an utterance yet not expressed by it. At one extreme we have Searle's notion of indirect content, which is the content of an indirect speech act in cases where a certain interchange of communicative intentions occurs. Then we have Grice's implicatures, both conventional and conversational, which the audience must derive in order to make the speaker's utterance meet the principles of cooperative conversation. Finally, we have regular implications, which follow from what is said but are not necessary for us to evaluate the audience as being cooperative.

[19]Fogelin, *Figuratively Speaking*, p. 40.

such a way that indirect content includes any implicatures the audience might wish to convey, both those that are required to bring the speaker's utterance in line with the cooperative maxims (i.e. Grice's implicatures) and those that do not. For example, although my telling my sister I am tired near bedtime may imply that I want to go sleep, it is not necessary for my audience to derive this implicature in order to grasp what was said. Thus Searle would classify this utterance as direct, but Fogelin's weaker conception would classify this speech act as indirect, with the proposition "I want to go to sleep" as its indirect content. Again, despite Fogelin's intention of being consistent with Searle, this does not fit into Searle's analysis of indirect speech acts. In addition, Fogelin's weaker requirements on the notion of indirect speech would have the unfortunate consequence of classifying all speech acts as indirect.

Another feature of Fogelin's analysis which makes it difficult to evaluate is his characterization of comparison statements as "factually lean or content-hungry." According to Fogelin, all comparison statements (i.e. literal and figurative) are *content-hungry* in that all they claim is that one thing is like another, without specifying the properties that make the utterance true or not. In other words, Fogelin holds that the content of "Steve is like a bulldozer" does not contain the features of Steve or bulldozers. However, Fogelin also believes that the purpose of a comparison statement is to attribute features of the object to the subject: "I say that Smith is like Jones in order to indicate that Smith (like Jones) is affable if not particularly bright."[20] To remedy the content-hunger of comparison statements, Fogelin proposes that the attribution of properties to the subject occurs in the indirect content of the utterance, implying that all comparison statements are indirect. The analysis of comparisons as content-hungry is needed in order to solve the problem which stumps most pragmatic theories of metaphor, the dilemma of how an utterance can have a truth value different from its literal interpretation without having a different meaning. In Fogelin's analysis, what differentiates the literal interpretation of an utterance of "Margaret Thatcher is like a bulldozer" (which is obviously false) from the metaphorical interpretation of the same utterance (which is possibly true), is not the content of the utterance but the criteria of evaluation. Thus Fogelin preserves the intuition of metaphorical truth *without* a shift in meaning or content. (Fogelin uses these two terms interchangeably.)

However, there are obvious problems with this analysis. One is that

[20]Ibid., p. 95.

Fogelin's conception of the content-hunger of comparison statements results in a conflict between Fogelin's notion of content and the (traditional)
notion of the proposition expressed by an utterance corresponding to the
meaning of that utterance, such that the content constitutes or determines
the truth conditions of that utterance.[21] That is, in his analysis, the content
of an utterance in a single context can have different truth conditions—
which goes against the beliefs of traditional semantics. Another difficulty
with this position is that it results in a fundamental difference between the
content of comparison statements (which are featureless) and that of other
types of statements. That is, if we adopt Fogelin's notion of content, the
term "bulldozer" would have one set of features in comparison statements
and a fundamentally different set in all noncomparative statements, a distinction which is challenged by the figurative nature of some noncompari-
son statements. My analysis of metaphor allows for the variability of features an entity might be said to have in different utterances or conversations, this variability being controlled by the notion of conceptualization.
In addition, I make a fundamental distinction between the feature space
that corresponds to an entity in literal references (which must remain true
to the standardized taxonomy and underlying metaphysics) and the feature space of entities in metaphorical references (which is allowed to vary
greatly from the standardized taxonomy but which varies in a systematic
way according to a role the entity in question is thought to play within a
system).

Another problem with Fogelin's notion of content is that he holds
metaphorical content to be indirect in at least two ways, one arising from
the figurativeness of the metaphor and the other from the fact that it is a
comparison. On the one hand, metaphors evoke properties not associated
with the literal meaning of the terms. As a result, the content of the metaphor must be indirect in that the audience must perform a corrective
judgment to alter their conception of the feature space. In this regard,
"Margaret Thatcher is like someone who pushes others around" is the in-

---

[21]Note that Fogelin has this difficulty because he has no vehicle to express metaphorical content other than the meaning of the sentence (which cannot change). Stern
avoids this difficulty by adopting Kaplan's double semantic structure in which character and content replace what Fogelin alternately calls either meaning or content.
See Josef Stern, "Metaphor as Demonstrative," *Journal of Philosophy* 82, no. 12
(Dec. 1985): 677–710. With Kaplan's content corresponding to the proposition expressed, one can accommodate a sentence type with different truth values (corresponding to different contents) in different contexts without any change in meaning
(i.e. character).

direct content resulting from a corrective judgment (via Grice's maxims) of an indirect speech act in which someone says, "Margaret Thatcher is like a bulldozer" in order to convey, indirectly, that Margaret Thatcher is like a pushy person. At the same time, since the metaphor is a comparison, the utterance is also indirect since the point of stating a likeness is merely to attribute certain properties to the subject. Thus, "Margaret Thatcher is a person who always gets her way" is the indirect content of a statement of likeness between Margaret Thatcher and a being with the properties cited. One problem with this description is the difference in how the notion of indirect content is used. Another is the model of metaphor comprehension that follows from this analysis, one requiring a minimum of two and perhaps three separate transformations. (I develop an objection to Fogelin's analysis as a "reinterpretation theory of metaphor" based on multiple transformations later.)

OBJECTION FROM INCOMPATIBILITY OF PERSPECTIVES

One of the most obvious arguments against the classification of metaphor as a literal indirect speech act stems from the fact that, in the traditional conception of indirect speech acts (which Searle articulates and Fogelin accepts), the speaker asserts *both* the direct and indirect contents of the utterance. Fogelin's analysis portrays the utterance of a metaphor as an indirect speech act, with the literal content being its direct content and metaphorical content being its indirect content. As a result, Fogelin must hold that in uttering a metaphor, the speaker intends to communicate what is said (literally) but also, primarily, something more, something contained in its indirect content (what we think of as metaphorical content). To see the consequences of this view, let us consider its application to Fogelin's example "Margaret Thatcher is a bulldozer."[22] In Fogelin's analysis, as an elliptical simile, the metaphorical utterance actually has as its true form, "Margaret Thatcher is like a bulldozer." In addition, as an indirect speech act, the utterance has both a direct and an indirect content. The direct content of the utterance, according to Fogelin, is its literal interpretation, that is, the proposition "Margaret Thatcher is like a bulldozer," where the identifying features of a bulldozer include being able to move large quantities of dirt quickly and efficiently and all other traits in its literal definition. However, its indirect content is its metaphorical content, which according to Fogelin is its literal content as judged by an al-

[22]Fogelin, *Figuratively Speaking*, pp. 87–88. Fogelin actually uses the concomitant simile as his example.

tered feature space. Thus the indirect content of the utterance, in Fogelin's view, would consist of the proposition "Margaret Thatcher has the salient features of a bulldozer," where the identifying features of a bulldozer include being able to get one's way even when other people are opposed, etc.[23] Since the utterance is figurative, it must be judged according to an altered feature space. As an indirect speech act, the speaker utterance meaning of the metaphorical utterance would include both of these. The conjunction of these two propositions would produce the following proposition: "Margaret Thatcher is like a bulldozer" where the identifying features of a bulldozer include being inanimate and moving dirt efficiently and being guided by a human and "Margaret Thatcher is a bulldozer" where the identifying features of the latter bulldozer include being able to get one's way even when other people are opposed, etc. However, this proposition is one which most people would hold to be either anomalous or false. One approach is to judge the proposition as false because no matter what perspective we take in judging the feature space, one of the clauses of the proposition will be false. That is, if we take a literal perspective and select a literal feature space (i.e. the features of bulldozers commonly listed in the definition of the term), the figurative portion of the content of the utterance will be false. On the other hand, if we take a figurative perspective (i.e. assume the metaphorical definition of bulldozer), then the proposition derived from a literal interpretation of the utterance is false, while the figurative proposition is true. Overall, only one of the propositional components can be judged true at one time given that each depends on different definitions of the terms as viewed from different perspectives. In other words, the proposition is anomalous because it is impossible to maintain two different feature spaces (literal and figurative) at the same time. Given either approach, Fogelin's analysis seems to contradict his own position in that he acknowledges the fact that given a metaphor, people generally do not judge the utterance to be obviously false on the basis of the falseness of the literal interpretation or anomalous on the basis of the incompatibility of judgment criteria. Instead, they judge it to

[23]One of the difficulties in expressing Fogelin's argument in formal terms is the question of how to represent the altered feature space. Although Fogelin claims that the altered feature space is different from the content, something that comes after in the evaluation of the utterance, he also claims that there is such a thing as a distinct metaphorical content, which would imply that the altered feature space is an identifying feature of the content, something the audience must use to derive the content and not merely evaluate it later. In my analysis, the feature space Fogelin talks about is part of the content, the result of conceptualization or reconceptualization.

be true or false depending on the truth or falsity of the metaphorical content (in this case, whether Margaret Thatcher is pushy or not). What this argument makes clear is that the literal interpretation of a metaphorical utterance is not part of the content expressed by the utterance, even if one attempts to account for the metaphoricity of the utterance by an altered feature space rather than through meaning. Neither can metaphorical utterances be classified as indirect speech acts with metaphorical content being their indirect content. Instead, the most natural classification of metaphorical content would be as the proposition expressed by the utterance (Claim 3).

ARGUMENT FROM MISSING THE POINT

In identifying metaphorical utterances as indirect speech acts in which the main point of the utterance lies in its indirect content, Fogelin leaves himself open to the following criticism. In indirect speech acts of the sort Fogelin mentions, the illocutionary force of the utterance is often different from the one of the apparent form of the utterance, as indicated by its grammatical structure (Searle's sentence meaning). For example, an utterance of "I am hungry now" typically has the illocutionary force of an assertion, the main point of the utterance being that of informing the audience of the facts conveyed by the direct content. However, in certain circumstances a woman might utter this sentence to her husband as a request to serve dinner.[24] In such a case the speech act would be indirect, the main point residing in the communication of the indirect content. Thus if the husband were to understand only that his spouse was hungry (i.e. grasping only Searle's sentence meaning), without taking the utterance as a request to serve dinner, we would say that he had missed the point of the utterance. In other words, in an indirect speech act the audience is expected to respond to the illocutionary force beyond that of the surface form of the utterance. However, even if the husband missed the point of the utterance and did not respond to the hidden request to be fed, we would not say that he failed to understand what was said. Instead we would say only that they had missed the result the speaker hoped to attain by uttering the sentence in question. In other words, the truth conditions of the utterance remain those of the direct content or surface form. Thus the truth value of the utterance above would depend only on whether or not the wife was hungry at the time of the utterance (the truth conditions). In the same

---

[24]We are assuming that this speech act meets the conditions Searle specifies and Fogelin accepts.

fashion, if asked what was said, most would agree that the content of the utterance is the statement of hunger on the part of the speaker. As a consequence, the illocutionary force of the utterance, whatever form it is considered to take, is not part of what is said.

However, this reasoning does not seem to apply in the case in metaphorical utterances. That is, if someone were to respond to a metaphorical utterance by grasping its literal sentence meaning and truth conditions only, without going beyond this, we would not assert that the person successfully grasped what was said but missed the main point. That is, if we assume that the truth conditions (and truth value) of metaphorical utterances are those of its surface or grammatical form, then certain difficulties arise. For example, suppose someone takes "Walter is a teddy bear" as the assignment of the individual Walter to the class of teddy bears referenced by the traditional taxonomy and word meanings, when the speaker intends that the audience assign a man named Walter to the class of beings with the characteristic of being lovable. In such a case, we would say not only that the audience missed the point of the utterance but also that they had failed to grasp what was said (i.e. the truth conditions of the utterance). Thus the metaphorical content of an utterance cannot be its indirect content and one cannot explain the metaphorical via the indirect. Again, the most natural classification of metaphorical content is as the proposition expressed by the utterance (Claim 3).

ARGUMENT FROM INDEPENDENCE OF SPEAKER INTENTION

Another argument that can be made against Fogelin's classification of metaphor as an indirect speech act stems from the fact that metaphor and metaphorical content are relatively independent of speaker intention. As Searle points out, indirect speech acts and metaphors are similar in that, in both of them, the extra meaning (or figurative meaning) is related in some way to the literal meaning of the utterance.[25] Partly as a result of this similarity, Searle (like Fogelin) classifies them both in the same category.[26] However, while both the indirect content of an indirect speech act and the metaphorical content of a metaphorical utterance are related to the literal meaning of the utterance, they are related to it in different ways. That is, in the case of indirect speech acts, the two propositions are only related in

[25]John Searle, "Metaphor," in *The Philosophy of Language*, ed. Martinich, pp. 408–29, p. 408.
    [26]Searle classifies them as utterances in which speaker utterance meaning and sentence meaning come apart.

that the information provided by one, when combined with contextual information (within the same perspective), and an attempt to ascertain why the speaker uttered the sentence, and the supposition that the speaker is being cooperative, leads the audience to derive a proposition other than the one expressed directly by a literal interpretation of the utterance. (Note that the proposition in question is often one that makes up for some deficiency of the first, such as its apparent lack of relevance.) However, in the case of metaphorical utterances, metaphorical content is more independent of speaker intention (in that speaker intention does not determine it).

For example, suppose Davidson's Saturnian, who, in learning the language, mistakenly believes that the Earth literally belongs in the extension of the word "floor" and utters, "The Earth is the floor." Although the speaker intends nothing more than to convey a certain proposition about the Earth (and perhaps to acquire or demonstrate linguistic competence), we can still say that the utterance metaphorically communicates the proposition it expresses, even if what determined the choice of words is linguistic error on the part of the Saturnian. What makes the utterance interpretable as a metaphor is the fact that we can reconceptualize the planet Earth as a floor in such a way as to derive a proposition that is possibly true, regardless of the purpose the Saturnian had in mind in speaking (e.g. to show off or to see if we were really listening). In contrast, in the utterance "I am hungry now" discussed above, if the audience (husband) failed to take the utterance as a request for dinner, Searle would not classify the utterance as an indirect speech act, *even* if the husband, in response to the wife's expression of hunger, were to start serving dinner. So, while being an indirect speech act is dependent upon one's intention to use one proposition to communicate another proposition or invoke a certain state of affairs and upon one's communication of this intention to the audience, being metaphorical is independent of these features. Therefore, we cannot explain metaphoricity as a matter of indirectness. In addition, if we hold that a dependence on speaker intention determines whether any given linguistic phenomenon should be studied by semantics or pragmatics, it seems that metaphorical content clearly falls into the realm of semantics (Claim 4).

ARGUMENT FROM INCONSISTENCY OF CONTENT

Fogelin's failure to show a parallel between elliptical utterances and metaphorical utterances can be extended to produce a criticism of his clas-

sification of metaphors as *literal* indirect speech acts. Fogelin uses a supposed parallel between elliptical utterances and metaphors to challenge
Searle's classification of metaphor as nonliteral by refuting what Fogelin
calls the hidden assumption that "the literal meaning of an utterance is
confined to the meaning of the words actually said."[27] According to Fogelin, given the elliptical utterance "In a little while," we can report that
what was said was the completed proposition "[the speaker] will be there
in a little while." Yet, as Fogelin says, the fact that the proposition does
not match the sentence meaning does not mean that the utterance ceases
to be literal. As a result, we cannot maintain that the literal meaning of an
utterance is confined to the words actually uttered. In the same way, argues Fogelin, we cannot say that the literal meaning of a metaphor is re-
stricted to the words actually uttered. In other words, the literal meaning
of "Sam is a pig" can be said to literally express the proposition "Sam is
like a pig." But here the difficulty arises. For Fogelin goes on from here to
claim that it is also all right to report the metaphor as saying "So-and-so
thinks that Sam behaves like (or looks like) a pig," on the ground that the
relevant basis for comparison is fixed by context.[28] As a result, according
to Fogelin, Searle's claim that we cannot possibly intend the literal interpretation of the metaphorical utterance since it is false is itself wrong.
That is, Fogelin believes that his argument shows that the literal content of
the metaphorical utterance is true. However, this argument provides at
least two problems with Fogelin's analysis.

On the one hand, the conclusion of this argument contradicts Fogelin's
explanation of metaphors as utterances with both a literal and a metaphorical meaning, utterances whose literal meaning (the literal comparison) is generally false.[29] That is, since the proposition above expresses a
literal comparison, and Sam is not literally like a pig, it is false. As a result,
Searle seems justified in saying that we do not intend that our metaphors
be taken literally. On the other hand, the assertion that the content of the
utterance is fixed by the context and may be different from the literal

---

[27]Fogelin, *Figuratively Speaking*, pp. 41–42.

[28]Note that the way this is presented implies that Fogelin believes that the relevant
aspects of the metaphor vehicle (as fixed by context) which are to be used in an
evaluation of its truth become part of the proposition expressed. This contradicts his
later claim that comparison statements are empty in content in that the literal and
metaphorical interpretation of an utterance produce the same content, though different truth conditions.

[29]Fogelin, *Figuratively Speaking*, p. 87.

meaning of the utterance contradicts Fogelin's content-lean notion of the content of comparison statements and his claim that the corrective judgment required in figurative speech acts affects the truth value of the metaphor without altering its literal content.[30]

OBJECTION FROM TRADITIONAL SEMANTICS

Perhaps the strongest argument against Fogelin's analysis (and one of particular interest to philosophers of language) is a conflict between Fogelin's analysis and traditional semantics. In order to eliminate the need for metaphorical meaning, Fogelin claims that the metaphorical content of a metaphorical utterance is its literal content (i.e. the proposition it expresses according to the rules of the language). At the same time, he claims that the truth value of the metaphorical utterance is different from that of its literal interpretation, when taken in certain contexts. In other words, in Fogelin's analysis the proposition expressed by an utterance (i.e. the content it expresses in a given context) is not equivalent to its truth or satisfaction conditions, something which goes against traditional semantics. As a result, two utterances with the same content can have different truth conditions when taken in different contexts, something clearly unacceptable to traditional semantics.

CONFLATION OF DISTINCTIONS

One final criticism of Fogelin's analysis is that he, like Searle before him, conflates the distinction between the literal and the nonliteral with that between the direct and the indirect, despite his stated intention to hold the two apart.[31] Given that Fogelin, like Searle, attempts to provide a pragmatic account of both metaphor and irony, it is not surprising that his analysis suffers from the same problem. For to attempt to explain the figurative pragmatically is an attempt to subsume it under the maxims of cooperative conversation and to eliminate it as a separate phenomenon. That this is Fogelin's goal is suggested by his description of the chart which classifies various types of speech acts under the two descriptions to get the four categories: Literal/Direct, Nonliteral/Direct, Literal/Indirect, and Nonliteral/Indirect.[32] (See Table 11.)

[30]This would not be a problem if Fogelin acknowledged a difference between meaning and content.
[31]Fogelin, *Figuratively Speaking*, p. 39.
[32]Ibid.

TABLE II

Fogelin: Distinctions and Classification

	Literal	Nonliteral
Direct	Saying, "The cat is on the mat," just meaning that the cat is on the mat	Reciting nonsense poetry
Indirect	Saying, "This hike is longer than I remember," meaning (primarily) that I need a rest	Saying, "You're a real friend," meaning you're a louse

While the inclusion of both distinctions in the chart seems to indicate that Fogelin preserves the separateness of the two distinctions, an examination of how various speech acts are classified show that this is misleading. This shows up in Fogelin's failure to assign any of the utterances we would normally consider to be nonliteral and direct to the category of Nonliteral/Direct. (In fact, the only thing he assigns to this category is nonsense poetry.) For example, if someone says, "There are icicles in here," with the sole intention of making conversation about how cold it is, Fogelin would assign this to the class of Literal/Indirect utterances on the grounds that since the speaker does not intend the literal meaning of the utterance, he must intend something beyond it. However, this classification leaves us without a way of distinguishing between different ways of using the metaphor above (i.e. to make an assertion as opposed to requesting something indirectly). Nor does it correspond to our intuition of what makes an act indirect. For example, suppose that the speaker who utters the comment about the icicles does so to get the person to close the window. In this case, the illocutionary force of the utterance would be different insofar as instead of making an assertion, the speaker would be making a request. In such circumstances, the utterance would be both metaphorical (in that the truth conditions of the proposition expressed are other than that of the literal interpretation of the utterance) and indirect (in that what is said is used primarily with the intention of conveying something else). However, Fogelin attempts to put these two utterances in the same category. His confusion in this matter is further reflected in his statement that there are few if any direct speech acts since we rarely "intend to convey no more information than what we actually state."[33] However, the distinction between direct and indirect was made, not to dis-

[33]Ibid., p. 40.

tinguish between acts in which what we intend to convey is solely the sentence meaning and those in which it goes beyond this, but rather to distinguish whether the type of purpose the act is used for (i.e. its illocutionary force) corresponds to the illocutionary force indicators of the grammatical form of the utterance.

In conclusion, despite Fogelin's claims to the contrary, it seems that an identification between metaphor and indirect speech acts cannot be maintained. That is, one cannot explain metaphoricity (or any other type of figurativeness) or the distinction between the literal and the nonliteral by appealing to indirect speech acts and the distinction between the direct and indirect. Nor can one account for metaphorical content by classifying it as literal indirect content. As Fogelin himself indicates, pragmatic theories of metaphor are particularly susceptible to the dilemma of accounting for metaphorical content and truth because in rejecting the possibility that metaphorical content can be the proposition expressed by the utterance, they lack the most natural vehicle to accommodate that content. While Fogelin attempts to handle this difficulty by analyzing metaphors as indirect speech acts and claiming that metaphorical content is the content of the indirect speech act, this attempt does not succeed. Given that Fogelin's notion of indirect content seems to correspond to that of Grice's conversational implicatures,[34] and given the criticisms of the analysis of metaphor as an implicature, it is not surprising that the attempt is unsuccessful.

Objections to Metaphor as an Elliptical Simile

We have shown that the analysis of the metaphorical in terms of the indirect and the attempt to subsume the metaphorical under the pragmatic is deeply flawed (Chapters 4–6). We have also already shown that both Searle's principles of how metaphorical content is generated and Davidson's vague explanation of metaphoricity in terms of bringing certain thoughts to mind are inadequate. It remains to be shown that the metaphorical content of a metaphorical utterance is produced by reconceptualization, rather than by some other means (Claim 5). That is, we have not yet defeated the comparativist's claim that the content of a nominative metaphor is the content of an elliptical simile.[35] Since many other prag-

[34]Ibid.

[35]Note that there are other possible analyses of metaphorical content, such as the one Searle describes. However, we already dismissed Searle's analysis of metaphorical content in Chapter 2, and most other theories of metaphor appeal to similarity (as comparativism does) in their attempts to account for metaphorical content.

matic theories of metaphor appeal to the similarity relation to explain how metaphorical content is generated, undermining the notion of metaphorical content as the content of an elliptical simile also lessens the value of those theories in accounting for metaphorical content within a pragmatic analysis (Claim 4). It also indirectly argues for an analysis of metaphor in terms of reconceptualization (Claim 5), since such an analysis remains true to Davidson's critique of semantic theories while accounting for the intuition of metaphorical content and truth (Criterion 3) and the relevance of the salience of features in the processing of metaphors.

ARGUMENT FROM FALSE PARALLEL

In defending his analysis of metaphor as an elliptical simile, Fogelin compares the case of metaphor with a situation in which, in response to an utterance of "Are you coming?," someone says "In a little while," and successfully communicates the proposition "{the person speaking} is coming in a little while," despite the grammatical incompleteness of the utterance.[36] In the situation described, not only is the utterance grammatically incomplete in that it lacks a subject and a verb, but this grammatical incompleteness results in an inability to produce a proposition. (That is, an utterance of it does not produce a Fregean thought, capable of being comprehended and evaluated.) However, without a proposition, not only can't the audience evaluate the utterance for truth value, but they can't even be said to have understood the utterance. As Fogelin says, however, the grammarian tells us that the missing information is inferred and plugged into the incomplete proposition to make a complete proposition. In the same way, Fogelin claims, the audience of a metaphor plugs the term "like" into the metaphor "Margaret Thatcher is a bulldozer" in order to produce the true form of the metaphor, "Margaret Thatcher is like a bulldozer."

However, the significant differences between the example above and the case of metaphor challenges Fogelin's identification between the two. We can summarize the differences between the processes of interpreting elliptical utterances and metaphors as follows: (1) in metaphors, until the audience attempts to evaluate the utterance in a context, there is no grammatical or obvious propositional inadequacy to indicate an ellipsis; (2) in metaphors, there is no gap in the original utterance to guide the search for the missing term; and (3) in metaphors, adding the term "like"

[36]Fogelin, *Figuratively Speaking*, p. 42.

does not solve the inadequacy (the blatant falsity) that prompted the search. As a result, it does not seem that the case of metaphor really parallels that of elliptical utterances, or that it solves anything to see metaphors as elliptical similes.

ARGUMENT FROM METAPHOR VS. SIMILE

Another simple argument for the disadvantages of a comparativist analysis of metaphor (and the advantages of an analysis in terms of reconceptualization) is that if one holds that the metaphorical content is that of an elliptical simile, then one is left without a means of accounting for a difference between metaphors and (figurative) similes. However, most people would agree that there *is* a difference between similes and metaphors even if the difference is a slight one. That is, most people would hold that it is slightly stronger to say that "Steve is a sheepdog" rather than "Steve is like a sheepdog."[37] Moreover, it is possible for someone to agree to the corresponding simile without agreeing to the metaphor whose content the simile is supposed to capture, a difference which must be reflected in the proposition expressed. That is, the proposition expressed by "Steve is like a sheepdog" must be different from that of "Steve is a sheepdog." If we define metaphors as elliptical similes, then there should be absolutely no difference between the two

SUMMARY

The strengths of Fogelin's analysis lie in his acknowledgment of (1) an understanding of the salience and selection of features as relevant to the processing of metaphors, (2) an awareness that this is the basis for figurativeness, and (3) an acknowledgment that context plays a role in the selection of features. However, our arguments have shown his pragmatic apparatus to be deeply flawed, as well as awkward.

While Fogelin's analysis of metaphor as an elliptical utterance fails in the ways described, it is helpful in other ways. For one thing, it clearly pinpoints the main dilemma for use theories of metaphor (that of accounting for the intuition of metaphorical content and truth) and it points to the need for some sort of vehicle for metaphorical content that allows us to preserve the notion that the proposition expressed is what is true or

[37]For a comprehensive argument against simile theories of metaphor based on our intuitions of a difference in strength between similes and metaphors, see Lynne Tirrell, "Reductive and Nonreductive Simile Theories of Metaphor," *The Journal of Philosophy*, 88, no. 7 (July 1991): 337–58.

TABLE 12

Evaluation of Fogelin's Analysis

Metaphoricity	OK. Accommodates our intuition that metaphoricity involves the shift in selection of relevant features. However, Fogelin also identifies the nonliteral with the indirect
Metaphor comprehension	Poor. Studies of the processing time of metaphors plus our intuitions of what we do when we process metaphors are incompatible with Fogelin's "multiple-interpretation" process of metaphor comprehension, which involves several steps of interpretation
The intuition of metaphorical content and truth	Well
Difficulty of specifying the satisfaction conditions of some metaphorical utterances	Well
The context dependence of metaphor	Very well
The ubiquity of metaphor (why metaphor is used)	Fair. Cannot explain why metaphors are used (rather than similes) since metaphors are essentially similes
The relationship between metaphor and simile	Fair. Accounts for the similarity between metaphor and simile but not the differences between them
Treatment of different types of metaphors	Does not handle non-nominative metaphors well since they are difficult to characterize as similes
The incorporation of metaphors into the language	Does not account for this
Consistency with the framework of semantics	Very poor. Requires a rift between the notion of content and truth conditions
Consistency with the framework of semantics	Fair. Fogelin seems to believe that what makes an act indirect is context (rather than the communication of the intention to be direct)
The dependence of the metaphorical on the literal	Fair. Accounts for this in that Fogelin considers the metaphorical meaning of the metaphor to be its literal meaning. However, as Davidson points out, the truth condition of X is a Y is different from X is like Y
The lack of conventionality of metaphor	Well
The fact that metaphors are about the world	Well
Independence of speaker aim and intention	Well. Does not mention but correctly attributes metaphoricity to the selection of relevant features rather than to speaker's intention

false while not falling prey to the notion of shifting meaning. Fogelin's analysis also seems to capture our intuition that when metaphorical utterances are processed, the features of the metaphor vehicle which are attributed to the subject of the metaphor are different from those used under a literal interpretation (Claim 2). In addition, it seems true that the selection of the features to be used in the evaluation is dependent upon context. However, while noting the importance of feature suppression and selection in the processing of metaphors and other figurative language, Fogelin fails to draw the natural conclusion but instead falls back on the pragmatic notion of indirect content to account for metaphorical content. That is, he fails to note that what is at work is reconceptualization. Given an account of metaphoricity based on reconceptualization, the different truth conditions of metaphorical and literal interpretations of an utterance and the different features used to evaluate figurative and literal comparisons naturally follows. In addition, the classification of metaphorical content as the proposition expressed by the utterance eliminates Fogelin's radical rift between content and truth conditions. Table 12 illustrates how Fogelin's analysis of metaphor fares against the cited desiderata when compared with previous theories of metaphor.

Arguments for Metaphor as Reconceptualization

We have shown that the analysis of the metaphorical in terms of the indirect is deeply flawed, which jeopardizes the classification of metaphor as a pragmatically defined phenomenon (Chapters 4–6). I will now present arguments for my claim that metaphoricity and metaphorical content are better explained via the notion reconceptualization, ultimately based on the premise that conceptualization underlies all language use.

Argument from Simplicity

One argument for an account of metaphor in terms of reconceptualization versus one that accounts for metaphor as an elliptical simile is an argument from simplicity. While my analysis of metaphor leaves the surface form of metaphors intact, so that nominative metaphors remain class-inclusion statements, the comparativist analysis of metaphor is forced to rewrite all metaphors. Since the grammatical form of most metaphors (i.e. of all nominative metaphors) is that of class inclusion, it is simpler to account for these utterances as such, rather than claim that each instance is, by design, missing a word critical to its interpretation (i.e. the word "like"). When we consider some of the results of taking metaphor as an elliptical simile, it becomes clear that the comparativist approach is far more complex than the proposed analysis, yet it offers no additional explanatory power. Fogelin, one of the major defenders of metaphor as an elliptical simile, attempts to compare metaphorical utterances to a case in which someone, in answer to a query about whether they are coming, answers, "In a little while."[38] However, this comparison seems faulty for the following reasons:[39] (1) in metaphorical utterances (unlike the ellipsis cited), until the audience attempts to evaluate the utterance in a context for relevance and informativeness, there often is no inadequacy (such as grammatical incompleteness or the incompleteness of the proposition expressed) to prompt a search for missing pieces; (2) in metaphorical utterances, there is no gap (comparable to the missing subject and predicate in the example) to guide the search for what is missing; and (3) in metaphorical utterances, adding the term "like" does not remedy the falsity (or irrelevance or lack of informativeness) of the utterance. That is, if one accepts a difference between literal and figurative comparisons (as Fogelin does), then a literal interpretation of an utterance of "Margaret Thatcher is like a bulldozer" is just as false (or irrelevant or uninformative) as "Margaret Thatcher is a bulldozer." As a result, after trying to remedy the supposed inadequacy of a metaphorical utterance by adding the term "like," we now are forced to find yet another method of remedying the inadequacy, this time by changing the features of the objects used in the evaluation of their comparison.[40] (Note that in Fogelin's relatively "content-free" view of the content of comparison statements, the content of a metaphor is the same whether it is taken literally or figuratively, though its truth conditions vary.) Given that the addition of the term "like" does not solve the supposed inadequacy of the metaphor, it does not seem reasonable to view its addition as similar to the addition of missing terms to an elliptical utterance (which are designed to fill the gap). In addition, if one accepts the difference between metaphors and their concomitant simile (which our intuitions say differ in strength and which some philosophers adamantly defend), the addition of the term "like" actually changes the truth (or satisfaction) conditions of the utterance,

---

[38]Fogelin, *Figuratively Speaking*, p. 42.

[39]See above, under Argument from False Parallel.

[40]Note that the "double inadequacy" of metaphor that results in Fogelin's analysis causes this analysis to fall under the category of an analysis of metaphor that has an *interpretation* theory of metaphor comprehension, a classification I explore below.

something which seriously calls into question whether adding the term "like" is a viable solution.

Given these findings, Occam's razor clearly dictates that we account for the metaphorical content of a nominative metaphor as a matter of class inclusion involving reconceptualization rather than as the content of its concomitant simile. In other words, it more reasonable to analyze "Steve is a sheepdog" as an utterance in which Steve is being assigned to the class of reconceptualized sheepdogs than to take the statement as a comparison between two classes in which the standards for similarity have been changed.

Argument from Inclusivity

Another defense of metaphorical content as the product of reconceptualization rather than the indirect content of an elliptical simile is that this approach handles a host of aspects of metaphor in a more intuitive fashion than the analysis of metaphor as an elliptical simile. For example, it seems that the process we go though in comprehending and evaluating nominative metaphors is most like the process we go through in selecting the features and the role of a class given the context (i.e. the process of reconceptualization). This can be most easily seen in cases where we either disagree with a metaphor or fail to understand a metaphor, and in the reasons we give in each case. Imagine a situation in which two students (Chris and Pat) are discussing what it takes to gain admittance to a certain school. Suppose that Chris says, "You have to be a very bright star to get into that school," and that Pat disagrees. There are at least two major different reasons why Pat might disagree. On the one hand, she might disagree because of her knowledge of a certain student who got into that school despite poor academic performance, average work experience, and average social skills, that is, without the qualities both she and Chris associate with "very bright stars." In this case, if Pat conveyed her reasons for disagreeing with Chris to him, Chris would probably change his mind about what is needed for admission to the school and retract his remark. On the other hand, Pat might disagree because she knew of someone who gained admission with average academic skills and no academic awards but excellent social skills and many accomplishments outside academics. In this case, if Pat conveyed this information to Chris, Chris might say that extracurricular accomplishments are as significant as academic records and stand by his original assessment of the admission policies of the school. The two scenarios differ in that, in the first case, the reason for the disagreement lies in Chris's and Pat's different understandings of the facts, despite their agreement on what it means to be a very bright star. This case is comparable to one in which someone, knowing that animals that suckle their young are mammals, doesn't know that whales suckle their young and thus says, "Whales are not mammals." In the second case, the two disagree because of their differing opinions about what it means to be a very bright star. This case is comparable to one in which a child, knowing that whales suckle their young but thinking that being land-bound rather than suckling one's young is a determinant of being a mammal, says "Whales are not mammals." What these cases show is that there are two processes that affect the processing and evaluation of class-inclusion statements (or statements that presuppose class inclusion): (1) the determination of the conditions for membership in the class and (2) the evaluation of whether the subject of the statement has the necessary qualities.[41]

The presence of these two distinct aspects of the processing of metaphorical utterances also shows up in cases where we fail to understand a metaphor. For example, if we fail to understand "My brother-in-law thinks that he is God on the second day of creation," the reason we would give would probably be that we don't know the conditions for being God on the second day of creation, that is, we don't know the identifying features of the category the metaphor vehicle represents. The fact that the processing of metaphorical utterances so clearly parallels the processing of class-inclusion statements is an argument for an analysis of metaphor in terms of reconceptualization.

Another reason for choosing an analysis of metaphor in terms of reconceptualization over one of metaphor as an elliptical simile is that it seems that this analysis intuitively handles the different content that is communicated when a metaphor is reversed. A particularly good example, given by Glucksberg, and Keysar, is the case of the reversal of "My butcher is a surgeon" to produce "My surgeon is a butcher."[42] To account for the different content expressed, on the basis of the different categories expressed by the metaphor vehicle, the comparativist viewpoint can only appeal to the differing salience of the features (such as the wielding of knives and the presence of spattered blood) on the basis of a difference in the context. As

---

[41]Josef Stern, "Metaphor as Demonstrative," also draws attention to the existence of two separate processes and this distinction figures prominently in his analysis.

[42]Sam Glucksberg and Boaz Keysar, "Understanding Metaphorical Comparisons: Beyond Similarity," *Psychological Review*, 97, no. 1 (1990): 3–18.

a result, it cannot account for the different content expressed by these two utterances in the same context of utterance. However, my analysis, which is based on reconceptualization, can easily account for these by pointing to the fact that surgeons and butchers play different roles in the systems within which we most commonly conceive of them. As a result, they evoke different categories when used as metaphor vehicles.

Argument Against Reinterpretation Theories

Yet another argument for metaphorical content as the product of re-conceptualization rather than the indirect content of an elliptical simile draws on the work of a growing movement in psychology against what has come to be known as the "reinterpretation" model of metaphor comprehension, which predicts that literal and metaphorical utterances are processed in fundamentally different ways.

A *reinterpretation* theory of metaphor comprehension is one that specifies that in comprehending a metaphor, the audience derives the metaphorical content only after deriving the literal content and being prompted by an anomaly (semantic or pragmatic). Thus the typical reinterpretation theory specifies that the first step is the derivation of a metaphor's literal meaning, which is thought to be determined solely by the rules of the language and unaffected by contextual information, pragmatic issues, or real-world knowledge.[43] Once it has been decided that the literal interpretation is not what the speaker intends to convey, the interpreter derives an alternative, perhaps figurative, content. As Glucksberg and Keysar point out, there are different versions of the reinterpretation view of metaphor comprehension, corresponding to whether the theory of metaphor holds the triggering condition for the derivation of the meta-

---

[43]Raymond Gibbs, who describes three versions of reinterpretation theory in his work on indirect speech acts, calls this the Literal First model and compares it with two others in "A Critical Examination of the Contribution of Literal Meaning to Understanding Nonliteral Discourse," *Text*, 2, nos. 1–3 (1982): 9–27. As Gibbs points out, the first official psychological version of this theory was presented by H. H. Clark and P. Lucy in 1975 ("Understanding What Is Meant from What Is Said: A Study of Conversationally Conveyed Requests," *Journal of Verbal Learning and Verbal Behavior* 19, pp. 56–72. However, the basic structure for this view of metaphor comprehension was held by H. P. Grice (1975; see "Logic and Conversation," in *The Philosophy of Language*, ed. Martinich, pp. 149–60), Monroe Beardsley (1962; see "The Metaphorical Twist," in *Philosophical Perspectives on Metaphor*, ed. Mark Johnson [Minneapolis: University of Minnesota Press, 1981], pp. 105–22), A. P. Martinich (1984; see "A Theory for Metaphor," in *Pragmatics*, ed. Steven Davis [Oxford: Oxford University Press, 1991], pp. 307–18), and Searle (1979; see.

phorical content to be semantic or pragmatic. That is, in a semantic theory of metaphor, semantic deviance is what decides that the literal interpretation is not what is intended and which triggers the search for an alternative interpretation. Beardsley's theory of metaphor is typical of a *semantic reinterpretation theory* of metaphor comprehension insofar as it holds that both metaphoricity itself and the process of comprehending a metaphor requires the recognition that the utterance is metaphorical, which is based upon a recognition of an "opposition" that is "within the meaning-structure itself."[44] Searle's analysis of metaphor,[45] which specifies that what triggers the search for a figurative content is a conflict between the *sentence meaning* and the presupposition that the speaker is following the maxims of cooperative conversation, is a prototypical case of a *pragmatic reinterpretation theory* of metaphor comprehension. However, since both theories specify that in order to produce a metaphorical interpretation of the utterance, one must first deduce its literal interpretation, find an anomaly (either semantic or pragmatic), and then deduce a metaphorical interpretation, both are reinterpretation theories. As a result, they share its assumptions, specifically, that (1) the literal interpretation of an utterance must always be derived first and (2) an anomaly of some sort (i.e. semantic or pragmatic) is required as a triggering condition in order for the metaphorical interpretation to be derived.[46]

While the reinterpretation view of metaphor is intuitively appealing, it has many difficulties, some of which are pointed out by psychologists and others by philosophers. Rumelhart (one of the first psychologists to criticize the reinterpretation model of metaphor comprehension), attacks the reinterpretation model on the basis of anecdotal evidence, observations of how children acquire language and of when they first appear to process and use metaphor, and psychological studies with results incompatible with the predictions of the reinterpretation model.[47] As he and other psychologists point out, the reinterpretation view of metaphor comprehension predicts processing behavior which simply does not occur. One notable example is that of processing time. The reinterpretation model of comprehension claims that the hearer first processes the literal meaning and then, upon discovering that the literal meaning is either false or inap-

[44] Beardsley, "Metaphorical Twist," p. 111.

[45] Searle, "Metaphor."

[46] Boaz Keysar and Sam Glucksberg, "Metaphor and Communication," *Poetics Today*, 13, no. 4 (1992): 633–58.

[47] David E. Rumelhart, "Some Problems with Literal Meanings," *Metaphor and Thought*, ed. A. Ortony (Cambridge: Cambridge University Press, 1979), pp. 78–90.

propriate, derives an alternative content. As a result, processing a metaphor should take more time than processing a literal utterance, regardless of the context in which it appears. However, this prediction is contradicted by studies performed by Gibbs, Keysar, Glucksberg, and many others. Gibbs's work shows that when metaphors are given in a context that encourages a metaphorical interpretation, it takes no more time to process a metaphorical utterance than a literal one.[48] For example, if the sentence "Regardless of the danger, the troops marched on" is given in a story context that favors a metaphorical interpretation (e.g. a description of children challenging their irate babysitter), it takes no longer to process it metaphorically than it takes to process a literal interpretation of the same sentence in a literal context (i.e. a description of a battlefield).[49] This and other studies by Keysar and Glucksberg (1) confirm the similarity in the processing times of literal and nonliteral utterances and (2) show an additional problem with the reinterpretation view of metaphor comprehension, something that conflicts with its additional assumption that a metaphorical interpretation is derived only once an anomaly has been detected.[50] That is, one of the studies Keysar and Glucksberg perform shows that when an utterance that has both literal and metaphorical interpretations is given in a context in which a literal interpretation would be true and a metaphorical interpretation would be false, readers take more time to verify the literal truth of the utterance than they do in the absence of a possible metaphorical interpretation.[51] In the absence of any other way of explaining the time lag, it seems reasonable to conclude, as they do, that interpreters have a tendency to derive the metaphorical interpretation of an utterance even without either a semantic or a pragmatic anomaly.

In addition to using the results of their studies to challenge the reinterpretation theory of metaphor comprehension, the psychologists cited also use them to claim that there is no difference between the nonliteral (or

[48]Gibbs, "Critical Examination."

[49]Ibid., p. 13. As Richard Gerrig points out ("Empirical Constraints on Computational Theories of Metaphor: Comments on Indurkhya," *Cognitive Science* 13 [1989]: 235–41, p. 23), similar processing time does not prove similar processes. It just eliminates models such as the Literal First model and puts the burden of proof, for accounting for the fact that literal and nonliteral utterances are processed in similar amounts of time, on those who believe the methods of processing are different for literal and nonliteral language.

[50]Note that the challenge to this assumption echoes the previous complaint of philosophers (led primarily by Ted Cohen), that metaphor cannot be a matter of semantic anomaly since there are metaphors that are not semantically anomalous.

[51]Keysar and Glucksberg, "Metaphor and Communication."

metaphorical) and the literal either (1) at the level of psychological processing, (2) within the types of knowledge and competence needed to process utterances during the various phases of comprehension, or (3) as a distinction in itself.[52] The first of these claims is clearly in accordance with my analysis. The second is in line with my discussion in Chapter 2 of the lack of modularity and linearity of language processing, incorporating both linguistic competence and pragmatic inferences, while acknowledging that metaphors do not invoke speaker intention the way indirect speech acts do. The third clearly contradicts one of my principal claims. Further examination of their work reveals, however, that the claim regarding the lack of distinction between the literal and the metaphorical does not arise from their studies alone, but also from several underlying assumptions, some of which are debatable. One such assumption is their acceptance of Searle's identification of indirect speech acts as nonliteral, an assumption we challenged in Chapter 5. One of the most direct results of this assumption is that these psychologists equate indirect speech acts with metaphors in that they identify both the indirect content of an indirect speech and the metaphorical content of a metaphor as speaker or conveyed meaning (an identification I dispute in Chapter 5 in my discussion of Searle). As a result, these psychologists tend to use indirect speech acts in their experiments and then generalize the results to metaphorical utterances. (Gibbs is particularly guilty in this regard.) However, given our resistance to this identification, the extrapolation does not follow.

Another difficulty (which accompanies the latter difficulty) is that most of the psychologists seem to follow Rumelhart in accepting Searle's notion of conveyed meaning (speaker meaning) as that which is relevant to psychological theories of comprehension. That is, their models of language comprehension are expressed solely in terms of conveyed meaning, which

---

[52]While all of the psychologists cited would agree with the first two of these claims, they might not agree with the third. Rumelhart comes the closest to actually saying this: "I argue that the classification of an utterance as to whether it involves literal and metaphorical meanings is analogous to our judgment as to whether a bit of language is formal or informal. It is a judgment that can be reliably made, but not one which signals fundamentally different comprehension processes." Rumelhart, "Some Problems," p. 79. Raymond Gibbs says, "The widely accepted distinctions between literal and metaphoric meanings and between semantics and pragmatics, have little utility for psychological theories of meaning and language use." "Understanding and Literal Meaning," *Cognitive Science* 13 (1989): 243–51. However, not all psychologists agree with this view. Marcelo Dascal argues for the relevance of the distinction between the literal and the metaphorical in psychological theories of comprehension in "Defending Literal Meaning," *Cognitive Science* 11 (1987): 259–81.

they contrast to sentence meaning and classify as pragmatic. In addition, on the basis of Searle's claim that an utterance is literal only when its conveyed meaning is the same as its sentence meaning, Glucksberg and Keysar contrast the conveyed meaning of an utterance with its literal meaning. As I noted in examining Searle's analysis of metaphor, the notion of conveyed meaning (or speaker meaning) is obscure. In addition, the identification of the literal with that in which sentence meaning is equivalent to the conveyed meaning is flawed, in part because it is unclear. For example, if the conveyed meaning is intended to contain all propositional content associated with the utterance, be it expressed or implied, then only utterances with no implicatures would be considered literal. However, this clearly goes against both our commonsense understanding of what is literal and the analysis presented in this book, in which literality stems from whether the entities are conceived of in accordance with the traditional taxonomy and metaphysics. In addition, the loss of a distinction between what is expressed and what is implied would seem to be an important one, and one with psychological impact. One of the consequences of the psychologists' adoption of the notion of conveyed meaning is that they view the distinction between meaning and use as the distinction between the process of comprehension and use. As a result, when they find that the processes of comprehension is the same for literal and metaphorical utterances, they conclude that the metaphorical is a matter of use.[53]

One final difficulty with the studies of these psychologists lies in the linguistic data used, the fact that many of the metaphors they use are almost completely dead (conventionalized, in their terms). In fact, the only study Gibbs performs using metaphors (instead of indirect speech acts) is one in which he argues that the conventionalized metaphorical meaning of an utterance (i.e. the metaphorical meaning of a dead metaphor) can be derived without accessing the literal meaning.[54] Since dead metaphors are thought to behave in comprehension as idioms or even as ambiguous terms whose formerly metaphorical meaning is now one of their literal meanings, Gibbs's conclusions would seem not to be about metaphors at all. However, studies performed by other psychologists (such as Keysar and Glucksberg) seem to use metaphors that are less conventionalized. As a result, their conclusion that metaphors need not (1) have their literal interpretation derived first and (2) have an anomalous triggering condition in order for a metaphorical interpretation to be derived seem to be valid.

[53]Keysar and Glucksberg, "Metaphor and Communication."
[54]Gibbs, "A Critical Examination."

In summary, the work of these psychologists shows that (1) the meanings of the terms often do not suffice to determine the proper interpretation in the absence of real-world knowledge or information provided contextually,[55] (2) people need not deduce the literal meaning of an utterance in order to deduce its conventionalized meaning or its metaphorical meaning (in cases in which the metaphor appears in a metaphorical context), (3) the metaphorical interpretation of an utterance can be derived without the triggering condition, and thus (4) the reinterpretation view of metaphor comprehension is inadequate. As a result of these findings, we can conclude that the view of metaphor as an elliptical simile is also inadequate, since it requires a reinterpretation view of metaphor comprehension. That is, since comparativism in general (and Fogelin's theory in particular) requires a reinterpretation view of metaphor comprehension, then comparativism is inadequate as an analysis of metaphorical content.[56]

In addition, the work of these psychologists fails to (1) show that the conveyed meaning of an utterance (i.e. its proposition expressed) is never the literal meaning of the utterance, (2) characterize metaphoricity, since Rumelhart's description of a partial fit applies to Donnellan's examples in which something true is said even if the description does not fit what is designated as well,[57] or (3) show that there is no distinction between the knowledge used in metaphor comprehension and the comprehension of literal utterances.

In contrast, the view of metaphorical content as stemming from reconceptualization does not require a reinterpretation view of metaphor comprehension. That is, since conceptualization and reconceptualization are essentially presemantic in that they precede the generation of the proposition expressed, there is nothing in my model to prevent the interpreter from taking the metaphorical vehicle as a prototypical representative of the ad hoc class in question *prior* to taking it as the representative of the class it literally designates. Therefore, my theory of metaphor in terms of reconceptualization accommodates the fact that one can interpret an utterance metaphorically without first interpreting it literally. In fact, in certain situations (e.g. when the speaker has been speaking metaphorically or

---

[55]Rumelhart, "Some Problems."

[56]Note that Fogelin's comparativist view seems to require a "multiple reinterpretation" view since it requires that we must first reinterpret the metaphor as a simile, then reinterpret it according to a different feature space, then derive its attribution of properties as indirect content.

[57]See Chapter 1, p. 00.

has a tendency to do so), the interpreter may have a bias toward deriving the metaphorical interpretation first and may even derive it when it is not intended. As a result, the argument against reinterpretation theories of metaphor comprehension is an argument against comparativism and in favor of my analysis of metaphor in terms of reconceptualization.

Argument from Contrast Between Metaphorical and Literal

One indication that what is at work in metaphors is reconceptualization lies in the contrast between literal class-inclusion statements and nominative metaphors. In both of these the form the utterance takes is "X is a Y." And in both cases, the structure causes the subject of the utterance to be assigned to the class mentioned in the predicate, invoking the subset relation and forcing the class referred to in the predicate to be conceived of at a higher level of abstraction than that designated by the subject of the sentence. In literal class-inclusion statements, X and Y are clearly at different levels in the hierarchy of abstraction (different levels in the taxonomic tree). For example, in the statement "That [pointing to some entity] is a mammal," the entity as indicated is clearly lower in the hierarchy of abstraction than the class indicated in the predicate, since any entity indicated by ostension is at the height of particularity or at the bottom of the hierarchy of abstraction. Even if we replaced the term "mammal" with "bear," then replaced "bear" with "brown bear," and so on, moving downward in the hierarchy of abstraction or taxonomic tree, the subject would remain lower than the class designated by the predicate. This occurs partly because of the nature of ostension, which singles out an individual in all of its particularity, and partly because of linguistic convention, which specifies that placing an article in front of a noun makes it more abstract.[58] In fact, even if we were to put aside the linguistic conventions, the nature of language (based on that of class inclusion) brings this about. That is, any entity or class that has a term that describes it (e.g. mammal, bear, brown bear), must be more abstract than any entity as indicated by ostension. So although we can vary the term in the predicate to refer to classes progressively lower in the hierarchy of abstraction, we cannot achieve the particularity of an entity indicated by ostension. (Note

---

[58]In fact, the only way to get a term in the predicate of a class-inclusion statement to approach the particularity of the subject of the class-inclusion statement is to use a proper name. For example, we could say "That is a Clinton." However, we can and will argue that this case is on the border on being metaphorical.

that when we indicate a particular entity using ostension, it seems that any feature of that entity we subsequently perceive as related to it can be assigned to that entity without disrupting the tie between language and that entity. This is not necessarily the case in any situation other than one of ostension. For example, if the thing I am pointing to and calling "gold" yields, upon investigation, a chemical composition other than Au, it becomes incorrect to call that entity "gold.") The other possible way of varying the literal class-inclusion statement to attempt to change the order of the subject and predicate class on the taxonomic scale is to vary the level of abstraction of the subject. For example, instead of saying, "That is a mammal," we can say "A bear is a mammal." In this case the class indicated by the subject is more abstract than that indicated by the term "that." However, even in this case, the predicate remains more abstract than the subject. In fact, if the predicate fails to be more abstract that the subject, as in an utterance of "A mammal is a bear," the utterance is judged false or anomalous.

Now let us consider the case of nominative metaphors. As I said earlier, the structure of class-inclusion statements seems to require that the class referred to in the predicate be at a higher level in the hierarchy of abstraction than the subject of the sentence or metaphor. However, in the case of metaphors, the class represented by the predicate, the class to which the metaphor subject is being assigned does not always appear to be at a higher level of abstraction. For example, consider an utterance of "A philosopher is really the city's pilot" or an utterance of "Juliet is the sun." In both cases it seems that the entity/class referred to in the predicate is at an equal level of abstraction with the subject or even at a lower level. How is it possible for metaphorical utterances to violate what seems to be an innate requirement of class-inclusion statements?

My theory of metaphor in terms of reconceptualization accounts for this apparent violation of an innate requirement of class-inclusion statements as follows. Although the predicate in a nominative metaphor may *appear* to be less abstract than that of the subject, the class to which the term "city's pilot" or "sun" is actually referring is more abstract. That is, because in metaphorical utterances the audience reconceptualizes the metaphor vehicle in terms of the role it plays in a system, producing a class that is more abstract than a literal interpretation would produce, the subset relation and the requirement that the subject be lower in the hierarchy of abstraction is met.

In literal utterances, all the audience has to do in processing a class-inclusion statement is to add X to the class that Y represents by virtue of linguistic convention and naive metaphysics. If we are linguistically competent, our linguistic knowledge steers us to the features the speaker is claiming the subject of the utterance has. However, if the utterance is not literal, things are not so straightforward. Before assigning the metaphor subject to the class and deciding which features in particular the speaker is interested in, the audience must derive the class to which the metaphor subject is being assigned, as represented by the metaphor vehicle.[59] That is, the audience must decide what kind of thing the metaphor vehicle is. The clues the audience has to work with include the fact that both the metaphor subject and the metaphor vehicle are members of the class in question, which rules out the standardized taxonomy evoked by linguistic convention and the role the metaphor vehicle plays in different systems in which it features prominently. In other words, in processing metaphors we are forced to go through a process almost identical (if not identical) with the process we go through when creating any class, a process which involves determining the features that the members of the class are likely to have and, perhaps, deciding which other members might be in the class. Since the notion of reconceptualization successfully resolves the apparent discrepancy in the hierarchy of abstraction *and* accounts for the process we go through in understanding metaphors, we have another argument for my theory of metaphor.

Argument from Failed Metaphor

Further evidence in favor of an analysis of metaphor in terms of reconceptualization can be found in an examination of the following failed metaphor. Suppose that we want to communicate the proposition that a whale is a mammal and that, although we can bring the class of mammals to mind and we remember that bears are prominent members of that class, we do not remember the name of the class (i.e. the term "mammal"). In an effort to communicate the desired proposition, we utter the sentence "A whale is a bear." Despite our intentions, this utterance would utterly fail to communicate the desired proposition, either literally or metaphorically. Nor would the audience be likely to take the utterance as a metaphor or to interpret the term "bear" metaphorically, even though the term clearly in-

---

[59]One might claim that it is precisely this requirement which explains the inadequacy of a computer or any other nonhuman entity to recognize and produce metaphors. This also provides an argument against the assumption of the tradition of language processing that claims that processing language is both a linear and a modular process, with semantic competence isolated from real-world knowledge.

vokes a few standard metaphorical readings (predicating aggressiveness etc.), as well as nonstandard ones (representing the class of mammals).

All the theories of metaphor we have critiqued are quite capable of explaining why the utterance fails to be taken as literal. In literal speech, the way one derives the class represented by the predicate is by using the meaning of the term as a list of features representative of the class. And whales lack most or all of the features listed. That is, most of the salient features of whales (under a standardized conceptualization) are incompatible with those of bears (also under a standardized conceptualization).

However, the failure of the utterance to be taken literally does not explain why the audience doesn't take the utterance as metaphorical. In fact, since the term "bear" is often interpreted metaphorically, the utterance's failure to be metaphorically true is all the more striking. Both Fogelin and Glucksberg and Keysar capitalize on the fact that the salience of features in an utterance depends upon features in the immediate context, *including* the subject and predicate. That is, merely by putting the term "whale" and the term "bear" in the same sentence prompts a search for similar and dissimilar features. However, as the principle of the irreversibility of metaphors makes clear, this is not the only thing going on. Glucksberg and Keysar account for the assymetry of metaphors by saying that the processing of metaphor requires that we conceive of the metaphor vehicle in terms of prototypicality, a relation it bears to a class the speaker intends to evoke. Yet their theories of metaphor do not explain why the audience does not take the utterance metaphorically. If processing figurative language simply involves creating an altered feature space (as Fogelin's model of metaphor suggests), when the audience concludes that the utterance, if taken literally, would clearly be false, why don't they make the necessary corrective judgment to suppress the irrelevant features of the bear so that it represents the class of mammals? Or, since one could argue that bears are prototypical representatives of the class of mammals, why doesn't the audience take the bear as a representative of the class of mammals and assign the whale to that class (as Glucksberg and Keysar's model predicts)? The failure of Fogelin's model shows that metaphoricity cannot be accounted for simply by specifying the creation of an altered feature space with which to evaluate similarity.[60] The failure of Glucksberg and Keysar's model shows that metaphoricity does not emerge solely from the use

---

[60]Fogelin's model seems to require that all obviously false statements be figurative, especially in cases in which the metaphor vehicle is a prototypical representative of the desired class.

of the prototypicality relation to represent the class to which we want to assign the metaphor subject. At the same time, this example confirms Davidson's intuition that what links a metaphor to what it expresses is not a matter of convention, even a convention based on prototypicality (such as the convention of taking a bear as a prototypical mammal). That is, the fact that a prototypicality relation exists between bears and mammals does not suffice to evoke metaphoricity or provoke a metaphorical interpretation.

What is missing in both Fogelin and Glucksberg and Keysar's analyses is the notion of reconceptualization in terms of the role the entity plays within a system. That is, what occurs in metaphor is not just an issue of whether certain entities possess certain features, whether different features are salient in different contexts, or whether a term (such as "bear") can acquire different readings. Instead it is a matter of reconceptualization, one which challenges the naive metaphysics. The notion of reconceptualization, as presented within my analysis of metaphor, accounts for both the variability of salient features an entity can be sensibly predicated to have *and* the fact that a given entity cannot be represented by just any set of features, especially within a certain context.

To understand why the utterance fails to be metaphorical, it helps to consider how it can be altered to succeed. For example, consider an utterance of "A whale can be a real bear." Although this utterance contains the same two entities as the previous one (whales and bears), it is more likely to be interpreted metaphorically. That is, the audience is likely to interpret the utterance as saying something like "A whale can be a very aggressive creature." Such an interpretation is made possible because that the term "real" causes the audience to examine what a bear "really" is, inviting them to let go of the features provided by the standardized metaphysics (whether they have the most complete knowledge of bears or the most minimal, having only seen them in movies)[61] and then reconceptualize the

---

[61]This point brings up the question for students of reference that Putnam has often addressed, that is, the question of how two people with vastly different levels of knowledge about an entity still manage to communicate about that entity and supposedly refer to the same entity. In my analysis, I explain this by claiming that in literal utterances, one speaks of the bear which is projected to be outside of ourselves, containing attributes which we may or may not know. Whether one be a scientist who studies bears or a Parisian courtier who has never left the city, in speaking literally about a bear one speaks of (or refers to) the bear that is part of the standardized metaphysics, that includes the entities one believes exists, regardless of how much or how little one knows about them. In contrast, in speaking metaphorically we release any attempt to capture all the features bears are thought to really have in this pro-

bear in terms of different roles. As it turns out, the term "real bear" tends to evoke the role characterized by the trait of aggressiveness, making it easy to generate a metaphorical reading of the utterance. As we we noted earlier, we call a metaphor "dead" when the features that the metaphor vehicle contributes to the proposition expressed are crystallized or formalized in a conceptualization that is part of the standardized taxonomy and naive metaphysics. Sometimes a metaphor is on its way to being dead because the conceptualization the metaphor is used to express already exists, regardless of whether it is associated with the term of the metaphor vehicle. Since one might argue that being aggressive is on its way to being one of the conventionalized meanings of the term "bear," the so-called "metaphorical reading" of bear might actually be on its way to being a literal meaning of the term. In any case, my analysis of metaphor can explain why this variation of the metaphorical utterance succeeds in provoking a metaphorical (if slightly conventionalized) reading of the term "bear."

Another way of varying the utterance to invoke a metaphorical reading is to alter the subject. Suppose, for example, that the speaker said, "Jerry is a bear," while pointing to a whale in a large tank. Although the audience might not know immediately how to interpret the utterance, it seems likely that they would attempt to interpret the utterance metaphorically, probably using questions to get more information about what was intended (e.g. "Do you mean that Jerry is aggressive and difficult to work with? or "Does Jerry sleep a lot or is he hard to get along with in the morning?"). The only difference between this utterance and the original is that the subject designates a particular entity rather than a class of entities. Since the entity in question is visible to both speaker and audience and is clearly *not* a bear, the utterance cannot be taken as literal. However, the fact that the subject is a particular and familiar entity rather than a class makes it clear that the speaker wants to say *something* about that bear (whereas in the utterance "A whale is a bear" the speaker may be trying to make a philosophical point about the nature of whales and bears that is too vague to be understood). Thus the audience is impelled to find another way of looking at bears that will generate a feature (such as aggressiveness or grouchiness) that can be attributed to the whale in question.

The final variation of the failed metaphor we shall consider is as follows: "Within the ocean kingdom, a whale is a bear." Again, while the

---

jected reality and attempt to capture it via the role it plays in some system, be it a cultural or subcultural role.

audience may seek more information in fleshing out a metaphorical interpretation of "bear" and the attribution of features to whales, they are
likely to interpret the utterance metaphorically. Here the difference between the successful metaphor and the failed original is that the former
describes the system within which the whale is being considered, provoking the audience to view the whale in terms of the role it plays within that
system and to search for the parallel system within which the bear plays a
role.

Thus our example of a failed metaphor and the three more successful
variations illustrate the way in which the various components of my theory of metaphor successfully predict the way metaphorical interpretations
are processed. These examples also confirm that the metaphoricity of an
utterance and the derivation of its metaphorical content are not determined by its purpose. In fact, a metaphorical utterance may have as its
main goal to attribute certain features to an entity, or to alter one's conception of the metaphor subject.

Argument from Extendability

One final argument that can be made for an analysis of metaphor in
terms of reconceptualization lies in the ability of this approach to explain
other linguistic phenomena, figurative and literal. For one thing, accounting for metaphor in terms of reconceptualization offers a method of
accounting for all figurative language. As I have shown, the notion of
reconceptualization can be used to explain both simile and metaphor, capturing our intuitions that each of these expresses a figurative content
which is judged according to an altered feature space. Since other types of
figurative speech are distinguished by the same features (i.e. a figurative
content evaluated using an altered feature space derived by the audience),
an analysis based on reconceptualization seems in order. For example,
consider a lengthy description of seven blindfolded Brahmins each of
whom describe the part of the elephant that they experience. Suppose a
preacher were to use this story to illustrate how it is that different religions
have such different notions of God, when there is only one God. What is at
work in this type of speech, what makes it possible for the audience to interpret the different descriptions of the elephant as an explanation of how
different religions emerge, is the fact that we are able to reconceptualize
things like elephants and our sensory experience of them in such a way as
to say something meaningful about our search for God, whom we ap-

proach blindfolded and have profoundly different, although equally valid
or truthful, experiences of.[62]

In addition, accounting for metaphor in terms of reconceptualization
accommodates current developments in linguistics which acknowledge
the limitations of formal mathematical logic for accommodating a whole
range of natural language phenomena. In response to the apparent inadequacies of formal logic in the face of phenomena indicating the context
dependence of semantic notions, there has been a trend toward embracing
a cognitive account of reference, a cognitive semantics. One of the prominent examples of this type is the work of Fauconnier, which specifies a
cognitive theory of mental spaces.[63] According to Fauconnier, reference
has its own cognitive structure in the form of mental spaces, separate from
that of other linguistic issues (i.e. accounts of predicate-argument structure, logical operators, etc.). Mental spaces consist of domains constructed during any discourse, according to guidelines provided by linguistic expressions. According to Fauconnier, language comprehension and
production is made possible by the creation and manipulation of
(personal) mental spaces (made up of roles and individuals), connectors
between referents (within and across spaces), and a few general principles.
For example, in an utterance such as "Harry thinks that Sally is quite unfriendly," the phrase "Harry thinks that" establishes a mental space M
which the audience constructs in processing the utterance, and the name
Sally sets up an element in that space, one which has the property of being
quite unfriendly. To comprehend the utterance, the audience would need
to establish such a space, with such elements and relations. Furthermore,
mental spaces are models that represent point of view. Thus the mental
space M would describe Harry's point of view in that utterance. In contrast, the utterance "Sally is quite unfriendly" would establish a mental
space R considered to represent the real state of things, yet still from the
speaker's point of view.

My account of metaphor in terms of reconceptualization seems compatible with Fauconnier's semantics. Both, as cognitive theories, proceed
from the assumption that language processing is not a matter of language

---

[62]It also seems quite likely that the notion of reconceptualization in terms of the
role an entity plays within a system can be used to account for statements concerning
fictional characters. One of the puzzles for traditional semantics has been accounting
for how statements about fictional or nonexistent entities manage to express meaningful and possibly true propositions.

[63]Gilles Fauconnier, *Mental Spaces* (Cambridge: Cambridge University Press,
1994).

decryption, a matter of unpacking content carried in the terms, but rather one of the creation and communication of cognitive structures or conceptualizations. Both acknowledge that something (be it point of view or conceptualization) underlies language use. In an attempt to capture the difference between the literal and the metaphorical, I have appealed to reconceptualization in terms of the role an individual plays, with the assumption that conceptualization underlies all communication. Fauconnier's term "mental spaces" gives a name to the domain which holds both the conceptualization used in literal language and the reconceptualizations I hold that conversants construct in processing metaphorical language. In both cases, the "pragmatic" or context-dependent aspect of grasping what was said lies not in the randomness of the goal a speaker might have in making an utterance but rather in the variability of point of view and the different ways of conceiving or representing an individual. Clearly much work remains to be done in the area of explaining how the two theories interrelate, but for our purposes here it suffices to point out that Fauconnier's semantics both seems to fit the requirements my theory of metaphor places upon semantics in acknowledging the significant role of conceptualization and reconceptualization in language use *and,* at the same time, provides a means for accounting for and unifying other linguistic phenomena unexplainable by a more traditional semantics (i.e. indexicals etc.).

In conclusion, expressing metaphor and other figurative language in terms of reconceptualization accounts for it in a way that links it to a phenomenon that underlies all language use, that of conceptualization and the creation of classes. Expressing metaphor and other figurative language in this way offers a means of unifying aspects of language currently considered disparate, unexplained by traditional semantics and considered secondary to language theory. As the group of phenomena that cannot be accounted for using a semantics based on formal logic grows, an account of language use that addresses these inadequacies becomes all the more attractive.

Summary

I have now conclusively argued for reconceptualization as a means of accounting for both metaphoricity and metaphorical content. I have also shown that my theory of metaphor, with its requirements for a theory of semantics, points the way toward a unified account of language use via a semantics based on conceptualization, perhaps a cognitive semantics such as Fauconnier develops. As we saw in Chapter 2, the distinction between semantics and pragmatics based on the distinction between meaning and use has been used to classify metaphor as a matter of either semantics or pragmatics. Yet, as I demonstrated in Chapter 3, metaphorical content cannot be explained by appealing to metaphorical meaning. Nor are the alternative pragmatic approaches proposed by Davidson (Chapter 4), Searle (Chapter 5), and Fogelin (Chapter 6) any more successful in accounting for metaphorical content. What seems to be indicated instead is a treatment, such as that of my analysis (and possibly Fogelin's), that incorporates semantic and pragmatic aspects of metaphor in much the same ways as treatments of literal utterances. My examination has shown that the variability in what is expressed by metaphorical content does not depend on the variability of what a speaker may intend to accomplish with the utterance. Rather, its variability depends on something of a different sort altogether, something related to reference rather than to speaker intention, on issues of what a thing is considered to be, and what relations it is considered to have with other entities, forming a system. Fauconnier's semantics calls this system or domain a "mental space" and develops the view that such domains are constructed during, and facilitate, both literal and figurative language use. My theory of metaphor accounts for the differences and similarities between the metaphorical and the literal, while providing evidence that metaphorical utterances honor such traditional linguistic distinctions as the distinction between what was said and what was implied and the relative independence of the content of an utterance on the speaker's intention. My final task is to see how an analysis of metaphor based on reconceptualization fares when evaluated using the criteria I have established for theories of metaphor.

7

Evaluation of the Analysis

Conditions on a Theory
of Metaphor

The best argument for my analysis of metaphor based on reconceptualization is that it meets the conditions on a theory of metaphor which we have established by reviewing existing theories of metaphor and the phenomena they describe. Thus our final step is to evaluate my account of metaphor in terms of reconceptualization using these criteria.

Metaphoricity

The main goal of any analysis of metaphor is to account for metaphoricity, that which allows us to distinguish between metaphorical and literal utterances. Some accounts of metaphor essentially explain metaphoricity away by arguing that the metaphorical is not fundamentally different from the literal. And indeed, as I have argued, the metaphorical and the literal form a continuum rather than existing as noncontiguous sets. Yet the continuity between the metaphorical and the literal does not eliminate the significant difference between the two. Other accounts of metaphor analyze metaphoricity in either semantic, pragmatic, or essentially nonlinguistic terms, seeing each as discrete systems. I explain metaphoricity in terms of reconceptualization, something which straddles the options previously considered in that while reconceptualization is essentially a prelinguistic phenomenon that underlies language use, a metaphorical utterance contains components (such as that of metaphorical content) which follow semantic and pragmatic rules. At the same time, the notion of reconceptualization is productive in that it can be used to explain both (1) other instances of figurative language (such as similes) and (2) metaphors which occur in realms other than the purely linguistic. That is, my notion of reconceptualization can also be used to explain "metaphors" that occur in paintings, works of music, and other art forms. Thus my analysis of metaphor in terms of reconceptualization accounts for Davidson's intuition that what is metaphorical need not be linguistic and that in processing metaphors we alter our conception of the world, not our conception of language.

Metaphor Comprehension

One of the most commonly stated goals of all theories of metaphor is that of accounting for metaphor comprehension. According to my analysis of metaphor, in comprehending a metaphor the audience must reconceptualize some or all of the entities referenced by the metaphorical utterance, either (1) by deriving the literal interpretation of an utterance, deciding that it is not appropriate within the context, and deriving an alternative, metaphorical interpretation (by reconceptualizing the metaphor vehicle in terms of the role it plays in the system and then reconceptualizing the metaphor subject in terms of that role) or (2) by deriving the metaphorical interpretation directly. In either case, the audience uses the satisfaction conditions of the ad hoc class the metaphor vehicle represents to evaluate the utterance, rather than those assigned to the metaphor vehicle by linguistic and taxonomic conventions.[1] My analysis in terms of reconceptualization not only accommodates our intuition that in processing metaphors we answer the question of what kind of thing the metaphor vehicle and subject are, but also accounts for the ways metaphors fail when they fail and for the existence of false metaphors. In the former case, metaphors can fail, on the one hand, because the metaphor vehicle does not evoke a role in a system that the audience can use for the reconceptualization. For example, in the utterance "Wallpaper is a table," the metaphor vehicle (table) does not evoke any particular system.[2] On the other hand, metaphors also fail when, despite the fact that the audience locates a role with which to reconceptualize the metaphor vehicle, that role is

---

[1]Note that even in the latter case, the audience must know the literal meaning of the term, even if they do not apply the full set of satisfaction conditions.

[2]Note that in certain contexts a table might evoke a particular system. For example, in T. S. Eliot's poem "The Love Song of J. Alfred Prufrock," "Let us go, then, you and I, when the evening is spread out against the sky, like a patient etherized upon a table," the term "the table" refers to is the operating table, which plays a certain role in a system made up of a surgeon, an operating table, and the patient. Examples like these show how dependent upon context the interpretation of metaphors is.

clearly incompatible with the metaphor subject. For example, consider the utterance "Wallpaper is a surgeon." Sometimes metaphors fail for a combination of both reasons. For example, in the utterance "A semicolon is a period," the only role and system the period evokes is within the linguistic system. However, the metaphor subject (i.e. the semicolon) evokes the same system and yet does not play the role the period does in that system. So while a period might effectively play the role of the metaphor vehicle in an utterance like "Her tasteless joke put a period on the conversation," it fails as a metaphor vehicle in the utterance "A semicolon is like a period."

Similarly, my analysis explains false metaphors by appealing to the fact that some metaphor vehicles strongly evoke a role in a system that is clearly incompatible with the metaphor subject. That is, whereas in some cases (such as "Shirley Temple is a bulldozer") the audience can reconceptualize the metaphor vehicle in terms of a role they play in a system, and there is no incompatibility between that role and the class to which the metaphor subject belongs (i.e. certain people play such the bulldozer role), the particular individual in question (the metaphor subject) does not belong to that class. For a metaphor to be false, rather than simply to fail to be metaphorical, it must be fairly easy to derive the role with which to reconceptualize the metaphor vehicle. One could argue that only metaphors that are on their way to being dead and thus part of the language succeed in being false metaphors.

Metaphorical Content and Truth

As the inadequacy of Davidson's analysis of metaphor shows, one of the most important features of any theory of metaphor is its ability to account for metaphorical content and truth. That is, any theory of metaphor must account for our intuition that the proposition expressed by a metaphorical utterance is not the proposition that is expressed according to the rules of the language (i.e. the literal interpretation of the utterance). The strongest feature of my analysis in terms of reconceptualization is its ability to account for metaphorical content and truth in a way that is consistent both with our intuitions of how metaphors are comprehended and with the framework and terminology provided by semantics.[3]

[3]Note that while Fogelin acknowledges the existence of a distinct metaphorical truth, he denies both metaphorical meaning and metaphorical content. That is, Fogelin claims that the content of a metaphorical interpretation of an utterance is the same as its content under a literal interpretation. What is different is the factors that are used in the evaluation of its truth. As I mentioned in Chapter 6, this has the particular

In order to determine what results a theory of metaphor should produce in terms of the content and resulting truth value of a metaphor, one must first ask oneself in what circumstances an utterance of "Steve is a sheepdog" would be judged to be true or false. Without deciding on a complete interpretation of the metaphor, most people would agree that the utterance would be true only if it were judged to be true that Steve is the kind of thing that a sheepdog is. That is, in order to evaluate the truth of the utterance, one must first determine what kind of thing a sheepdog is (in this context). In ordinary (literal) class-inclusion statements, what a sheepdog is is determined by the rules of the language, the taxonomy underlying the terms. That is, the properties that determine the class of "a sheepdog" are those which are required for a literal application of the term "sheepdog" to an object. As a result, to determine the truth of the utterance, we must compare the attributes of the object being assigned to the class (i.e. the subject of the metaphor) with those specified by the rules of the language. However, in the case of metaphors, the attributes of a sheepdog are not given by the rules of the language (or its underlying taxonomy) but rather must be derived by the speaker in seeking a new conceptualization or ad hoc category of which a sheepdog is a prototypical representative. In addition, one must first determine what attributes make up the class it is intended to represent by deciding on various ways one can conceptualize a sheepdog.

In my analysis, the content of the utterance is different under a metaphorical interpretation than it is under a literal interpretation because the class to which the subject of the metaphor is assigned by the metaphorical utterance is different from that to which the metaphor vehicle literally refers. As a result, the truth value of the utterance is quite different depending on whether the utterance is interpreted literally or metaphorically. Furthermore, the account my analysis provides of the metaphorical content itself (i.e. its truth conditions) seems to correspond to an intuitive account of metaphorical content (i.e. what a given metaphor says). To see this, consider a metaphorical interpretation of the sentence "Margaret Thatcher is a bulldozer," uttered by one person to another in reaction to a news story claiming that Margaret Thatcher overrode the wishes of a certain committee to have a poll tax enacted. In my analysis, the metaphorical content is dependent upon a reconceptualization of some or all of the entities, states, or events referred to in the utterance. Given the metaphor

---

result that one proposition can have different truth conditions and value, something clearly incompatible with traditional semantics.

in question, since the part of the sentence that is metaphorical (i.e. consti-tutes the metaphor vehicle) is the term "bulldozer," this is what we must reconceptualize by specifying the role the bulldozer plays with a system. In doing so, we must reflect on what properties of bulldozers are salient in the context. In this case, it is how bulldozers interact with the objects around them that is relevant.[4] As a result, the properties that characterize the ad hoc class to which the metaphor subject is assigned attempt to de-scribe this type of interactive role. (For example, we might say that when Margaret Thatcher is moving toward a certain goal she reaches it, even if others get in her way.) In addition, the metaphorical content expressed by the utterance will attribute just these characteristics to Margaret That-cher, and not those specified by a literal interpretation (and the standard-ized conceptualization) of bulldozers. Yet this content describes what most people would say they grasp when they understand the metaphor. As a result, it seems that my analysis satisfies the condition of accounting for our intuition of metaphorical content and truth.

Difficulty of Specifying the Truth Conditions of Some Metaphors

Another aspect of metaphor that an analysis of metaphor must address, one that Davidson uses in his arguments against the notion of metaphori-cal meaning, is the fact that it seems difficult or even impossible to para-phrase some metaphors. As I said earlier, how one answers the question of metaphor's paraphrasability depends on how one interprets this notion, for there is more than one conception of what it means to be paraphras-able. According to one conception, one utterance is a paraphrase of an-other if and only if it expresses the same proposition as that utterance (i.e. has the same truth conditions). According to another (more narrow) con-

---

[4]Note that metaphors are often used to express the relationship between the sub-ject of the metaphor and other entities in their environment. This is probably because (1) relational properties of entities are either not salient or not specified within the taxonomy underlying the language and (2) the contrast between the individual prop-erties of the metaphor subject and vehicle (such as concreteness vs. abstractness, ani-macy vs. inanimacy, etc.) causes these to be omitted in the ad hoc category that is constructed. This aspect of metaphor (i.e. its facility for suppressing certain proper-ties of objects and emphasizing others) is one that has made it so appealing to educa-tors like Plato whose goal is to help students look past the material aspects of things in order to truly understand them. In addition, the ease with which it expresses the relational aspects of objects makes it useful both for learning and for communication. (I explore these issues below.)

ception, an utterance is a paraphrase of another if and only if, in addition to expressing the same proposition, it has the same effect, which can include such things as the emotional response on the part of the hearer, the behavior of the hearer in response, the connotations associated with the utterance by the culture, etc. Given the second (more narrow) conception of paraphrasability, the fact that it is difficult to paraphrase a metaphor would not be sufficient to distinguish it from literal utterances, since these, too, would be difficult or impossible to paraphrase. (The variability of connotations associated with different terms, if nothing else, would prevent this.) According to this conception of paraphrasability, it is unclear why we would want to demand paraphrasability either of literal or of metaphorical utterances.

However, given the first (broader and hence more plausible) conception of paraphrasability, it does seem that it is more difficult to paraphrase metaphorical utterances than literal utterances. For example, when Socrates calls the philosopher the pilot of the city, while it is clear that being in command of a ship is not a specification of the truth conditions, it is less clear whether the philosopher must be acknowledged to be a navigator of sorts by those he directs (as in the case of actual pilots) or not. Whereas this example is a simple one, some poetic metaphors are so difficult to unravel that it is unclear whether one ever sorts out their truth conditions. For example, consider the utterance of "Let us go then, you and I, when the evening is spread out against the sky like a patient etherized upon a table."[5] Competent speakers of the language faced with this kind of complex metaphor may *never* figure out what is being said, let alone whether it is true or not. In contrast, competent speakers faced with a literal utterance generally know the conditions under which it would be true, even in cases in which a want of world knowledge prevents them from knowing whether the utterance is true.[6]

Nonetheless, although it may be difficult to give the truth conditions of some metaphors, there doesn't seem to be any reason why they cannot, in principle, be given. To see this, it is helpful to consider a metaphorical utterance of "Juliet is the sun." As was discussed in Chapter 3, Romeo might instead have said, "Consider the class of things that are the center of certain systems, like the sun at the center of the universe. Notice that without

[5]T. S. Eliot, "The Love Song of J. Alfred Prufrock," in *T. S. Eliot: Selected Poems* (London: Faber and Faber, 1954), p. 11.

[6]Note that, in accordance with Putnam's argument, the competence required might be different for an ordinary speaker and a scientist. Hilary Putnam, "Meaning and Reference," *Journal of Philosophy* 70 (Nov. 8, 1973): 699–711.

the sun, animate things cannot grow, reproduce, or even subsist. Notice that the day begins when the sun appears and ends when it leaves. Notice that seedlings struggle to break through the earth to find the sunlight and, when they succeed, orient their bodies so that their leaves face the sun. Notice that all planetary activity centers on the sun. For me, Juliet is in this class of things." Intuitively, it seems that this description successfully paraphrases the metaphor in question, especially if Romeo mentions all the properties of the sun he wishes to attribute to Juliet. Thus it seems that although some metaphors are difficult to paraphrase, it is not impossible to specify the truth conditions they communicate.

In my analysis of metaphor in terms of reconceptualization, the difficulty (vs. impossibility) in expressing the truth conditions of metaphorical utterances (as opposed to literal utterances) is explained by the fact that while the truth conditions of a literal utterance are given by the taxonomy and naive metaphysics underlying the rules of the language, this is not the case for most metaphors. In my analysis of metaphor, the fuzziness of some metaphors, the difficulty of specifying their truth conditions, stems from the fact that the class to which the subject is assigned either (1) is not captured (formalized) in the language (in cases where the new conceptualization or ad hoc category is somewhat established) or (2) is newly created in the metaphor. In either case, the exact truth conditions of the utterance may not be known in that they are not provided by the rules of the language and its underlying taxonomy, as is customary in the case of literal class-inclusion statements. But the difficulty in paraphrasing the metaphor lies not in a lack of linguistic competence or knowledge of specific properties of the entities in question but rather in the difficulty of abstracting from the metaphor vehicle to the role intended by the speaker, one which, if it were obvious, would probably be incorporated into the language.

In addition, it seems that if a literal paraphrase of the utterance (such as the description above) successfully captures the truth conditions of the metaphor in question, it does so for the reasons cited in my analysis. That is, according to my analysis of metaphor, a metaphorical utterance of the form presented (i.e. nominative) is true if and only if the subject of the metaphor belongs to the class to which it is assigned within the metaphor, a class the metaphor vehicle represents via the role it plays in the system it evokes. The paraphrase of Romeo's utterance claims the existence of such a class, goes on to describe the conditions for membership, and then claims that Juliet (the metaphor subject) belongs in this class. In addition, in the description certain properties of both Juliet and the sun are emphasized, while others are left out. Since this intuitive description corresponds to our analysis of the processes underlying metaphor comprehension, it would seem to confirm it as well.

The Context Dependence of Metaphor

One of the features of metaphor that leads Davidson to dismiss semantic theories of metaphor is its context dependence, the fact that in order to interpret (or even recognize) many metaphors the audience must know features of context not encompassed in linguistic competence. According to my analysis, the heightened dependence of metaphor on the context, in comparison to the relative context independence of literal utterances, derives from the fact that in the case of literal utterances, most of the features being assigned to the subject of the utterance are provided by the standardized taxonomy evoked by the term's meaning. In contrast, in processing metaphorical utterances, the audience must construct the class through reconceptualization, using features from the context to determine what aspects or dimensions of the entities referenced are to be considered relevant. For example, in a conversation about interactive styles, calling a person a certain type of animal indicates that interactive styles are relevant while details of genus and species are not. In other words, in my analysis contextual clues are required to allow the audience to determine what features count or are relevant.

The Ubiquity of Metaphor
(Why Metaphors Are Used)

Another aspect of metaphors that an analysis of metaphor must accommodate is the fact that they are used so often in education, literature, science, and rhetoric. One of the most obvious virtues of metaphor is that it allows us to describe entities for which we have no name in a way that (1) fits the entity into an existing framework and (2) conveys a great deal of information about the entity, which aspects of it are important and which are not. Metaphors also allow us to recategorize existing entities. (We have already discussed its use in the designation of manufactured objects.)

One factor underlying this aspect of metaphor is that metaphors usually describe an abstract category (such as time) in terms of a more concrete category (such as rivers). Since the concrete is easier to understand, to remember, and to manipulate than the abstract, expressing a concept in these terms is of great value. The usefulness of this can be seen in the fact that we so often make diagrams to help us solve mathematical problems and to illustrate complicated theories. If the concrete model is synchronized with the issue at hand in an understandable way (note that the color of diagrams and their position on the page are deemed irrelevant) and if it captures all of the relevant properties, then we can manipulate the model and use it either as a basis for speculation concerning the abstract concept or even as a means of deriving conclusions about it. The identification of Juliet with the sun is a case in point, since the sun is a concrete object that plays a certain role within a structured group of entities which most people think they can characterize via a series of simple relationships. That is, we can characterize the sun as that which emits light and is the center of a solar system within which every other entity rotates around the sun (which can be taken to symbolize power). Along the same lines, we can characterize the moon as that which emits no light and which rotates around the earth (showing devotion). In addition, other entities within the system can be characterized according to their relationship to the other entities in the system, and while the number of major players in the solar system is limited, the system allows for the introduction of others (for example, as meteorites or comets). As a result, this particular metaphor serves as a valuable tool for describing systems of relationships such as that between Romeo, Juliet, and the people in their environment.

Another reason for the rhetorical power of metaphor lies in its emotive power, as can be seen in an example in which two people discuss a third person known to both. "He's pushy," says the first; "he's a bully." "You don't understand," says the second; "he's pushy but he's a sheepdog." If the second person succeeds in convincing the first that the person in question is a sheep dog rather than a bully, she will have changed the first person's conception of the person in question. However, it seems that there should be no difference between viewing the person as a bully and viewing him as a sheepdog, especially since both people agree that the person being categorized is pushy. The discrepancy between the beliefs of the two conversants emerges from (1) the emotive power of metaphor and (2) the dependence of metaphorical content on the context. The emotive power of the metaphor, as Henle points out,[7] stems in part from the emotions evoked by the metaphor vehicle. That is, part of what differentiates the

[7]Paul Henle, "Metaphor," in *Language, Thought and Culture*, ed. Paul Henle, (Ann Arbor: University of Michigan Press, 1958), pp. 173–95.

class of bullies from that of sheepdogs is that we tend to feel positive feelings about sheepdogs but negative feelings about bullies. By ignoring context dependence, we fail to acknowledge the fact that the two classes of bullies and sheepdogs are, to a certain extent, defined within the context in such a way that while each (in a different context) might be used to describe someone who is aggressive, in a context in which they are being contrasted, the categories they designate are taken to specify more than aggressiveness so that the difference between the two lies in the properties providing the further specificity.

Yet another aspect of metaphor that makes it such a useful device is that metaphor involves a certain amount of abstraction and construction of new categories. That is, the fact that processing a metaphor requires the audience to reconceptualize some or all of the entities involved, abstracting away from the metaphor vehicle to find a super-ordinate category to which the metaphor vehicle is predicated to belong, makes metaphor a powerful tool both for education and for science. This aspect of metaphor serves education because much of learning is abstraction. It also serves science, because much of science is the creation of new categories, new entities, and the reconceptualization of existing entities in order to explain the phenomena in a way consistent with other phenomena.

Besides offering an abstraction process that serves these general purposes, metaphor can be used specifically to cause an audience to abstract away from certain aspects of a thing, making it appropriate for literature, education, rhetoric (i.e. persuasion), and science. Socrates' use of metaphor is prototypical. Ostensibly Socrates uses metaphor to aid in the classical search for the real which is thought to be concealed behind the appearances, which, for him, constitutes the search for the universal behind the particular. Because metaphor, in putting entities of different material properties in the same class forces an abstraction away from the particular and a reconceptualization that produces a super-ordinate class, it is ideal for Socrates' goals. At the same time, once one accepts the metaphorical identification (for example, of the philosopher and the pilot) on the basis of a few common properties, then it is easy to attribute other properties to the metaphor subject without the close scrutiny that would otherwise be required. As a result, metaphor also helps Socrates in his attempts to persuade his audience of what he thinks is right.

One final reason metaphor is so useful to both education and rhetoric is that in processing most metaphors the audience must actively participate in the creation of content in a way that is not required in the case of literal utterances. That is, as educators, rhetoricians, and psychologists have shown, when someone actively engages in processing the information they receive (as they do in processing metaphors in drawing connections, selecting properties), they are much more likely to pay attention, to evaluate what they learn critically, and to remember what they learn later on.

Metaphor Versus Simile: Similarities and Differences

Another condition for a successful theory of metaphor is that it account for both the similarities and the differences between metaphors and similes. The first step is to characterize similes. Given (1) a tradition in which similes (along with metaphors) are thought to be figurative and (2) a recognition of similes as comparison statements, similes can be identified as figurative comparison statements. Given the assumption that there is a difference between figurative and literal comparison statements, it seems that the way of accounting for the difference between them is in terms of the figurativeness of the former. Literal and figurative comparison statements are often distinguished from each other in terms of the relative likeness of the objects they are comparing. That is, a comparison statement is considered to be literal if the objects being compared are considered to be similar, figurative if they are not.[8] However, there is another way of describing the difference, one which is compatible with our view that the metaphoricity of an utterance (and perhaps figurativeness in general) is not attached to sentence types or even utterances of sentence types, but rather to ways of interpreting utterances. In other words, I claim that just as there are both literal and figurative interpretations of class-inclusion statements, there are literal and figurative interpretations of comparison statements. In my analysis of metaphor, through a literal interpretation of a comparison statement, the features of the metaphor vehicle that are compared with those of the subject of the metaphor are those which are assigned to it by the rules of the language and its underlying taxonomy. For example, a literal interpretation of "A nectarine is like a peach" would place the salient features of peaches in comparison with the salient features of nectarines,[9] where the salience of the features is determined ac-

---

[8]Note that this assumption conflicts with the idea of literal but false comparison statements.

[9]Note that in some cases one might not know the salient features of nectarines. That is, how comparison statements are processed depends, in part, on the purpose for which they are used. In certain cases, comparison statements are used as a means of attributing certain features of the subject of the comparison. In these cases, instead

cording to the taxonomy underlying the language. In contrast, in a figurative interpretation of the same statement, the features of peaches to be used would be those they possess when reconceptualized.[10] Of course, certain sentences might be more suited to being interpreted figuratively rather than literally and vice-versa, owing partly to the details of the context. For example, the comparison given above favors a literal reading in situations in which the audience does not know what a nectarine is like but wants to know so that they can look for it at the market. This is not to say, however, that in this account the knowledge of the audience *determines* whether the utterance is metaphorical or not or what proposition the utterance expresses. It simply influences how the audience is likely to interpret the utterance and thus is one of the factors a competent communicator (as opposed to someone who is just linguistically competent) will take into account when choosing how to express the proposition they desire to communicate in order to achieve the desired effect.

Similarities

In my analysis, then, figurative similes and metaphors are similar in that in both cases ad hoc or new categories are invoked, via their prototypical representatives, with the result that different properties of the metaphor vehicle and subject are taken into account when processing them. In the case of metaphors, the subject is assigned membership in the category represented by the metaphor vehicle. In the case of similes, the subject is declared to have similarity to the metaphor vehicle, an object from which it is ordinarily considered to be very different. What makes them both figurative is that in both cases the participants must make their perspective on the entities in question such that the features that are salient and thus used in the processing and evaluation of the utterance are those of a new conceptualization or ad hoc category rather than the category literally designated by the term used metaphorically.[11]

---

of comparing the features of each and evaluating the utterance on the basis of this comparison, the audience attributes the features of the vehicle of comparison to the subject. However, the variety in purpose for which comparison statements are used does not affect its content or its truth conditions.

[10]This account of similes is similar to that of Fogelin in that it accounts for their figurativeness in terms of the features used in the evaluation of the truth of each of the different interpretations.

[11]Note that even given literal interpretations of comparison statements, in different contexts, different properties are salient and are used as the basis for comparison. For example, in a context in which students are comparing schools for their general

Differences

In addition to being able to account for the similarity between metaphor and similes, a theory of metaphor should be able to account for the difference between the two. That is, a theory of metaphor should account for the intuition of most speakers that although metaphors and figurative similes are similar in effect, in general a metaphor seems more powerful than its corresponding simile. For example, to say "Margaret Thatcher is a bulldozer" seems more powerful and definitive than to say "Margaret Thatcher is like a bulldozer." In fact, this difference in strength may even correspond to a difference in propositional content in that it seems possible to assent to the proposition that Margaret Thatcher *is like* a bulldozer while denying that she *is* a bulldozer (much in that way that we can assent to the proposition that a nectarine is like a peach while rejecting the proposition that it actually is a peach).

In my analysis of metaphor, the difference between metaphor and simile can be accounted for, in part, by appealing to the relationship between class inclusion (also referred to as categorization or grouping) and similarity. Put simply, the grounds for declaring a similarity between objects seem not to be the same as the grounds for group membership, so that we can say two objects are similar without considering the two to be in the same class. This fact is tied to how we form the ad hoc categories with which we reconceptualize the vehicle of comparison. In theory, any given entity has an infinite number of properties and one can reconceptualize or categorize that entity according to any one of those properties. For example, to be the sun might mean to be very large, to be very bright, to be very hot, to be yellow, to be at a certain location in the galaxy, to be a certain distance from the Earth, to be very far away, to have a certain chemical composition, etc. However, while any one of these properties might serve as the basis for a comparison (especially to the degree that they are salient in the metaphor vehicle in the context), taken independently they may not characterize the sun in such a way that one would agree that to be the sun is to have that property. (That is, they may not describe a class of which

---

academic ranking, Stanford and Harvard might be ranked similarly. However, in a context in which architectural students are discussing architecture, the same two schools would be considered very different. As a result, the fact that different properties are used in the evaluation of a comparison statement need not mean that in one context the utterance is metaphorical. However, there is a difference between the contextual variation of literal and metaphorical comparisons in that, in the former, while different attributes are used in the evaluation, all the attributes used appear in the underlying taxonomy, but in the case of metaphor this is not so.

the sun is a prototypical exemplar.) For example, in a situation in which a person's habit of getting up early in the morning is salient, as is the sun's rising, one might say that the person in question is like the sun. However, the same speaker who announces this similarity might be reluctant to assign that person to the same class as the sun. In other words, the features that make up the ad hoc category in question should characterize the metaphor vehicle. As a result, while someone might agree that Juliet is like the sun in that her smile is very bright, they might be unwilling to say that she is the sun, since Juliet may lack the rest of the traits that characterize the sun.

Treatment of Different Types of Metaphors

Another major challenge for theories of metaphor is to provide an analysis of metaphor which is able to account for different types of metaphors, ranging from metaphors as common and "dead" as "Man is a wolf," to those as novel and rich as the metaphor "For mortal beings, such as ourselves, time is a river." In addition, the theories must account for metaphors that are novel and yet mundane, such as the utterance of Rumelhart's son to his mother, "Mom, I have a hangnail."[12] Clearly, different theories of metaphor seem to be better suited to different types of metaphor.[13] For example, Goodman's theory of metaphor, which explains metaphor by appealing to the transfer of a schema, seems better able to account for metaphors which seem to convey many connections between the metaphor subject and vehicle than for metaphors of the sort produced by Rumelhart's son.[14]

One of the ways metaphors seem to vary is that while some seem to attribute but a single property to the subject of the metaphor, others provide a rich analogy between the metaphor subject and vehicle which both seems to provide a better way of characterizing the metaphor subject and allows one to draw a number of conclusions about the metaphor subject. For example, a metaphor that puts time in the same category as a river allows us to infer a great deal about the nature of time (that it moves continuously, in one direction) and allows us to speculate concerning whether

[12]David E. Rumelhart, "Some Problems with Literal Meanings," in *Metaphor and Thought*, ed. A. Ortony (Cambridge: Cambridge University Press, 1979), pp. 78–90.
[13]Ina Loewenberg, "Truth and Consequences of Metaphor," *Philosophy and Rhetoric* 6 (1973): 30–45, p. 36.
[14]Nelson Goodman, "Metaphor as Moonlighting," in *Philosophical Perspectives on Metaphor*, ed. Mark Johnson (Minneapolis: University of Minnesota Press, 1981), pp. 221–27.

it has enough in common with time to be able to serve as a model for studying time. (For example, we might wonder whether the dynamics of a river in reaction to irregularities in its bed is duplicated by the flow of time in reaction to some yet unidentified entity.) In my analysis, the difference between metaphors of this sort and of the sort produced by Rumelhart's son is to be found in the richness of the role played by the metaphor vehicle and the status of the new conceptualization or ad hoc category underlying it. If the ad hoc category underlying the metaphor is one which is of great value in that the properties it assigns to the metaphor subject allow a greater understanding of it (or communication of that understanding), then the metaphor is richer than one in which the ad hoc category serves the purpose of attributing a certain feature to the metaphor subject but not much else. The quality of the proposed reconceptualization also affects the cognitive impact of the metaphor. That is, the cognitive impact of a metaphor includes the reconceptualization or category scheme proposed by the metaphor, as well as the proposition expressed. This would explain the seemingly unique cognitive impact of metaphors that causes Davidson to want to dismiss their importance as being propositional in nature.

Another distinction used to characterize types of metaphor is that distinction between novel and common metaphors. In my analysis, the difference between the processing of the two is based upon both the novelty of the new conceptualization or ad hoc category (produced by reconceptualization) underlying the metaphor and the use of the metaphor vehicle as a means of referring to that category. That is, a metaphor might be designated novel in that it is the first time that the ad hoc category is used or it is the first time the metaphor vehicle functions as a prototypical representative of that category. In the case of Rumelhart's son's utterance, the metaphor is novel in that the ad hoc category he employs is probably new. At the same time, it is also novel in that he refers to it via the prototypical exemplar of a hangnail, which is usually not thought to designate any ad hoc category. However, there are metaphors in which a familiar ad hoc category (or even a category that is not ad hoc but common) is employed using a new prototypical exemplar. For example, consider an utterance of "Would you like to get together after the meeting for a little discreet interfacing?"

Another way of distinguishing between types of metaphors is according to their degree of metaphoricity. One of the most accepted kinds of metaphors is that of dead metaphors. Although the descriptions of a dead metaphor vary according to the theory at hand, dead metaphors are thought to be those in which the referent the term once used to pick out only metaphorically is now properly (i.e. according to linguistic and taxonomic convention) within the extension of the term. Given a diachronic view of the language, a dead metaphor is an expression which, having at one time been metaphorically applied to some object, through a shift in meaning can now literally be applied to the same object. For example, the expression "hood" seems to be an expression which at one time could be applied only metaphorically to the part of the car which covered the engine, but which now properly applies to that same part.

My analysis of metaphor accounts for both dead and live metaphors (and the differences between them) by appealing to the status of the ad hoc category as a means of conceptualizing the entities in question and the relationship between the ad hoc category the metaphor accesses and the term being used to access it. For example, if the ad hoc category becomes incorporated into the existing category scheme in that it becomes a standard way of conceptualizing the metaphor vehicle, then the principle of functionality dictates that it become incorporated into the language and the principle of economy dictates that it should be named. In many such cases, the category in question is named by the term previously used metaphorically so that the term (i.e. the metaphor vehicle) becomes ambiguous as to whether it is used in its previous literal sense or its metaphorical sense and it now applies literally to both.[15] To the extent that this process occurs (i.e. the incorporation of the ad hoc category and its representation by the metaphor vehicle), the metaphor is thought to be dead and one need not reconceptualize the entities referred to in the metaphorical utterance in order to comprehend it since the concept that underlies the terms (as specified by the rules of the language) is adequate.

The Incorporation of Metaphors into the Language

Another aspect of metaphors noted by psychologists, linguists, and philosophers alike is that some metaphors seem to become incorporated

[15]Note that the term in question need not invariably be ambiguous, in that instead its meaning might be extended to include new applications within the original meaning. For example, one might argue that the term "wing" is not ambiguous, since its application to bird parts and plane parts results from the same meaning rather than from two different meanings. In this case, either the meaning of the term did not specify animacy on the part of the bearer of the wing when it originated, or when other possible applications were found (such as airplane parts), the animacy condition was dropped and the category "wing" became slightly super-ordinate to its previous definition.

into the language through time. In other words, while a particular term may be applied only metaphorically to a given object when first used, over time the meaning of the term changes so that it can be literally applied to that object. That is, the term in question seems to become ambiguous over time is such a way that the term acquires another meaning through which it can be applied literally to the object to which it used to apply only metaphorically. Terms that have undergone this process are considered to have become incorporated into the language itself. To return to our earlier example, although the application of the term "hood" to a certain car part must have been metaphorical when it first occurred since that term originated and was defined, prior to the creation of the particular car part, the term "hood" now literally refers to the car part indicated.

One way to uncover such terms is by uncovering traces of their original application and both the contrast between different objects in the same class and the grounds for their similarity (i.e. the reason for grouping them together). The term "hood of a car," then, is a case in point.[16]

Another place to look for such terms is categories of objects that have been newly created (artificial objects such as cars and their various parts) or objects that have been redefined as our theories of what exists in the world. Thus both manufacturing and the sciences tend to abound with the use of metaphorical terms, though for slightly different reasons. Manufacturing tends to have an abundance of metaphors, for it needs terms to refer to the new objects it is creating, preferably terms that relate the new thing to something already familiar. On the other hand, science needs new terms (1) to refer to objects whose existence seems required in order to explain certain phenomena or their behavior or (2) to refer to different aspects of existing and named entities, or (3) to change the way of looking at different entities so as to incorporate it into a different perspective.

If we accept that some metaphorical uses of language cease to be metaphorical in that they become incorporated into the language, the question arises why some metaphors become part of the language while others do not. If we assume that both language and categorization are ultimately functional in nature, the answer to this question probably lies in the func-

---

[16]Note that the use of the term "hood" in this way serves as a paradigm for the notion that metaphor is an extension of meaning of a term, an interpretation of metaphor derived from a strict translation from the Greek *metaphora*. However, Davidson's criticism of meaning-shift theories of metaphor applies here in that if the meaning of the word is actually extended so that the term properly applies to the object in question, then the term is no longer metaphoric.

tionality of the ad hoc category being used metaphorically and of the use of the term to designate this category. (Note that these issues are distinct in that although a given ad hoc category may become incorporated into the language, it may be designated by a different term.) On the one hand, the need for efficiency would seem to argue that if a certain ad hoc category becomes part of the language, it makes sense to refer to it using one term rather than a description (the economy factor). In other words, the same factors that cause most of the categories we create to acquire names (e.g. camping gear) would also seem to encourage the use of a single term for the ad hoc categories that metaphorical terms designate. At the same time, it would seem that in many cases the best term to use to designate the category in question would be the metaphorical term, especially if (1) its use is established, (2) it is the most prototypical exemplar of the category in question, and (3) the connotations it carries are appropriate.[17]

As to which ad hoc categories become incorporated into the language, they would seem to be the categories that (1) mirror the correlational structure of the environment,[18] (2) are clearly delineated from other categories, (3) serve a useful purpose in naming something frequently referred to by many people (e.g. a certain car part), (4) fit well into the existing taxonomies, and (5) cannot be replaced by another category (either one more abstract or more concrete which possesses most of the same features as the ad hoc category although it may contain a few more or less).[19] To see how the first factor affects the incorporation of certain uses of terms into the language, one need only consider the multiplicity of objects that are clearly delineated in time and space whose names were probably

[17]As we shall see when we discuss the effectiveness of metaphor in education and persuasion, one reason for using the metaphor vehicle to designate the ad hoc category is the concreteness and simplicity it may bring to an otherwise abstract and obscure object.

[18]Barsalou is mistaken when he asserts that all ad hoc categories violate the correlational structure of the environment. While some ad hoc categories (such as the ones he cites) do violate the correlational structure in that they group things together irrespective of their shape, size, etc., others (such as "part of the car that covers the engine," actually corresponds to something that is concretely delineated) do mirror the correlational structure of the environment. Lawrence Barsalou "Ad Hoc Categories," *Memory & Cognition* 11, pp. 211–27.

[19]This list is not intended to be comprehensive but rather to serve as a general characterization of the factors that affect the incorporation of categories into our taxonomies and language. In addition, some of the factors are interrelated. For example, if something mirrors the correlational structure of the environment, it is probably clearly delineated from others and should not conflict with existing taxonomies.

metaphorical when first used (e.g. car hood, car muffler, airplane wing, hangnail, bobby sock). The justification for the fourth factor is that if a certain category conflicts with existing taxonomies, it would be more difficult to retain in memory and thus more difficult to incorporate into the language.

To see how these factors interact to determine whether a given metaphorical use becomes incorporated into the language, it helps to consider an example. Rumelhart's son's reference to a protuberance on his sock as a hangnail should be likely to be incorporated into the language, since the category in question (1) mirrors the correlational structure of the environment, (2) is clearly delineated, and (3) serves a purpose (i.e. knitted garments like socks often acquire protuberances of the sort the boy describes and these protuberances need to be dealt with, for the sake of both comfort and the durability of the sock, and (4) does not conflict with existing taxonomies (i.e. while hangnails belong to animate objects, the suspension of this feature of their characterization in order to include protuberances on socks does not seriously affect their characterization since belonging to an animate object is not critical to their recognition). That this use has *not* been incorporated into the language can be explained by the fact that the functionality of the proposed ad hoc category is already captured by another category that is fairly well established. That is, the protuberance on the boy's sock falls under the more general category of protuberances of knitted garments, which are commonly called pills. In addition, the greater specificity of Rumelhart's ad hoc category in being attached to garments for the feet does not add to the general functionality in this particular use and keeps it from being useful to designate protuberances on sweaters. That is, the category designated by the term "pill" contains all the functionality of the boy's hangnail and more. As a result, it makes sense that this particular metaphorical use did not become part of the language and probably never will.

Consistency with the Terminology of Semantics and Pragmatics

Another condition on an analysis of metaphor is that it account for metaphor in a way consistent with the terminology it borrows from semantics and pragmatics. As we discussed in Chapters 1 and 2, many semantic theories of metaphor fail to meet this condition because they use the term "meaning" inconsistently, and accordingly they prove inadequate. That is, in referring to the metaphorical content we associate with metaphors as a matter of meaning (i.e. determined by the conventions of the language), these theories (such as that of Black) in effect deny the very metaphoricity of metaphors. For the matter of meaning they refer to is not such that a term in its metaphorical application ceases to be metaphorical once that term becomes a matter of meaning.

In my analysis of metaphor I assume a distinction between meaning and content (in the manner of Kaplan and Moravcsik[20]) that allows us to speak of the metaphorical content of an utterance (i.e. the proposition it expresses) without assuming a metaphorical meaning that has the characteristics we ordinarily associate with meaning (such as conventionality, context independence, etc.). In fact, in my analysis metaphorical content is not determined by any kind of meaning, be it metaphorical or literal. In this respect it departs from traditional, Fregean semantics, although it is related to it. Instead, metaphorical content relies, in part, on the reconceptualization of the metaphor vehicle to produce a class not determined by metaphorical meaning. My view of the role of linguistic competence reflects this view in that I hold that although the audience must know the meaning of the term in that they must know the relevant properties of the class it designates (relevant in this context), this knowledge is not sufficient to allow them to derive the metaphorical interpretation. In addition, the audience must have the ability to reconceptualize, that is, to take the metaphor vehicle as the prototype of a class and to determine what that class is, something which may emerge from knowledge of cultural stereotypes (in the case of dying metaphors), contextual information, or a general ability to abstract by selecting relevant properties and suppressing irrelevant properties.[21]

At the same time, my analysis of metaphor may be considered semantic in that I respect the difference between what is said and what is implied and I hold that the metaphorical content associated with metaphors is the proposition expressed by the metaphorical utterance, rather than a pragmatic or use-based phenomenon. However, in maintaining that the proposition expressed by a metaphorical utterance is context-sensitive, my

[20]David Kaplan, "Names and Demonstratives," in *The Philosophy of Language*, ed. A. P. Martinich (Oxford: Oxford University Press, 1990), pp. 316–29; Julius Moravcsik, "Between Reference and Meaning," *Midwest Studies in Philosophy* 14 (1989): 68–83.

[21]That is, when children produce what seem like metaphors owing to their flawed understanding of the terms they use, these do not count as metaphors.

analysis challenges the framework provided by traditional semantics.[22] It also challenges the traditional relationship between semantics and pragmatics.

In this new conception of the contribution of semantics to the study of language, the relationship between semantics and pragmatics shifts slightly from the one painted by Morris and unconsciously assumed by many philosophers of language.[23] That is, according to this conception, the proposition expressed by an utterance is dependent upon context and thus is not a property of sentence types. Therefore, if one wants to maintain that propositions are the domain of semantics, one can no longer picture the relationship between semantics and pragmatics as one in which semantics studies sentence types (in the absence of context) and pragmatics studies the use of these types as they occur in context. One alternative, proposed by theorists such as Stern, Recanati, Sperber, Wilson, and Carston, is that what semantics studies is not the determination of content (the proposition expressed), but rather the contribution the notion of meaning and the concomitant semantic competence make to the determination of content. Sperber and Wilson describe the role of pragmatic processes as follows:

> By 'pragmatic processes' we mean the processes used to bridge the gap between the semantic representations of sentences and the interpretations of utterances in context. . . . Pragmatic processes are involved in every aspect of utterance interpretation: in the recovery of explicit propositional content, implicit import, and illocutionary force.[24]

The difference between semantics and pragmatics in such a view does not lie in a difference of subject matter (for they both study all utterances in a language), or a difference in context dependence (for the utterances they both study are context-dependent), but rather a difference in their approach to the phenomena to be studied, the level at which they analyze the phenomenon in question. While pragmatics conceives of human communication as a subclass of human action, to be studied in terms of such things as intentions and beliefs, semantics studies the role that linguistic competence plays in the determination of what is said.

[22]Many current theorists challenge the context independence of the proposition expressed, including Robyn Carston and François Recanati.

[23]Note that while many philosophers of language do not explicitly specify a relationship between pragmatics and semantics, they assume a piggy-back relationship of the sort described by Morris.

[24]Deirdre Wilson and Dan Sperber, "Pragmatics and Modularity," in *Pragmatics*, ed. Steven Davis (Oxford: Oxford University Press, 1991), pp. 581–95.

Despite the differences between my analysis and the traditional view of the relationship between semantics and pragmatics, my analysis does not rule out the notion of metaphorical meaning, as long as that meaning is not conventional in the way of literal meaning.[25] Nor is my analysis of metaphor tied to either an extensionalist or an intensionalist theory of meaning (as long as one is willing to accept the notion of proposition expressed, which can be characterized in terms of fact that utterances have satisfaction conditions and need not appeal to intensional notions). That is, my analysis of metaphor is compatible with the analysis of Goodman, who holds an extensionalist theory of meaning.[26]

The Dependence of the Metaphorical on the Literal

One of the conditions Davidson (and Stern) consider essential to a theory of metaphor is that it account for a dependence of the metaphorical on the literal. For Davidson this dependence consists in the fact that the audience must derive an image based on a literal interpretation of the utterance. In my understanding, the metaphorical is dependent upon the literal in that to derive the metaphorical one must know the literal meaning of the metaphorical term and must know the entity or class referred to by the term, even if one does not have a complete grasp of all the properties of the class. For example, to grasp the features of the class "sun" which is referred to in the utterance "Juliet is the sun," one must know the meaning of the term "sun" and grasp the entity referred to by that term (whether or not one grasps all the properties that entity is thought to possess). In my analysis, the metaphorical is dependent upon the literal in that one must be able to derive the entity represented by the metaphor vehicle in order to derive the class it is thought to represent (prototypically) and the properties of that class.

The Lack of Conventionality of Metaphor

In examining Davidson's argument against metaphorical meaning based upon dead metaphors, we found that one of the requirements of

---

[25]For an account of metaphorical meaning that is compatible with this analysis, see the work of Josef Stern, specifically his analysis in "What Metaphors Do Not Mean," *Midwest Studies in Philosophy* 16 (1991): 13–52.

[26]Goodman, "Metaphor as Moonlighting."

metaphorical meaning (and content, if you accept this distinction) is that it not be tied to the term by conventional means. In my analysis of metaphor, the lack of conventionality of metaphorical meaning and content stems from the fact that they are based upon a reconceptualization of some or all of the entities referenced in the metaphor. Since this reconceptualization is not determined by linguistic convention but rather affected by cultural stereotypes and contextual information, it is not conventionalized. Nor is the resulting content.

The Fact That Metaphors Are About the World

One of Davidson's fundamental insights was that in processing metaphors we learn something new about the world, rather than about language. In my analysis this phenomenon is accounted for by the fact that, in order to process a metaphor, we must reconceptualize some or all of the entities referenced in the utterance. However, the act of reconceptualization involves changing our conception of something in such a way that we disregard features previously thought essential and highlight others thought unessential. As a result, reconceptualization clearly involves learning about the world, even if the properties we attribute to the metaphor subject are not new (although they may be).

The Relative Independence of Speaker Intention

One of the main difficulties with pragmatic theories of metaphor is that they attempt to explain metaphorical content as determined by speaker intention. In my analysis, while the speaker's intention to speak metaphorically or to utter a certain proposition is a factor that can be used by the audience to ascertain what was said, it does not determine either metaphoricity or the proposition expressed. Instead, the speaker is responsible for controlling such things as linguistic competence, knowledge of shared beliefs and cultural prejudices, and publicly accessible aspects of the context so as to express the desired proposition in the desired manner (i.e. metaphorically or literally). In figurative utterances, as in other utterances, a speaker sets out with the intention of achieving a goal by communicating certain propositions and a certain attitude (e.g. one of belief) toward that proposition. However, the speaker's ability to communicate those propositions is limited by their mastery of the language; their awareness of the audience's linguistic, cultural, and personal background; their awareness of information in the immediate circumstances; their ability to determine what information needs to be communicated in order to express the desired proposition (and desired perspective) with the appropriate attitude; and, finally, their ability to bring all these factors together to achieve their goals. At the same time, since what is said is the result of contextual information available to all parties, the speaker is responsible for proper use of this, as well as for linguistic competence. For example, if the speaker says something about "that woman" while looking directly at a woman in a group, what is said will be considered to be about the woman he is looking at. In other words, successful communication depends upon more than linguistic competence (or the mere intention to communicate), even in literal language use, and the speaker is held responsible for these factors as well. In addition, while figurative language brings the additional burden of being able to invoke reconceptualization, the way in which it depends upon speaker intention is not fundamentally different from the way in which literal language depends upon speaker intention.

Other

One final virtue of my analysis is its ability to accommodate the fact that so many metaphorical utterances can be recognized as metaphorical and interpreted metaphorically with some degree of accuracy in the absence of information about the context in which they appear, something which appears to contradict our contention that metaphor is context-dependent. One way of explaining this apparent contradiction is to say that certain knowledge most of us share allows us to infer a standard context. However, we can also use the terminology of my analysis to explain this apparent contradiction in another, perhaps clearer way. That is, given my analysis, we would explain our ability to interpret so many metaphors in the absence of the context in which they are uttered as due either to our familiarity with the category the metaphor vehicle is used to represent and the conception of the metaphor vehicle as a prototypical member of that category or to our ability to derive the category in question by way of our knowledge of stereotypes and so forth. Of course, some of the specific properties attributed to the metaphor subject through assignment to the ad hoc category will be dependent upon the context. For example, in a conversation about appetites, being a pig will emphasize the size of one's appetite more than the sound one makes or how neat one keeps one's room.

TABLE 13

Evaluation of My Analysis

Metaphoricity	Very well. Explains the metaphoricity of metaphors and similes and opens an avenue for explaining nonlinguistic metaphors
Metaphor comprehension	Fair. Doesn't go into great detail but is compatible with (1) the findings of psychologists regarding processing time and (2) with our intuitions about how metaphors are processed
The intuition of metaphorical content and truth	Very well. Builds this analysis around the notion that the proposition expressed by a metaphor is its metaphorical content
Difficulty of specifying the satisfaction conditions of some metaphorical utterances	Very well
The context dependence of metaphor	Very well. Explains by appealing to the fact that hearers must construct the categories metaphorically accessed and use context-dependent information to do so
The ubiquity of metaphor (why metaphor is used)	Well
The relationship between metaphor and simile	Very well. Doesn't account for the figurativeness of similes or the falseness of some similes
Treatment of different types of metaphors	Well. Can accommodate all types
The incorporation of metaphors into the language	Very well
Consistency with the framework of semantics	Well
The dependence of the metaphorical on the literal	OK[27]
The lack of conventionality of metaphor	Well
The fact that metaphors are about the world	Very well
The independence of speaker aim and intention	Very well

[27]In some respects Davidson's analysis handles this condition quite well in that he claims that the content of the metaphor is its literal content and this literal content generates the image that constitutes metaphoricity. Yet Josef Stern points out that Davidson's analysis is weak in that all that is required for Davidson's analysis is the literal meanings of the principle and subsidiary subject. That is, Davidson's analysis has no way of distinguishing between metaphors and similes. Since I address this point elsewhere and this condition is not one of those I am focusing on, I won't go into this here. For more on this topic, see Josef Stern, "What Metaphors Do Not Mean," *Midwest Studies in Philosophy* 16 (1991): 13–51.

Summary

In summary, I have argued for an analysis of metaphor in terms of reconceptualization rather than as the content of a simile. In addition, I have evaluated my analysis of metaphor using the criteria established in previous chapters, producing the results listed in Table 13. Much work remains to be done in this area, including a more rigorous inquiry into the correlation of my analysis of metaphor with featural semantics, an exploration of the ramifications of adopting such a theory of semantics, and an application of my theory to other types of figurative language.

Index

Index

content, 43; definition of, 12, 22; indirect, *see* indirect content; literal (definition of), 14; metaphorical, *see* metaphorical content
content-hunger, of comparison statements, 171, 175, 176, 190
context, metaphorical, 15, 20; definition of, 14
context dependence: definition of, 89; of irony, 152; of metaphor, *see* metaphor, context dependence of; postsemantic, 90; presemantic, 90; semantic, 90
context independence, 61
conventionality, 21, 40, 70, 71. *See also* unconventionality, of metaphor
conversational implicature, *see* implicatures
conversational maxims, 125, 126, 127, 134
Cooperative Principle, 125
corrective judgment, 169
correlational structure, *see* structure, correlational
criteria for a theory of metaphor: Criterion 1, 7; Criterion 2, 7; Criterion 3, 7, 21, 43, 60, 61, 99, 141, 165, 186; Criterion 4, 7, 79; Criterion 5, 7, 91, 97; Criterion 6, 7; Criterion 7, 7; Criterion 8, 7; Criterion 9, 7; Criterion 10, 21, 59, 97, 99, 137; Criterion 11, 75, 97, 99; Criterion 12, 21, 71, 75, 97; Criterion 13, 21, 71, 75, 97; Criterion 14, 21, 123, 148

Davidson, Donald, 20, 45, 46, 47, 48, 49, 50, 53, 55, 60, 113–21, 102, 165, 168, 171, 173, 181, 185, 186, 208
Davis, Steven, 24
definition of terms, 12–17
designata, 57
distinction: conflation of, 144–45, 196; direct vs. indirect, 144, 166, 174; literal vs. nonliteral, 144, 166; meaning vs. content, *see* meaning, vs. content; meaning vs. use, *see* meaning, vs. use; what is said vs. what is conveyed, *see* what is said, vs. what is conveyed; what is said vs. what is implied, *see* what is said vs. what is implied
Donnellan, Keith, 22, 23

education: use of metaphor, 3, 216–18
emotive power, 3, 6

explicatures, definition of, 125
extension, 10, 16, 23, 35; extensional component, 32, 34; extensional theory of meaning, 87, 230; extensionality, 25

falsity, types, *see* metaphor, failed
Fauconnier, Gilles, 58, 59, 95, 206, 207, 208
feature salience, 172
feature selection, 16, 171, 172, 173, 189
feature space, 171, 176, 178, 198, 205; altered, 178, 202; and relevance, 170, 172; as criteria of evaluation, 167; figurative, 170; literal (definition of), 178; vs. content, 175
features of my analysis, 40
figurative comparisons, definition of, 170
figurative content, *see* metaphorical content
figurative language: as an altered feature space, 170–71; as reconceptualization, 10; via a corrective judgment, 169
figurative meaning, *see* meaning, figurative
figurative predications, definition of, 170
first meaning, 48. *See also* secondary meaning
focus, *see* metaphor vehicle
Fogelin, Robert, 13, 20, 45, 47, 129, 131, 132, 147, 154, 155, 156, 164; adoption of Grice's framework, 167, 169
Frege, Gottlob, 12, 22, 43, 48, 54, 56
Fregean thought, *see* thought, Fregean
functionality, 37; of categorization, 37, 39

Gibbs, Raymond, 24
Glucksberg, Sam, 15, 21, 30, 202, 203
Goodman, Nelson, 43, 54, 63, 73, 75, 76, 80, 84, 85, 87
graded structure, of categories, 39; definition of, 35
Gray, W. D, 35
Grice, H. P., 12, 21, 24, 50, 51, 52, 100, 104, 105, 113, 114
Gricean framework, 124, 167, 169
Gricean implicature, *see* implicatures

Heidegger, Martin, 10
Henle, Paul, 43

illocutionary force, 146, 159 (*see also* metaphoricity, as illocutionary force); definition of, 102

This book was typeset in Sabon, with Adobe Garamond
superscript numbers and chapter numbers.
Sabon was designed by Jan Tschichold and issued in 1964;
Adobe Garamond was designed by Robert Slimbach and
issued in 1989. The two typefaces are based broadly on the
work of the sixteenth-century typographer Claude Garamond
and his pupil Jacques Sabon.